Exploring the Basic Income Guarantee

Series Editor
Karl Widerquist, Georgetown University in Qatar, Doha, USA

Basic income is one of the most innovative, powerful, straightforward, and controversial proposals for addressing poverty and growing inequalities. A Basic Income Guarantee (BIG) is designed to be an unconditional, government-insured guarantee that all citizens will have enough income to meet their basic needs. The concept of basic, or guaranteed, income is a form of social provision and this series examines the arguments for and against it from an interdisciplinary perspective with special focus on the economic and social factors. By systematically connecting abstract philosophical debates over competing principles of BIG to the empirical analysis of concrete policy proposals, this series contributes to the fields of economics, politics, social policy, and philosophy and establishes a theoretical framework for interdisciplinary research. It will bring together international and national scholars and activists to provide a comparative look at the main efforts to date to pass unconditional BIG legislation across regions of the globe and will identify commonalities and differences across countries drawing lessons for advancing social policies in general and BIG policies in particular.

All proposals submitted to the series undergo documented single-blind peer review by subject-matter experts (SME). In addition, all manuscripts are reviewed by SME prior to acceptance through a documented single-blind process.

Jong-sung You • Nam Hoon Kang •
Seungju Lee

# UBI from Idea to Reality

A Blueprint for Basic Income in Korea

palgrave
macmillan

Jong-sung You
Korea Inequality Research Lab
Yonsei University
Seodaemun-gu, Soul-t'ukpyolsi, Korea
(Republic of)

Seungju Lee
Department of Social Welfare
Daegu University
Gyeongsangbuk-do, Kyongsang-bukto,
Korea (Republic of)

Nam Hoon Kang
Hanshin University
Seoul, Soul-t'ukpyolsi, Korea (Republic of)

ISSN 2662-3803 ISSN 2662-3811 (electronic)
Exploring the Basic Income Guarantee
ISBN 978-3-032-26199-1 ISBN 978-3-032-26200-4 (eBook)
https://doi.org/10.1007/978-3-032-26200-4



This Palgrave Macmillan imprint is published by the registered company Springer Nature Switzerland AG
The registered company address is: Gewerbestrasse 11, 6330 Cham, Switzerland

# Foreword

The Republic of Korea is ready, able, and willing to introduce a basic income, setting a standard for the rest of the world to follow. A basic income is not adequately understood by many commentators and critics. It would be a system in which every legal usual resident in the country would receive a modest amount from the state each month, paid without conditions, paid individually to all men and women equally, with a different amount for children, paid to the mother or surrogate mother.

It would be an *economic right*, not a form of charity, intended to give everybody equal basic security, and thus involving supplements for those with disabilities that involve extra costs of living. It would not be a substitute for other forms of benefit or social services, and would not prevent anybody from earning from labor or business activity.

Although it would reduce income poverty and inequality, the primary justifications for building a basic income system are *ethical*, not instrumental. First of all, it is a matter of *common justice*. Consider the commons. They are what belongs to everybody as Korean citizens, that is, all that is inherited from the numerous generations of ancestors, ever since the country was established in BC2333 on the wonderful principles of *hongik ingan*.

The commons includes all the land, all the vast sea and seabed area, and the minerals under the land and seabed belonging to the country.

It also includes all the social institutions constructed for the public and bequeathed to Koreans and legally resident others.

So, in terms of common justice, everybody should receive a share from this accumulated common wealth, a sort of common dividend. If the state allows the private inheritance of private wealth, as it does—in which those fortunate enough to inherit have done nothing to earn it—then one should surely accept the legitimacy of a shared inheritance of public common wealth. And since we cannot possibly estimate whose ancestors contributed more or less, the only just system would be to provide equal common dividends to everybody.

A basic income is also a matter of *ecological justice*. The rich pollute much more than the poor, and therefore it would be justifiable to tax the causes of pollution and common resource depletion, such as by a carbon tax, and recycle the revenue as equal common dividends. While this would compensate the poor, it would also reduce income inequality, needed at a time of rapid growth in inequalities.

While being a source of justice, a basic income—however modest an amount initially—would also enhance three forms of *freedom*—freedom to choose and to say 'no' to forms of exploitation, freedom to be moral, and freedom from domination by figures in positions of unaccountable authority.

Third, basic income would enhance *basic security*. This is a fundamental human need. We want it for ourselves and for our families, and we should want it for everybody else. Basic security is a public good, in that if some people have it, that would not deprive others from having it as well.

Today, we are threatened by environmental decay, natural disasters and a growing risk of economic and social shocks. We are living in an era of *chronic uncertainty*. We face uninsurable risks that make most of us feel insecure, lacking Robustness (immunity from being hurt, financially or otherwise) and lacking Resilience (a strong ability to cope with shocks and to recover from them).

In those circumstances, a basic income would be the equivalent of a **social vaccine**. Most sensible people believe they and their children should take vaccines to protect against illnesses, giving greater immunity and greater ability to cope with and recover from such illnesses should we contract them. And if everybody takes such vaccines, that will lessen the likelihood of pandemics.

So, why should we not want a social vaccine to protect everybody from economic and social shocks and hazards? The evidence from around the world shows that economic insecurity increases morbidity, stress and deaths from despair. Basic security would reverse all that and lessen the demands on public healthcare services.

This role for basic income is particularly important for the growing precariat in the Republic of Korea and globally. The precariat faces constant uncertainty and a life of intense insecurity. In that context, a basic income is becoming not only a social vaccine but also a *political imperative*. Chronic insecurity is known to cause people to support populists and those promising unrealistic return to some mythical past. It is the relatively uneducated part of the precariat—the faction I call *Atavists*—which supports the likes of Donald Trump. A basic income would encourage more people to be altruistic, tolerant and a society in favor of empathy and social solidarity.

We should be confident that the new government in this dynamic country will move to phase in a real basic income, as the anchor of a well-functioning social protection system. Elsewhere, I have explained how it could be funded sustainably, based on a Commons Capital Fund. It would also lead to more effective education, as shown in my new book.

I am enormously encouraged by the fact that this book's authors not only understand basic income but also propose practical equitable ways of funding it. Those ways are among others. There is a debate to be had about whether children under a certain age should receive a higher or lower level than provided to adults. The authors favor a higher amount, because they wish to provide a pro-natalist incentive, given Korea's very low fertility rate. An alternative view is that the basic income should be lower for children, because less income is needed for them and because the basic income should give equal basic security for everyone. It would also be unfair for those without children, and if the government wished to promote higher fertility that should be done by other policies. Clearly, this is a controversial issue to be resolved objectively.

The government should convene a meeting of experts to decide the best way forward. Above all, we should be encouraged by the fact that in 2025 a President was elected who understands basic income. I have had the great privilege of meeting him on several occasions, and believe he is committed to this potentially transformative policy. It is an exciting time to be a Korean.

Honorary Co-President, Basic Income Earth Network Guy Standing
Professorial Research Associate,
SOAS University of London

# Foreword

Fifteen years ago, when what I call "the third wave of the Basic Income movement" started to take off, Korea's part in the international movement for Basic Income was hardly noticeable. But beginning in 2014, the Republic of Korea quickly sprang onto the scene not only to take a noticeable role but to become one of the leading countries in the movement.

In 2014, delegates from the Republic of Korea secured the endorsement of the Basic Income Earth Network (BIEN) to host the network's Sixteenth International Congress in Seoul, Korea two years later. As chair of BIEN at the time, I was invited to visit the Congress site in 2015 (a year in advance of the international Congress). I found a very knowledgeable and dedicated group of individuals who had organized a national conference that rivaled some of BIEN's international Congresses for size and activity. I knew then that the 2016 BIEN Congress in Seoul would be a success, and my expectations were exceeded.

The 2016 Congress was so successful that in 2023, Seoul became the first city in the world to be asked host the BEIN Congress twice. Along with India, the Republic of Korea is one of only two Asian nations that have ever hosted a BIEN Congress.

Not only do Korean Basic Income activists have outsized influence within the Basic Income movement, but they have helped to make Basic Income more relevant in national politics in the Republica of Korean than it is in national politics almost anywhere else in the world. Citizens are getting the message, and politicians are listening. Even President Lee Jae-myung supports a version of Basic Income. Whether Lee Jae-myung's proposal will be introduced remains to be seen, but if you're wondering how Basic Income supporters got the issue on the national agenda, this book shows you.

This book has thorough, cross-disciplinary scholarship, which is both well-versed in research that has been conducted on Basic Income around the world over the last half century and fully embedded in the contemporary political and economic situation in the Republic of Korea. It carefully develops a finely tailored proposal that is economically and politically feasible in the Republic of Korea right here and now. It is a blueprint for the introduction of Basic Income in the Republic of Korea and a model for how to build proposals that can get Basic Income on the table elsewhere.

Professor of Philosophy,
Georgetown University-Qatar

Karl Widerquist

# Preface

Today, humanity faces three major challenges: the AI revolution, the climate crisis, and population aging. Amid these challenges, together with rising economic inequality and insecurity, the twentieth-century welfare state model is reaching its limits. While we do not claim that basic income is a panacea, we believe it must serve as a central pillar in building a new twenty-first-century welfare state paradigm in this era of great transition.

South Korea, which joined the ranks of developed nations through compressed economic growth in the late twentieth century, has rapidly—albeit belatedly—expanded its welfare model over the past few decades. Korea has now reached a point, however, where it can no longer postpone the choice between maintaining the existing welfare model and transitioning to a new paradigm.

In 2026, Korea is making notable strides—surpassing the KOSPI 5,000 milestone and aiming to become one of the world's top three powerhouses in AI—yet it is also grappling with "K-shaped" growth. This phenomenon is characterized by shrinking youth employment, widening polarization between industries, and deepening inequalities in both income and wealth. While it remains difficult to predict the precise extent of job displacement and labor-market polarization brought about by AI, basic income is increasingly approaching us not as a matter of choice, but as a necessity.

The global community also faces the urgent and critical task of transitioning to renewable energy to avert a climate catastrophe driven by carbon emissions. Carbon taxes represent a market-friendly instrument for enabling a swift and efficient energy transition. While carbon taxes accelerate the shift to renewables by raising the price of fossil fuels, they also raise energy costs and can inadvertently reduce households' real incomes. We believe that basic income is one of the most effective ways to facilitate this energy transition while at the same time maintaining households' real incomes.

The year 2026 marks a significant turning point, as South Korea officially enters a super-aged society. Although population aging in Korea began later than in the West or Japan, the old-age dependency ratio—the ratio of the elderly population to the working-age population—is projected to exceed the OECD average beginning this year. By the 2060s, Korea is expected to become an unprecedented case globally, with the elderly population outnumbering the working-age population and the elderly dependency ratio rising above 100%. Meanwhile, the crises of population decline and regional extinction caused by ultra-low fertility are emerging as existential threats to Korea, alongside the shared global climate crisis. This is precisely why we place as much emphasis on "sustainable efficiency" as on the realization of substantive freedom and equality.

In this book, we seek to demonstrate that basic income is an effective, market-friendly policy that can advance demographic sustainability by addressing the low-birth-rate crisis; foster ecological sustainability by contributing to carbon neutrality and the mitigation of the climate crisis; and promote economic sustainability by overcoming the long-term inefficiencies that often result from the short-term focus of selective welfare models. Amid the great transitions of the Fourth Industrial Revolution—driven by AI, low fertility, population aging, and the climate crisis—we argue that basic income must become a vital pillar of the twenty-first-century welfare state.

Since 2018, we have engaged in eight years of collaborative research in preparation for this book. Specializing in public policy, economics, and social welfare, the authors have wrestled with how to translate the ideals of basic income into a policy design that is practically implementable within South Korea's institutional context. As a result, the proposals in this book place significant emphasis on new institutional forms—such as a negative income tax (NIT)-type basic income and a universal earned income tax credit (EITC)—in addition to the common wealth-dividend-type universal basic income long advocated in UBI circles.

We affirm that the universal right to basic income is grounded in the duty to pay taxes, thereby addressing the "free-rider problem." Recognizing that a full basic income capable of meeting all basic needs is not feasible at this stage, we propose instead a "partial basic income" at a meaningful level. Rather than dismantling the existing social security system, we advocate a partial replacement of social assistance, combined with universal EITC-style support for social insurance contributions by working people, in order to close coverage gaps.

Financially, the bulk of the total benefit expenditure is funded through tax increases and the partial replacement of existing social assistance benefits. We keep the net fiscal requirement within 0.3% of Gross National Income (GNI), ensuring sustainability both now and in the long term. This model not only avoids an increase in national debt but also bolsters the long-term fiscal sustainability of social insurance funds through indirect support. Under this plan, nearly 70% of the population would become net beneficiaries. The top 30% would be net contributors, but even for the top 10% the net contribution would not exceed 10% of disposable income. In this way, without imposing an excessive burden, the model substantially reduces income inequality and poverty by raising the disposable income of low-income groups by more than 30%.

This work was supported by the Laboratory Program for Korean Studies through the Ministry of Education of the Republic of Korea and the Korean Studies Promotion Service of the Academy of Korean Studies (AKS-2018-LAB-1250002). The Korea Inequality Research Lab (www.kirl.re.kr; Director: Jong-sung You) is a collaborative research project involving sixteen domestic and international scholars. It began at Gachon University in December 2018 with support from the Academy of Korean Studies and has continued as a Yonsei University affiliate since 2024. This large-scale project will produce ten English-language research volumes and thirty-eight papers in international journals (SSCI or SCOPUS indexed) on the measurement, causes, and consequences of inequality, as well as on social policies to alleviate inequality. The present volume is one of the ten books in the series on social policies for reducing inequality.

Throughout the research and writing process, we presented interim findings at the Lab's monthly seminars and manuscript workshops, receiving invaluable critical feedback from our fellow researchers. We would like to express our deepest gratitude to our co-researchers: Professors Byung

You Cheon, Timo Fleckenstein, Eunyoung Ha, Stephan Haggard, Jun Ho Jeong, Woo Chang Kang, Nak Nyeon Kim, Soohyun Lee, Sophia Seung-yoon Lee, Cheol-Sung Lee, Sung Ho Park, Jung Wook Son, and Frederick Solt. We are especially grateful to Stephan Haggard, who served both as a co-researcher and as a mentor, providing insightful comments on drafts of this book and several other volumes of the project. We also thank Professors Minhye Kim, Sam Ock Park, and Byung-Deuk Woo, who collaborated with us despite not being formally affiliated with the Lab. We further acknowledge the contributions of Professors Inkwan Chung and Sangyong Son; Drs. Yuhwi Kim, Jeong-eun Koo, and Dongjin Kim; and Ju-seong Jeong, Joonyoung Seo, Haeeun Choi, Dabin Lim, and Subin Lee, who have worked with us as post-doctoral researchers or research assistants. Finally, we owe a special debt of gratitude to Suzin You, formerly a data researcher at the Lab and now leading AI and data-science projects at the international development organization IDinsight, for developing the simulation app (basicincome.jongsungyou.com/en) for our proposed "Korean-style basic income."

We presented portions of our early drafts and related papers at numerous domestic and international conferences and received invaluable comments from a wide range of experts. This book has benefited greatly from the discussions and feedback generated at several key events: the international webinar in February 2022; the early-draft workshop at the BIEN Congress in Seoul in August 2023; the international conference hosted by the Korea Inequality Research Lab at Yonsei University in August 2024; the BIEN Congress in Brisbane, Australia, in 2024; the Sydney workshop in 2025; online presentations at the 2025 BIEN Congress; and the English- and Korean-draft workshops in March 2025.

We are deeply grateful to the international scholars and activists who participated in these discussions and provided critical insights: Marc de Basquiat, Jurgen De Wispelaere, Emma Hansma, Troy Henderson, Torben Iversen, Elise Klein, Eunro Lee, Soomi Lee, Anni Miller, Tadashi Okanouchi, Scott Santens, Ben Spies-Butcher, Guy Standing, Malcolm Torry, Philippe Van Parijs, Karl Widerquist, and Almaz Zelleke.

Our dialogues and debates with a wide network of Korean scholars and civic activists were also instrumental in shaping this book. We would like to thank Hyosang Ahn, Seung-ho Baek, Hee-yeon Cho, Jieun Choi, Young Jun Choi, Yiyoon Chung, Min Geum, Jang-Pyo Hong, Chang Lyul Jeong, Seunghee Jeong, Gangsoo Jun, Byung-Goo Kang, Shin-Wook Kang, Won Don Kang, Kyoseong Kim, Seungyun Kim, Taeil Kim,

Inhoe Ku, No Wan Kwack, Jeong-im Kwon, Jin-Kwan Kwon, Chongkoo Lee, Han-joo Lee, Il-Young Lee, Jae-wook Lee, Jinsu Lee, Jun-young Lee, Sangho Lee, Wonjae Lee, Wonjin Lee, Gi-up Nam, Hoyoung Oh, KeonHo Oh, Kyongcheol Park, Kibaeg Park, Ki Seong Park, Sang-Min Rhie, Jaerin Ryu, Kwang-Yeong Shin, Ahyoung Song, Jae-jin Yang, Gun-min Yi, Young Seong Yoo, HyeongJoong Yoon, and Dongchul Yu.

In particular, the sharp comments from Torben Iversen, a preeminent scholar of comparative political economy who maintains a critical distance from the basic-income community; the debate with Jae-jin Yang, a leading Korean social-welfare scholar critical of basic income; and our discussions with Ki Seong Park, who developed the Safety Income model—the prototype for Seoul's Stepping-Stone Income—and Nak-Hoe Kim, one of the five former economic officials who proposed an individual-level negative income tax model, provided the intellectual friction that helped refine our arguments. We also extend our deepest gratitude to senior scholars who offered us invaluable encouragement and advice, including Sang-mok Suh, President of the International Council on Social Welfare; Joung-Woo Lee, Professor Emeritus at Kyeongbuk National University; and Jin Soon Lee, former President of the Korea Development Institute.

Last but not least, we would like to express our special gratitude to Karl Widerquist, editor of the *Exploring the Basic Income Guarantee* series at Palgrave Macmillan, who took part in the initial draft workshop at the Seoul BIEN Congress in 2023 and encouraged us to publish our work in this series.

Two of us served on the Basic Income Committee and the Basic Society Committee in the policy camp of then-presidential candidate Lee Jae-myung during the 2022 election. We played a role in having "rural basic income" adopted as an official campaign pledge—a policy that had not been part of the initial platform. We regarded rural basic income, which covers all residents in rural areas rather than only farmers, as more consistent with the principles of universality and unconditionality and as a potential stepping stone toward nationwide universal basic income.

Beginning this year, a two-year pilot project for rural basic income is under way, with expectations of nationwide expansion. Two of us are currently members of the research team charged with evaluating this pilot. We hope that rural basic income will expand beyond individual villages to entire rural counties and eventually evolve into a national universal basic income. We further hope that South Korea's innovations as one of the world's top three AI powers will be accompanied by the expansion of basic income. One of us has been appointed Vice-Chair of the Presidential Commission on Basic Society, chaired by President Lee Jae-myung himself. The "basic society" envisioned by the Lee administration encompasses a wide range of social services—including housing, healthcare, education, care, finance, transportation, communications, energy, and culture—far beyond basic income alone. While all of these services are crucial, it is clear that basic income must serve as the core foundation.

Seoul, Republic of Korea
Spring 2026

Jong-sung You
Nam Hoon Kang
Seungju Lee

# Contents

# List of Figures

# List of Tables

CHAPTER 1

# Introduction

One: Our capitalist societies are replete with unacceptable inequalities.
Two: Freedom is of paramount importance.

(van Parijs, 1995: 1)

In 2022, South Korea (simply Korea, hereafter) almost became the first country in the world to implement universal basic income (Standing, 2022; You and Choi, 2022). During the 2022 presidential election, Lee Jae-myung, the ruling liberal Democratic Party candidate, pledged to implement a modest basic income for all citizens. He proposed a nationwide basic income, alongside youth and rural basic incomes, financed by a land value tax and a carbon tax. However, this did not happen as he lost to Yoon Seok-yeol of the conservative People Power Party by a narrow margin of 0.7% points.

Following the subsequent presidential election held after the impeachment of former President Yoon Suk-yeol due to the unconstitutional declaration of martial law, Lee Jae-myung was elected and inaugurated as the President for a new five-year term. President Lee is currently pursuing 'Basic Society' policies, which include the provision of basic income and basic services (such as basic housing, care, finance, transportation, medical care, and telecommunications). Current basic income initiatives include rural basic income at the county level and 'Sunshine Income,' with policies also extending Child Basic Income (child allowances) up to age 12.



J. S. You et al., *UBI from Idea to Reality*, Exploring the Basic Income Guarantee,
https://doi.org/10.1007/978-3-032-26200-4_1

Notably, the carbon dividends based on a carbon tax, land dividends based on a land value tax, and the Youth Basic Income pledged during the 2022 campaign have not yet been revisited.

Starting in 2026, ten counties have been selected to provide a monthly rural basic income of 150,000 KRW to all residents. After a two-year pilot phase, this program is expected to expand to 69 counties designated as depopulation areas. Furthermore, since 2026, a project to establish approximately 500 'Sunshine (Wind) Income Villages' annually has been underway. The Sunshine Income (Sunshine Dividend) policy involves local governments and cooperatives securing equity by providing land or investing funds in solar and wind power generation, then distributing dividends to residents in the form of basic income or participation income. Sunshine and Wind Income could become a vital funding source for rural basic income. Due to high preference among local residents, these policies hold the potential for rapid expansion across all rural areas.

Meanwhile, Seoul Mayor Oh Se-hoon of the People Power Party promoted a policy known as 'Stepping Stone Income,' a form of negative income tax (NIT). A three-year randomized controlled trial (RCT) of this policy was conducted for Seoul residents. In contrast, Gyeonggi Province Governor Kim Dong-yeon of the Democratic Party has pursued 'Opportunity Income,' a form of participation income.

Whether a universal basic income covering the entire population will be implemented during President Lee Jae-myung's term remains uncertain. Land dividends based on a land value tax may be rediscussed if real estate prices continue to rise. Carbon dividends are also essential for an energy transition that does not exacerbate inequality. A bill to expand Child Basic Income up to age 12 has already passed the National Assembly. The proliferation of rural basic income and Sunshine Income may catalyze demands for a nationwide universal basic income. Additionally, the 'AI Sovereign Wealth Fund' currently being promoted by the Lee administration could serve as a funding source for basic income if a portion of the fund's profits is distributed to all citizens. Above all, given the urgent need for tax and pension reforms, discussions on universal basic income, negative income tax, and participation income are expected to continue steadily.

This book outlines the normative and practical benefits of a basic income approach to income security and proposes a realistic BI plan for Korea that is feasible financially, administratively, and politically. While the three of us co-authors are known to be advocates of UBI, we have studied the advantages of NIT and PI, as well as UBI, for the last several years and designed a package incorporating programs of UBI, NIT, and PI, based on the principles of UBI.

Basic income has been advocated as a means to achieve both freedom and equality without compromising economic efficiency, while negative income tax has been promoted as a way to eradicate poverty and reduce the disincentive to work associated with existing social assistance programs. Despite their different philosophical backgrounds, basic income and negative income tax can be designed to produce the same redistributive effects and can, in some ways, be considered the same policy.

We compare the principles, advantages, and disadvantages of basic income and negative income tax, exploring the feasibility of a 'negative income tax-type basic income' that leverages the advantages of both policies. We also explore the potential for a 'common wealth dividend' basic income, which would distribute equally the profits or rents arising from the broadly or narrowly defined common wealth. In addition, we consider the introduction of a 'universal earned income tax credit' (universal EITC) as a form of participation income provided to all working persons.

While our theoretical discussion of universal basic income (UBI), negative income tax (NIT), and universal EITC can be applied to any country, we will focus on Korea as an example of a place where there has been an actual discussion of the issue. It is important to note that we are not designing a new system in a vacuum but are instead building on the existing one and replacing parts of it. We will also consider the fiscal, administrative, and political feasibility of our proposals. While our proposed policies have been tailored to specific circumstances in Korea, we believe that the fundamental ideas and many aspects of our proposal can also be applied to other countries.

We do not claim that basic income is a panacea capable of solving all the problems facing humanity, nor do we argue for a wholesale replacement of the existing welfare state with basic income. Nor do we assert that our proposal can fully realize the ideals of basic income. However, we believe that our proposed policies will take a significant step toward realizing the ideals of universal basic income in an era of increasing inequality and insecurity, with looming threats of ecological and demographic unsustainability. We will demonstrate that our proposed reforms will not only promote both equality and freedom but also enhance sustainable efficiency. Sustainable efficiency refers to promoting long-term economic efficiency rather than short-term economic efficiency, as well as ecological and demographic sustainability. Demographic sustainability is a particularly serious issue in Korea, with the looming threat of population extinction due to an extremely low total fertility rate of around 0.7.

In designing a new income security system that promotes equality, freedom, and sustainable efficiency, we present an analytical framework that integrates taxation and benefits (public transfers). To facilitate broader understanding, we are providing a free online application that allows individuals and households to simulate the amounts of benefits they would receive, as well as the taxes they would be required to pay, under our policy alternatives (basicincome.jongsungyou.com/en).

## 1.1 Basic Income for Freedom, Equality, and Sustainable Efficiency

Basic income is an income paid to everyone (universal), without any conditions attached (unconditional), on an individual basis (rather than on a household basis), and in regular, fixed amounts of cash. Advocated by Thomas More (1516), Thomas Paine (1797), and others, interest and support for basic income today extend far beyond the traditional ideological spectrum of left and right. This is due to its practicality in realizing both freedom and equality and its potential as an alternative social security system that overcomes the limitations of traditional welfare states in addressing growing inequality and insecurity around the world. We will show why traditional welfare states are ineffective and inefficient in reducing inequality and poverty and why basic income can effectively and efficiently tackle the problem of inequality and poverty and enhance real freedom for all. In addition, we will discuss its potential to help address the socioeconomic crisis caused by climate change and the demographic crisis of low birthrates and aging.

A basic income promotes "real freedom" by providing a consistent income floor for all. According to van Parijs (1995), real freedom goes beyond "formal freedom" - the absence of coercion or violation of one's rights to self-ownership - to the realization of opportunities, including the material means, to do what one might want to do. A basic income provides the material means essential for substantive freedom in a way that does not compromise formal freedom. Receipt of a basic income is not subject to any means-testing or strings attached, making it truly liberating, unlike means-tested and conditional benefits.

In addition, a basic income provides a constant share of "equal distribution" to everyone, which can be understood as an equal share of part of the national income derived from the common wealth (collective wealth of a society) in a broad sense, such as land, the natural resources and environment, and the knowledge and institutions accumulated and developed from the past. Depending on the social consensus, this could be 5% of national income, or 25% of national income.

Herbert Simon, Nobel laureate in economics, argued that 90% of today's social production in advanced countries is not the result of individual efforts, but is instead derived from accumulated knowledge, technology, information, and institutions from the past. Therefore, he suggested that morally speaking, a tax rate of 90% would be appropriate, but proposed imposing a tax rate of 70% and using half of the revenue to provide a basic income to everyone (Simon, 2000).

A basic income promotes equality of opportunity and, at the same time, equality of outcome to a certain extent. Basic income prioritizes equality of opportunity, which is necessary for real freedom, but it also reduces excessive inequality of outcomes, which undermines formal equality of opportunity.

Basic income provides a new alternative social security in response to the increasing inability of traditional welfare states to address the growing income and wealth inequality and poverty in their countries. Especially in the era of deindustrialization, when the share of the precariat, or precarious working class, is increasing (Standing, 2017), and in anticipation of further job losses and precariousness with the advent of the AI revolution, the need for basic income becomes even more important. Basic income can be an effective and efficient alternative to social assistance, which, along with social insurance, comprises the two main pillars of the existing welfare state income security system.

Means-tested social assistance, by requiring continual proof of poverty, generates stigma, discourages both work and saving, and ultimately traps recipients in poverty. By contrast, basic income is granted as a fundamental social right available to all, thereby providing genuine freedom. Social assistance is typically provided on a household basis, which creates advantages for smaller households and thus encourages household separation and, in some cases, marriage avoidance. It can also result in unfair distribution among household members. Basic income, however, is paid to individuals, thereby eliminating these problems. Moreover, because existing social assistance benefits are reduced as additional income is earned, beneficiaries are incentivized to conceal income, seek work in the informal sector, or reduce their labor supply. Basic income avoids such distortions, thereby preserving economic efficiency.

There are three general conceptions of distributive justice: desert, need, and equality (Miller, 1992). The principle of desert indicates that people deserve rewards according to their contributions. The capitalist market economy is a system of mechanisms that rewards people based on their contributions to social output. However, it is impossible to accurately measure each person's contributions. As a result, social conflicts arise, accompanied by both excessive and inadequate compensation. Can we say that unpaid labor, such as housework or care work, has zero share of social contributions? Distributive justice: cannot be fulfilled by the principle of desert alone.

Social assistance is a system that provides aid to individuals on the margins of the capitalist market economy, such as the poor and disabled, who are unable to meet their basic needs through the principle of desert. The problem lies in the negative effects of means-testing to identify those in need. These effects include stigma, destruction of freedom and dignity, disincentives to work, poverty traps, low participation rates, and administrative costs. It produces two types of errors: the inclusion of the undeserving poor and the exclusion of the deserving poor. Therefore, means-tested social assistance should be a last resort for correcting market distribution. Once we recognize the fundamental impossibility of accurately measuring individual contributions and needs, we can accept that a portion of social production should be distributed equally to all.

Next, basic income is emerging as an alternative income security system as social insurance becomes increasingly inadequate in the changing labor market of the twenty-first century. Social insurance has traditionally been based on the employment relationship, with premiums shared by workers and employers, and designed to protect male breadwinners in the event of income loss due to illness, work injury, unemployment, or old age. However, with the decline of the male breadwinner model based on the standard employment relationship of industrial capitalism and the rise of precarious workforces, social insurance has created increasingly large blind spots. As a result, those most in need of protection, such as precariously employed workers and micro-entrepreneurs, are left unprotected or only weakly protected. A universal basic income could be considered a primary social insurance that provides a minimum level of protection even to those who are excluded from the protection of existing social insurance programs.

Imagine, as in John Rawls' thought experiment, that we choose the principle of distribution under a veil of ignorance, where we have no idea what physical condition or social position we will occupy from our original position (Rawls, 1971). It is conceivable that individuals who do not know whether they will become disabled or incapacitated would choose to distribute at least some portion of social output as a basic income based on the principle of equality, rather than basing all distribution on the principle of desert or contributions alone (capitalism) or on the principles of desert and need alone (welfare capitalism). If those individuals in the original position are risk-averse, they will prefer a high level of basic income that requires equal distribution of a significant portion of national income, but they will not choose a level that is too high, as that could hinder economic growth and cause the size of basic income to shrink over time. Van Parijs argues that implementing the highest sustainable level of basic income is consistent with the Rawlsian "difference principle," which aims to maximize the benefits to the least advantaged (van Parijs, 1995).

Furthermore, a basic income could help overcome the demographic crisis of population decline and rural extinction caused by extremely low birth rates and urban migration. South Korea's total fertility rate fell to 0.72 in 2023, the lowest in the OECD and only about one-third of the 2.1 needed to reproduce the population. The urbanization of the population has pushed rural areas to the brink of extinction due to depopulation. Unlike social assistance, which incentivizes the breakup of households, basic income promotes household formation and can contribute to higher marriage and fertility rates by providing income security for young people. By providing higher utility to residents of areas with relatively low living costs, such as housing, basic income can ease urbanization and prevent the extinction of rural municipalities. If the national basic income is delayed or started at a very low level, this effect can be strengthened by providing a rural basic income to rural residents (You & Choi, 2022).

## 1.2 Negative Income Tax for Efficient Poverty Alleviation

A negative income tax (NIT) refers to the payment of a negative tax, or cash benefit, by the state to low-income earners below a certain income threshold. In other words, the government imposes a positive tax on those earning above the threshold but pays a negative tax to those below the threshold, rather than simply exempting them from paying taxes. It is like a refundable tax credit: the lower the market income, the larger the negative tax or cash benefit.

The NIT has gained traction beyond the ideological spectrum on the left and right since neoliberal economist Milton Friedman proposed it as an efficient alternative to existing welfare programs for poverty alleviation in his 1962 book, *Capitalism and Freedom*. Friedman (1962, 1966) emphasized that an NIT could eliminate the inefficiencies of the existing welfare state and reduce overly bloated welfare budgets. Many progressive economists also advocated for an NIT, including James Tobin, who emphasized that it could be a progressive alternative by eliminating not only the inefficiencies but also the large blind spots of existing social welfare (Tobin et al., 1967). In early 1968, 1,200 economists signed a statement calling for the adoption of an NIT. The Rev. Dr. Martin Luther King Jr. also called for a NIT, or a guaranteed minimum income, before his assassination. In 1969, Republican President Richard Nixon proposed an NIT-type Family Assistance Plan. Nixon's proposal passed the House of Representatives in 1970 but failed to cross the Senate threshold.

With respect to work incentives, Friedman and other economists have emphasized that NITs are less disincentivizing than traditional social assistance. This is because social assistance typically reduces benefits by a dollar for every dollar of additional earned income (i.e., a marginal tax rate of 100%), so there is no incentive to work at all, whereas an NIT only reduces benefits by a fraction of dollar (e.g., 50%) for every dollar of additional earned income, so there is an incentive to work. However, the working poor who were previously not on the welfare rolls would have less of an incentive to work under a NIT, as it would cut around 50% of their earned income. In microeconomic terms, this is equivalent to a reduction in wages of around 50%, resulting in a 'substitution effect' as the utility of labor relative to leisure decreases. In addition, as household income increases, labor participation may decrease due to an 'income effect' (Kang, 2019a).

The U.S. government conducted large-scale policy experiments on NITs starting in 1968, and neighboring Canada also experimented with NITs. The results of these randomized controlled experiments found significant work disincentive effects. The primary earner, the breadwinner of the family, reduced their working hours by 0.5–9%, the secondary earner by 0–27%, and single mothers by 15–30%. These effects on labor supply could be perceived as either small or large. While the ultimate labor market effect will be determined by supply and demand response, the experiments showed only supply response. The demand response could mitigate the negative labor supply effect. The substantial reduction of work hours by the secondary earners could be interpreted as liberating them to care for their children. However, politicians and the media interpreted the results negatively. In addition, the finding of increased divorce among the NIT recipients further discredited the policy (Widerquist, 2005).

Ultimately, the U.S. Congress rejected Nixon's Family Assistance Plan, a negative income tax policy, but instead introduced a variant of a negative income tax, the earned income tax credit (EITC), in 1975. The EITC is a type of negative income tax in that it provides subsidies to low-income workers. However, unlike the negative income tax, under the EITC, benefits are zero at zero earnings and increase as earnings increase, up to a certain point, to incentivize low-earning workers to work.

Although negative income tax has not been fully adopted in the United States or elsewhere, the study and discussion of negative income tax proposals in academia and politics has been influential in the introduction and spread of workfare taxes, as well as the reform of social security systems in many countries (Myles and Pierson, 1997).

Notably, the negative income tax debate has overlapped with the basic income debate, sparking discussions about the possibility of introducing a basic income in the form of a negative income tax, or a negative income tax in the form of a basic income. James Tobin proposed a negative income tax as a way to implement a universal basic income, but with additional taxation on all other income (Tobin et al., 1967). In the 1972 presidential election, Democratic candidate George McGovern proposed a negative income tax in the form of a basic income of $1,000 per year for all Americans, following James Tobin's recommendations. Milton Friedman also wrote that "a basic income, when combined with a positive income tax with no tax exemptions, is another way of introducing a negative income tax" (Suplicy and Friedman, 2000).

## 1.3 Similarities and Differences Between Basic Income and Negative Income Tax

Basic income is universal by definition. Along with unconditionality, universality is a key element in the definition of basic income. While negative income tax can be seen as a violation of the universality of basic income in that it distinguishes between those who receive benefits and those who pay taxes, it can also be seen as effectively the same as a combination of universal basic income and universal taxation.

Let us consider an example in which a basic income policy and a negative income tax policy produce the same redistributive outcome. Table 1.1 shows a hypothetical economy with 11 people. People have market incomes ranging from $0 to $100,000, with an average income of $50,000. This is the same as the case presented by Mankiw (2016).

First, let's look at the basic income policy that pays everyone an income of $10,000. The amount needed to pay 11 people is $110,000. This can be raised by taxing everyone's market income at a rate of 20%. People's disposable income is their market income plus the basic income minus the tax.

Next, let's look at a negative income tax with a threshold (breakeven) income of $50,000 and a payment of $10,000 minus 20% of market income for those below the threshold (guaranteed income = $10,000, clawback rate = 20%). Those above the threshold are taxed at a 20% rate on market income above the threshold. For example, Person 2, who has a market income of $20,000, would receive $10,000 - ($20,000 * 0.2) = $6,000, resulting in a disposable income of $20,000 + $6,000 = $26,000. This is the same result as if they received a basic income of $10,000 and paid

**Table 1.1** Basic Income and Negative Income Tax

| *Market State (Mean income = 50,000)* | | *Basic Income (Basic income = 10,000, Tax rate = 20%)* | | | *Negative Income Tax (Guaranteed income = 10,000, Break-even income = 50,000, Withdrawal rate = Tax rate = 20%)* | | |
|---|---|---|---|---|---|---|---|
| *People* | *Market income* | *Basic income* | *Tax* | *Disposable income* | *NIT payment* | *Tax* | *Disposable income* |
| Person 0 | 0 | 10,000 | 0 | 10,000 | 10,000 | | 10,000 |
| Person 1 | 10,000 | 10,000 | 2,000 | 18,000 | 8,000 | | 18,000 |
| Person 2 | 20,000 | 10,000 | 4,000 | 26,000 | 6,000 | | 26,000 |
| Person 3 | 30,000 | 10,000 | 6,000 | 34,000 | 4,000 | | 34,000 |
| Person 4 | 40,000 | 10,000 | 8,000 | 42,000 | 2,000 | | 42,000 |
| Person 5 | 50,000 | 10,000 | 10,000 | 50,000 | 0 | | 50,000 |
| Person 6 | 60,000 | 10,000 | 12,000 | 58,000 | | 2,000 | 58,000 |
| Person 7 | 70,000 | 10,000 | 14,000 | 66,000 | | 4,000 | 66,000 |
| Person 8 | 80,000 | 10,000 | 16,000 | 74,000 | | 6,000 | 74,000 |
| Person 9 | 90,000 | 10,000 | 18,000 | 82,000 | | 8,000 | 82,000 |
| Person 10 | 100,000 | 10,000 | 20,000 | 90,000 | | 10,000 | 90,000 |
| Total | 550,000 | 110,000 | 110,000 | 550,000 | 30,000 | 30,000 | 550,000 |

$4,000 in tax, which is 20% of their market income. Person 7, with a market income of $70,000, would pay $4,000 in tax, which is 20% of the $20,000 market income over the $50,000 threshold, resulting in a disposable income of $66,000. This is the same result as receiving a basic income of $10,000 and paying $14,000 in tax, or 20% of market income.

Under the two seemingly very different policies, everyone's disposable income is exactly the same. Gregory Mankiw notes that basic income and negative income tax have the same outcome. He points out that when analyzing a policy, both the money paid (taxes) and the money received (benefits) should be considered simultaneously, and that many academic papers and news articles draw incomplete or erroneous conclusions by considering taxes and benefits separately. A common misconception is that a basic income would have no redistributive effect because everyone would receive the same amount, and that a policy of differential payment through means testing, such as a negative income tax, would be more progressive (Mankiw, 2021). He also points out that a basic income is easier to implement administratively than a negative income tax, which requires an income test. In addition, unlike negative income tax, basic income has the advantage of not having a stigma effect because it does not distinguish between those who pay taxes and those who receive benefits.

However, there is a downside to basic income. In the example above, the gross cost of a negative income tax is $30,000, while that of a basic income is $110,000. The net cost is 0 for both policies, and the redistributive results are the same, but basic income has the disadvantage of appearing to be more costly. The rich pay much more in taxes than they receive in basic income, but those who do not understand this mechanism often question why the rich should be given basic income.

While basic income and negative income tax can be designed to have the same redistributive effect, as in the example above, they are often designed quite differently. In the example above, basic income is funded solely by income tax, and both basic income and negative income tax have a single tax rate of 20%. However, most negative income tax proposals have a relatively high guaranteed income and a high marginal tax rate (clawback rate) of around 50% for those receiving benefits. In contrast, while some proposals for a full basic income aim at a level sufficient to meet basic needs or to fully replace existing social assistance, many others advocate for a partial basic income set at a more modest level. Fundamentally, basic income does not necessarily imply covering all basic needs, but rather providing a foundational floor of income upon which other sources of earnings can be added.

Additionally, the breakeven income threshold is often set differently. In basic income, the threshold is usually the average income or higher, while in negative income tax, the threshold is typically the median income or lower. Furthermore, basic income is paid to individuals, whereas many proposals for negative income tax are structured on a household basis. Basic income can also be based on sources other than income tax, such as in Alaska, where a fraction of the fund generated from oil revenue is distributed to all residents at a rate of 1/n.

These differences in the design of basic income and negative income tax stem from the distinct backgrounds and primary objectives of the two policies. Basic income is founded on the principle of equal rights to the common wealth shared by all (Ranalli, 2021) and seeks to enhance the real freedom of every individual (Van Parijs, 1995); therefore, it is in principle oriented toward individual-based payments. In contrast, negative income tax is generally household-based, as its primary aim is the efficient alleviation of poverty. This reflects the view that it would be unfair to make payments on an individual basis when, for example, the children or spouses of wealthy individuals lack personal income but are not genuinely in need. However, in the case of basic income, the taxes paid by a wealthy household head would exceed the basic income received by the spouse and children, so that in effect the outcome would be equivalent to that of a household-based negative income tax.

The differences in benefit levels and breakeven income also stem from the different main purposes of promoting real freedom versus alleviating poverty. Basic Income is based on the principle of distributing a portion of national income equally to everyone, considering it as the profit of the common wealth. A simple way to achieve this is through a basic income system funded by a flat rate income tax. If the basic income is fully financed by a single flat rate income tax, the threshold income would be the average income. The levels of benefits and tax rates would be determined by the percentage of national income distributed equally. If a progressive income tax funds the basic income, even individuals with above-average incomes can benefit.

In a negative income tax that applies the same tax rate to those below and above the threshold income, the average income becomes the threshold income, too. If such a negative income tax is implemented on an individual basis, the result is the same as a basic income with a flat tax. In this

**Table 1.2** General Design Differences Between UBI and NIT

| | Universal Basic Income | Negative Income Tax |
|---|---|---|
| **Unit of Payment** | Individual | Individual or Household |
| **Level of Guarantee** | Relatively Low | Relatively High |
| **Tax Rate (Clawback Rate)** | Relatively Low | Relatively High |
| **Threshold (Break-even Point)** | (Above) Average Income | (Below) Median Income |

case, both the amount of basic income and the amount of guaranteed negative income tax payment are the same. Individuals with below-average incomes become net beneficiaries, while those with above-average incomes become net contributors. Average income is generally higher than median income, so more than half of the population would be net beneficiaries.

However, negative income tax proposals often take a household-level payment and set both the guaranteed income level and the clawback rate high, with the threshold at or below the median income. The tax rate on income above the threshold is typically lower than the clawback rate on the negative income tax payment. The key design differences can be summarized as Table 1.2.

A basic income may be favorable if the goal is to promote real freedom and reduce inequality, while a negative income tax may be favorable if the goal is to reduce poverty. It is important to note, however, that a negative income tax with an excessively high clawback rate may be effective in reducing poverty in the short run, but not necessarily in the long run, as it reduces incentives to work and encourages individuals to underreport income. A household-based negative income tax may also encourage household disintegration because splitting a household could result in a higher amount of negative income tax payment.

## 1.4 Negative Income Tax-Type Basic Income

There have been proposals to implement basic income as a negative income tax and proposals to implement negative income tax as a basic income. Proposals to implement basic income as a negative income tax are based on the assumption that framing it this way may be easier to garner majority support for the introduction of the policy. While UBI may have advantages in maintaining popular support in the long run because it makes a majority of the population net beneficiaries, a UBI scheme requires a much larger total budget than an NIT scheme with the same redistributive effects, even when both schemes are fiscally neutral or require the same amount of net cost. Many people may think it too costly a policy and a waste of resources to distribute basic income to the rich. On the other hand, proposals to implement the negative income tax as a basic income method are based on administrative expediency. It may be administratively cumbersome and costly to conduct frequent income tests to determine eligible recipients and the amounts of the NIT benefit payment. It is administratively easier to use the basic income method by giving everyone a certain amount of money without income tests and then collecting a certain rate of tax on all income.

Professor Mankiw asked Harvard undergraduates about their preferences for a negative income tax plan, which would provide more support for low-income people and tax income above a certain threshold, versus a basic income plan, which would provide a certain amount of income for everyone, regardless of income level, but tax all income. Mankiw found that 90% of students chose the negative income tax option, even though the two schemes had the same redistributive effect (Mankiw, 2021). This example suggests that, in terms of political feasibility, it may be better to frame it as a negative income tax to gain support from the general public.

The debate over basic income in Korea's 2022 presidential election was dominated by opposition rooted in traditional notions of need-based social welfare as well as fears that a large tax increase would be necessary to fund the program. The argument that basic income is a waste of precious resources on people who do not need help was quite persuasive. Many people incorrectly believed that basic income would not be redistributive because it provides the same amount of money to everyone, regardless of their income level. Therefore, to increase the political feasibility of implementing a basic income, it may be a helpful strategy to propose a negative income tax that achieves the same redistributive effect as the desired basic income.

There are important issues to consider when designing an NIT-type basic income. While negative income tax is often designed at the household level, it should be designed at the individual level, consistent with the principles of basic income. Providing a basic income or negative income tax on an individual level would enhance individual freedom and encourage household formation rather than dissolution. However, from a poverty reduction perspective, a household-level negative income tax may be more efficient, at least in the short term (not considering the long-term effects of household dissolution or disincentives to work). People familiar with traditional needs-based welfare principles may prefer a household-level negative income tax over an individual-level one. Therefore, it is important to clarify the benefits of individual-level income security policies in addressing the demographic crisis of low birth rates and increasing freedom and autonomy.

Although NIT is often considered to require frequent income tests and is therefore administratively costly, this problem can be avoided by administering it as a refundable tax credit. Taxpayers can claim NIT-type basic income as a refundable tax credit in their annual tax return, including the benefits for their dependents. Everyone who is not claimed as a dependent should file a tax return to receive NIT-type basic income, even if their income is minimal or zero. This method has the advantage of making the total budget much smaller than an equivalent UBI.

Fundamentally, we need to make it clear that everyone has the right to a basic income of the NIT type, but this right is based on the obligation to pay taxes. Free-riding can be prevented by ensuring that all individuals pay taxes on their income and wealth. In years when individuals earn no or little income, they will receive a NIT-type basic income payment, but in other years when they earn a high income, they will pay a positive tax. Most people will become net beneficiaries at times and net contributors at other times, such as during childhood, old age, and sickness.

## 1.5 Effective Tax Rate, Participation Tax Rate, and Effective Marginal Tax Rate

The most important decisions to make when designing a NIT-type basic income are the amount of the 'basic guaranteed income' (amount of benefit for those with no market income), the threshold income or break-even point, and the clawback rate below the threshold and the tax rate above the threshold. These variables are interrelated, and there are trade-offs among them.

To eliminate relative poverty, it would be desirable to set the basic guaranteed income at or above the relative poverty line, or 50% of median income. However, to avoid creating a fiscal deficit, the higher the level of basic guaranteed income, the higher the tax rates should be, both below and above the threshold.

For example, if the threshold income is set at the average income, a 20% flat tax rate is required to provide a basic guaranteed income of 20% of the average income, and a 30% flat tax rate is required to provide a basic guaranteed income of 30% of the average income. If the threshold income is set at or below the median income, a higher clawback rate is required to provide the same level of basic guaranteed income.

However, it is important to note that we are not designing a new policy in a vacuum. We need to decide whether to maintain the existing income tax and social insurance contribution system, adding a NIT-type basic income payment below the threshold and an additional income tax above the threshold, or to completely overhaul the income tax system.

We also need to decide whether to maintain the existing social security benefits or fully or partially replace them. It is important to consider how the actual benefits and burdens change depending on the relationship with the existing system. Of particular importance are the effective tax rate, participation tax rate, and effective marginal tax rate.

The effective tax rate is distinguished from the nominal tax rate and takes into account not only the positive taxes such as income tax and social security contributions but also the negative taxes such as public transfers. If the amount of money that you receive in public transfers is greater than the amount of money that you pay in taxes and social security contributions, your effective tax rate is negative.

A negative income tax aims to alleviate poverty by making the effective tax rate for low-income earners negative so that their disposable income (market income + public transfers - taxes and social security contributions) is greater than their market income. A negative effective tax rate in the lower income brackets and a positive effective tax rate in the higher income brackets mean a progressive income redistribution. The progressivity of the effective tax rate is important from an income redistribution perspective. The more progressive the effective tax rate, the greater the redistributive effect.

A flat-tax-based NIT-type basic income has a nominal tax rate that is proportional but an effective tax rate that is progressive. When income approaches zero, the effective tax rate is highly negative; as income approaches the break-even level, the effective tax rate converges toward zero. Once income exceeds the break-even level, the effective tax rate turns positive and gradually increases as income rises and eventually converges to the nominal flat tax rate.

The participation tax rate is the proportion of earned income that goes to taxes, social security contributions, and reductions in public transfers when someone not participating in the labor market starts participating. The higher the participation tax rate, the lower the incentive to participate in the labor market. People may choose to avoid working completely or work in the informal sector to avoid income exposure.

The effective marginal tax rate is the ratio of the increase in taxes and social insurance contributions and reduced public transfers to a small increase in income due to an increase in hours worked or a rise in wages. The higher the effective marginal tax rate, the weaker the incentive to work more or increase one's earned income. When participation tax rates and effective marginal tax rates are high, they not only undermine economic efficiency by discouraging labor supply but can also be seen as restricting real freedom by limiting people's ability to escape poverty through work.

In analyzing the shortcomings of the existing income security system and designing alternative policies, we will focus on the effective tax rate, the participation tax rate, and the effective marginal tax rate. These rates will be examined under both the current system and our proposed policies, disaggregated by income group, household type, and social assistance recipient status. In designing an NIT-type basic income, we aim to strengthen the overall progressivity of the effective tax rate while at the same time lowering the excessively high participation tax rates and effective marginal tax rates imposed on social assistance recipients.

We first concluded that it is neither realistic nor desirable to replace the entire existing income tax system, social assistance, and income-security social insurance (such as employment insurance and public pensions) with an NIT-type basic income. Employment insurance and public pensions provide more than a minimum level of benefits; they also serve to maintain an adequate level of income to smooth consumption during periods of unemployment or retirement. We believe it is preferable to address coverage gaps rather than replacing these programs with an NIT-type basic income.

Next, we examined the option of fully replacing the current income tax system and social assistance with an NIT-type basic income and found it to be unrealistic. Full replacement of existing social assistance in Korea would require a basic guaranteed income of around 40% of average personal income and a tax rate of around 40%; adding roughly 20% in social insurance contributions would bring both the participation tax rate and the effective marginal tax rate to about 60%—assuming that all other public goods and administrative expenditures were financed entirely from sources other than income tax. We believe that the labor-supply-reducing effects of 60% participation and effective marginal tax rates combined with the basic guaranteed income cannot be ignored.

Consequently, we propose maintaining the existing income tax system and social insurance contributions while replacing only part of social assistance with an NIT-type basic income. For advocates of a full basic income, our proposal may seem too modest, but we regard it as a way to enhance real freedom: by strengthening the progressivity of the effective tax rate without letting participation and effective marginal tax rates rise excessively, thereby minimizing disincentives to work, and by reducing reliance on means-tested social assistance.

The definition of income, along with the frequency of income calculations and payments, should also be important considerations when designing a policy. Generally, the concept of income used in tax administration is quite narrow. When introducing an NIT-type basic income, a more comprehensive definition of income should be applied. It is necessary to use a comprehensive concept of income that includes non-taxable income, capital gains, and imputed rents, but there are challenges in implementing it administratively. The frequency of income calculations and payments, whether monthly or annually, can also significantly impact policy effects and administrative burdens.

## 1.6 Reforming Regressive Tax Expenditures Into Universal Refundable Tax Credits

By converting means-tested social assistance programs into an NIT-type basic income, it is possible to reduce excessively high participation tax rates and effective marginal tax rates. In addition, rather than requiring complex paperwork and imposing stigma tied to means testing, benefits could be paid through a simple procedure at annual income tax filing as a refundable tax credit. Those whose income exceeds the threshold would simply settle the tax due on their excess income. Income would be assessed on an annual basis, but recipients could choose to receive benefits either as a lump sum or monthly or quarterly. However, for individuals whose income suddenly drops compared to the previous year, they should be allowed to report the change on a semiannual or quarterly basis and apply for the NIT-type basic income benefit as a refundable tax credit.

Refundable tax credits also offer an effective way to reform regressive income deductions that exist in many countries. Moreover, by universalizing refundable tax credits, benefits can be extended to people who have been excluded under existing deduction schemes.

Tax relief generally takes two forms: income deductions and tax credits. In a progressive income tax system, income deductions are regressive. Even for the same amount of deduction, high-income taxpayers in higher tax brackets receive a greater tax reduction than low-income taxpayers in lower tax brackets.

In contrast, an equal amount of tax credit provides the same reduction in tax liability for all taxpayers. However, when the tax due is smaller than the tax credit amount, the taxpayer can only benefit up to the tax due. By comparison, an equal amount of refundable tax credit reduces tax liability even when no tax is owed, or when the tax credit exceeds the tax due, thus generating a negative tax liability—in other words, a refund. If refundable tax credits were extended universally, they would effectively function as a negative income tax-type basic income.

Tax benefits such as income deductions or tax credits are called "tax expenditures" as opposed to direct cash welfare spending. Tax expenditures are a hidden form of welfare and, unlike cash transfers, often have regressive characteristics (Howard, 1997). Tax expenditures are harder for the general public to understand and typically attract less scrutiny than direct spending. Therefore, we must recognize that reforming regressive tax expenditures is at least as important as reforming cash assistance programs. In particular, converting tax deductions into refundable tax credits and expanding their coverage as broadly as possible can be a useful strategy for introducing basic income. For example, the basic personal deduction available to taxpayers and their dependents could be converted into a universal refundable tax credit for everyone. This would, in effect, amount to a universal basic income.

## 1.7 Introducing a Universal Earned Income Tax Credit as Participation Income

In existing social assistance programs, the participation tax rate and effective marginal tax rate for low-income workers can reach or even exceed 100%. As earned income increases, not only do social assistance benefits decrease or eligibility for benefits disappear, but recipients also lose other benefits provided by the public and private sectors. Although the tax rate (clawback rate) in negative income tax is set lower than in traditional social assistance programs, a fairly high rate is still necessary if the guaranteed income level is set high. Combined with existing income tax and social security contributions, this can result in very high effective marginal tax rates and participation tax rates.

In contrast, the earned income tax credit (EITC) is a refundable tax credit that aims to incentivize work by providing low-income earners with a negative or zero marginal tax rate. Under the negative income tax, the smaller the market earnings, the larger the benefit, whereas under an EITC system, the benefit is zero at zero earnings and increases as earnings rise up to a certain level. This is called the phase-in range (marginal tax rate < 0). After that, the benefit remains constant until a certain income level, which is called the plateau range (marginal tax rate = 0). Beyond that point, the benefit decreases as earned income increases, and individuals above a certain income level lose eligibility for the EITC benefit. This is called the phase-out range (marginal tax rate > 0).

When the EITC was first introduced in the United States, it started at a very low level. However, the EITC has expanded over the years, and since 1996, it has become the largest social assistance program in the United States. The EITC program has also spread to countries such as Canada, the United Kingdom, and Sweden, as well as Korea, where the EITC system was introduced in 2008 and significantly expanded during the COVID-19 pandemic. The rapid expansion and development of in-work subsidy systems in various countries over the past decades can be attributed to their ability to gain widespread political support due to their effects of promoting labor incentives and alleviating poverty.

However, the EITC system is criticized for its complex structure, which consists of phase-in, plateau, and phase-out ranges, making it difficult for people to understand. It is also operated on a household basis, potentially leading to incentives for household dissolution. In Korea, where income tax is levied on an individual basis while the EITC is executed on a household basis, the impact of the EITC on participation tax rates and effective marginal tax rates varies depending on household income and assets as well as household composition. The EITC is more favorable to households with fewer members, effectively creating a marriage penalty. In addition, the EITC increases the marginal tax rate in the phase-out region, undermining work incentives.

Recently, there have been proposals in the United States to eliminate the phase-out of the EITC and reform it into a universal EITC system operated on an individual basis (Burman, 2020; Leff, 2020). The proposal aims to make the in-work subsidy system similar to a basic income. It is not truly universal because it only covers those in paid work, but it is universal in the sense that it does not exclude anyone with earned income. Under this system, a fixed proportion of earned income is paid as a benefit up to a certain threshold, after which the benefit remains constant. In other words, it consists only of phase-in and plateau ranges, with no phase-out range.

While the idea of a universal EITC may be controversial, we believe it is desirable to introduce a universal EITC by transforming the regressive tax breaks for employment income in Korea. The 'employment income deduction'(근로소득공제) and 'employment income tax credit'(근로소득세액공제) provide generous tax breaks for workers in Korea. The total amount of tax breaks due to these deductions and credits are many times the total amount of the Korean-style EITC, known as the "Work Incentive Payment" (WIP, 근로장려금). The amount of tax breaks for regular workers continuously increases as earnings rise to a very high level. Most non-regular workers and the self-employed are not covered by these tax breaks, and only a minority receive Work Incentive Payments. The tax benefits of the employment income deduction and the employment income tax credit, as well as the current WIP (Korean-style EITC), can be integrated and converted into a refundable tax credit that covers all workers, including the self-employed, with a cap set at a level lower than the current tax benefits for high-income earners. We could call this "universal EITC," distinct from the current Korean-style EITC.

This reform will have the following advantages. First, it will transform the regressive 'tax expenditures' for mostly regular workers into a progressive system for all working individuals. This reform will significantly improve the progressivity of the income tax system in Korea. Secondly, it will contribute to lowering the participation tax rates and effective marginal tax rates for low-income earners. The universal EITC has only a phase-in range (marginal tax rate < 0) and a plateau range (marginal tax rate = 0), which reduces the effective tax rate, as well as the participation tax rate and effective marginal tax rate, for low-income workers.

Thirdly, it will enable many low-income workers to enroll in social insurance programs such as employment insurance and the National Pension. Currently, many low-income and precarious workers fall into the blind spots of social insurance programs. The refundable tax credit could be used by low-income earners to pay the social insurance premiums. Fourthly, capital income and capital gains are often exempted from taxation or lightly taxed compared to earned income. The universal EITC in the form of refundable tax credit will help correct the unfair disadvantage of earned income compared to capital income and capital gains in taxation. It will promote productive activities rather than rent-seeking activities. Fifth, whereas the current Korean EITC system is difficult to understand and suffers from a low take-up rate—thereby limiting its effectiveness in encouraging work—a universal EITC would be simple for everyone to grasp and could be expected to generate a substantially stronger incentive to work.

All these advantages may not apply to other countries, but they will be significant in Korea. In fact, we considered reforming the employment income deductions and employment income tax credits into a NIT-type basic income in the form of a universal refundable tax credit(Kang, 2019a; You, 2018). However, we found significant resistance from workers to the idea of extending the coverage of tax benefits to the non-working population. We also realized various advantages of reforming them into a universal EITC as mentioned above.

Universal EITC can be viewed as a form of participation income. Participation income was first proposed by Anthony Atkinson (1996). Unlike basic income, participation income is given to working-age adults on the condition of 'participation'. 'Participation' refers to a broad definition of social contribution, including paid work, self-employment, caregiving, certified volunteer activities, as well as education, training, and job-seeking activities. Illness or disability can be recognized as an exception.

Atkinson proposed participation income in response to the criticism against unconditional basic income that it allows free riding. The main criticism against participation income was the administrative difficulty in determining eligibility for participation (De Wispelaere and Stirton, 2007). In response to the criticism regarding administrative difficulty, Heikki Hiilamo (2022) proposed local-level administration and active promotion of various opportunities for participation, such as local community development projects, ecological care services, training opportunities, and other activities.

While universal EITC discussed above covers only those in paid work, it could be designed to support not only paid work but also socially meaningful unpaid work at the local level, as Hiilamo (2022) suggested. This program can address the concern that basic income may encourage individuals to free ride without contributing to society.

## 1.8 Common Wealth Dividend Basic Income

Basic income can be seen as a way of distributing a portion of the national income derived from the common wealth, which refers to the collective wealth of a society in a broad sense. We could also promote the concept of a common wealth dividend in a narrower sense. It may be easier to gain public agreement on the idea that natural resources and the environment, such as sunshine, wind, the ozone layer, and land, should be considered common wealth than on the broader concept of common wealth.

Basic income can be a valuable tool for equitably distributing profits generated from natural resources and ensuring sustainable preservation of the environment. The value of land is influenced more by its location than by the development efforts of private owners. Therefore, it would be just to allocate a significant portion of land profits to all individuals as a land dividend basic income, funded by a tax on land value. Implementing a land value tax would also encourage efficient utilization of land and discourage speculation in real estate.

Carbon tax is considered the most effective and efficient tool to achieve carbon neutrality and preserve the ozone layer in response to the climate crisis. If a carbon tax is introduced, however, the burden on households increases due to a rise in energy prices, which often creates public resistance. A carbon dividend basic income policy that distributes the carbon tax revenue equally among citizens can create a majority of net beneficiaries and secure political support (Economists' statement, 2019). While a land dividend basic income can promote economic efficiency as well as fairness, a carbon dividend basic income can enhance ecological sustainability in a fair and efficient way.

We could also establish a common wealth fund by reclaiming development gains from the state's land development and social overhead capital investment, as well as profits from state-invested and R&D-supported companies, including renewable energy companies. We could distribute a portion of the fund's profits to all citizens, similar to how the Alaska Permanent Fund operates. Basic income financed by land value tax, carbon tax, and the common wealth fund can be referred to as a 'common wealth dividend basic income' to differentiate it from a negative income tax-type basic income. The proposal to transform the basic deduction in income taxation into a universal refundable tax credit can be regarded as a broad form of a Common Wealth Dividend basic income.

## 1.9 Our Proposal

We propose a new system of income security that combines common wealth dividend basic income, NIT-type basic income, and universal EITC, to pursue equality, freedom, and sustainable efficiency. Every citizen has both the duty to pay taxes and the right to receive a basic income, which is to be designed and operated on a fiscally neutral basis.

Our proposal does not provide a high level of basic income or guaranteed income on a household basis to achieve short-term poverty reduction, imposing high participation and effective marginal tax rates. This is because high tax rates can restrict the real freedom of recipients and increase the risk of trapping them in poverty by diminishing their motivation to work. To promote the real freedom of individuals, we adhere to the principle of providing basic income on an individual, rather than a household, basis.

Under this principle, the level of the basic guaranteed income—the sum of the common wealth basic income and the NIT-type basic income —is set so that participation tax rates and effective marginal tax rates do not become excessively high. This does not amount to a "full basic income" that would cover basic needs and completely replace existing social assistance. Rather, it takes the form of a "partial basic income" at a meaningful level, replacing a substantial portion of existing social assistance, expanding real freedom, and enhancing equality. In addition, the universal EITC reforms the regressive earned income deduction and supports social insurance contributions for low-income workers. In doing so, the basic-income-style income security system becomes a central pillar of social protection, closing gaps in social insurance while reducing reliance on means-tested social assistance.

**Basic principles:**

1. Eligibility for basic income is a right for all citizens, based on the obligation to pay taxes.
2. The introduction of a basic income system is designed to be fiscally neutral. It will not generate fiscal deficits.

3. Two types of basic income will be introduced: a common wealth dividend-type and an NIT-type. In addition, a universal EITC will be introduced for all working people.
4. The level of the basic guaranteed income constitutes a meaningful partial basic income. Considering the severity of low fertility, population aging, and elderly poverty, the income provided for children and the elderly is set at a level approaching that of a full basic income.
5. Social assistance based on means testing should be replaced as much as possible by basic income, and social assistance should function as a last-resort safety net.
6. Basic income does not replace earnings-related social insurance programs, but is limited to guaranteeing a minimum income floor for all. Contribution-based social insurance, such as public pensions and unemployment insurance, should automatically enroll all adults to eliminate blind spots, and a universal EITC should help low-income workers to cover social insurance contributions.

**A package of two basic income and a participation income programs:**

1. **Common wealth dividend basic income:**
   a. Introduce a land value tax to replace the existing comprehensive real estate tax, and implement land dividend basic income with the increased tax revenue.
   b. To achieve carbon neutrality in response to the climate crisis, establish a carbon tax and implement carbon dividend basic income using the carbon tax revenue.
   c. Form a 'common wealth fund' with the profits from land development and social overhead capital investment by the government, and R&D-supported companies, and distribute the fund's profits equally to the entire population.
   d. The amount of common wealth dividends basic income, which combines land dividend, carbon dividend, and dividends from other sources of common wealth, will vary each year depending on fluctuating tax revenue and fund profits without specifying a fixed amount.
   e. Introduce a broad definition of common wealth dividend basic income by replacing the basic deduction in the existing income tax.

f. The combined common wealth dividend basic income could provide payments equivalent to approximately 3% of per capita GNI (around 1.65 million KRW in 2026).
g. The common wealth dividend basic income can be treated as taxable income, allowing lower-income individuals to effectively receive greater benefits than high-income individuals through the application of lower tax rates.

2. **Negative income tax-type basic income**:
   a. Provide a basic guaranteed income of 12% of per capita GNI (approximately 6.6 million KRW in 2026) for children and the elderly, and 6% of per capita GNI (about 3.3 million KRW in 2026) for adults.
   b. Set the threshold (break-even) income at roughly 60% of per capita GNI (around 33 million KRW in 2026), which corresponds approximately to the mean personal income.
   c. Apply clawback rates of 20% for children and the elderly, and 10% for adults.
   d. Including the common wealth dividend basic income, children and the elderly with no market income would be guaranteed a minimum income of 15% of per capita GNI (about 8.25 million KRW in 2026), and adults would be guaranteed 9% (about 4.95 million KRW in 2026).
   e. Impose a "basic income tax" of 10% on income exceeding the threshold income (around 33 million KRW in 2026) in addition to the existing income tax, while abolishing the current basic deductions and child tax credits. Alternatively, the basic income tax rate could be lowered to 3–5% with the revenue supplemented through higher VA and corporate tax rates and reductions in general expenditures.
   f. Fully replace child and parenting allowances as well as the basic pension, and partially replace cash benefits of the National Basic Livelihood Security System (livelihood and housing benefits) within the scope of the NIT-type basic income.

3. **Universal EITC:**
   a. Provide every working person, including the self-employed, with a payment equal to 12% (or 10%) of earned income up to 50% of per capita GNI, and, for earned income above that threshold, a

flat amount equal to 6% (or 5%) of per capita GNI (about KRW 3.3 million or 2.75 million in 2026).

b. Abolish the current employee income deduction, employee income tax credit, and the work incentive payment (the Korean EITC), and integrate them into a universal earned income tax credit—effectively a form of participation income.

## 1.10 Financial Feasibility Study and Estimation of Expected Effects: Methods and Data

Our proposal aims for fiscal neutrality, meaning that revenues and expenditures must be balanced. In other words, the total expenditure for the two types of basic income payments combined with the universal earned income tax credit must match the resources generated from additional tax revenues (such as the basic income tax), reductions in existing social security benefits, and other fiscal savings. Fiscal neutrality must also remain sustainable over the long term, taking into account the increase in benefits for the elderly due to population aging, and the system must be designed to minimize any reduction in productive activity caused by weakened work incentives.

The proposed common wealth basic income, NIT-type basic income, and universal EITC are all designed to be fiscally neutral or close to it. The common wealth basic income does not set its payment amount in advance but allocates funds annually on a per-capita (1/n) basis within available resources, ensuring no fiscal burden arises. The NIT-type basic income can also be operated on an almost fiscally neutral basis through additional revenues from the basic income tax, the abolition of personal and child tax credits under the income tax system, and the partial replacement of social assistance. The funding for the universal EITC can also be covered mostly by abolishing the existing employment income deduction and employment income tax credit, as well as by reallocating the current Work Incentive Payment (Korean-style EITC) budget.

We set the limit for additional resources that can be secured through reductions in general fiscal expenditures within 1% of gross national income (GNI), aiming to bring the net fiscal cost close to zero. This approach reflects the fact that, although Korea's public social security spending is still significantly below the OECD average, it is projected to surpass the average and reach one of the highest levels by around 2060, even if the current social security system is maintained without expansion due to rapid population aging. In particular, we will assess the medium- to long-term fiscal implications of our proposed basic income system, including replacing the current Basic Pension with an NIT-type basic income.

To assess the fiscal feasibility and income redistribution effects of these three policies, we will conduct a static micro-simulation analysis drawing on the most recent nationally representative microdata on income, taxation, and social security benefits. For our micro-simulation analysis, we primarily utilize data from the Survey of Household Finances and Living Conditions (SHFLC) conducted by Ministry of Data and Statistics. We will also use the OECD's tax-benefit model for Korea to evaluate the impact on labor supply and household formation incentives by analyzing changes in participation tax rates and effective marginal tax rates.

Our analysis indicates that the net fiscal cost of the proposed policies would remain well within 1% of GNI, both now and in the medium to long term. Nearly 70% of the population would be net beneficiaries, resulting in a substantial reduction in inequality and poverty. The negative impact on labor supply would be minimized, while the potential positive effects could be considerable. In addition, the marriage penalties and incentives for household dissolution embedded in the current social assistance system would largely be eliminated, while incentives for household formation — including marriage and childbearing — would be substantially strengthened.

## 1.11 The Plan of the Book

This book is composed of four chapters in Part I and six chapters in Part II. Part I includes the introduction (Chapter 1) and three chapters discussing the theoretical foundations of NIT-type basic income, Common Wealth Dividend basic income, and the universal earned income tax credit. Part II begins with a critical analysis of the Korean welfare state and includes chapters on our proposals, fiscal feasibility, expected effects, the political viability, and concludes with Chapter 10.

Chapter 2 discusses the need to replace existing social assistance as much as possible through the introduction of NIT-type basic income. It first demonstrates how the high participation tax rates and effective marginal tax rates generated by existing social assistance restrict individuals' real freedom and weaken labor incentives. While targeting support to the poor may appear efficient in the short term, it proves to be inefficient in the long term. The chapter shows that social assistance programs can be replaced by Pareto-superior basic income or NIT-type basic income, where no one loses while some individuals achieve better outcomes. It then highlights the advantages of a flat-rate (single-rate) basic income or NIT, arguing that they can enhance freedom and contribute to economic efficiency with relatively low participation and effective marginal tax rates. Regarding NIT-type basic income, a full basic income is practically unfeasible; instead, a meaningful partial basic income that partially replaces social assistance is recommended.

The chapter also compares household-based versus individual-based NIT or basic income. While household-based NIT may be more efficient for poverty reduction, it creates incentives for household dissolution, marriage avoidance, and lower fertility. Considering the need for differential payments by age, individual-based NIT-type basic income emerges as the preferable policy. The administrative challenges of implementing NIT-type basic income can be addressed through a refundable tax credit approach. Finally, important design and implementation issues are discussed, including the definition of income, the calculation and payment cycles of income and benefits, and the relationship with existing tax and transfer systems.

Chapter 3 discusses the necessity of Common Wealth Dividend basic income. After a theoretical review of the concepts of common wealth, natural commons, and rents from the commons, it argues that a substantial portion of the income generated from natural commons should be distributed equally to everyone based on equal rights. Universal basic income can be viewed, in a broad sense, as a form of common wealth dividend. Specific examples of natural commons dividends include land dividends based on landholding taxes, carbon dividends based on carbon tax revenues, and "sunshine dividends" based on profits from government investments in renewable energy, such as solar power. Initially, renewable energy dividends could serve as a main source for rural basic income and may also compensate for the gradual reduction in carbon dividends as carbon emissions decrease.

Chapter 4 examines refundable tax credits as a practical mechanism for implementing NIT-type basic income that partially replaces social assistance, as well as a means to introduce broad common wealth dividend basic income and reform regressive tax expenditures. First, it discusses how converting income tax basic exemptions into universal refundable tax credits in various countries can eliminate the regressivity that provides larger tax benefits to high-income earners and effectively create a nationwide basic income with a broad common wealth dividend character. Next, it explores reforming Korea's most significant regressive tax expenditure—earned income deductions—into a universal earned income tax credit combined with the current earned income tax credit and earned income subsidy, presenting the rationale for implementing a Universal EITC. The chapter introduces the concept of participation income and U.S. scholars' proposals for a universal EITC, and discusses the advantages of implementing a universal EITC as participation income in countries like Korea and Japan, where generous earned income deductions currently exist.

Chapter 5 critically analyzes the current Korean welfare state at a crossroads. It first examines the deepening income and wealth inequality, high elderly poverty, and the inability of existing social assistance and social insurance systems to effectively address these issues. It then diagnoses the excessively high participation and effective marginal tax rates created by the National Basic Livelihood Security System, income reversals between recipients and non-recipients, and the inadequacies of contribution-based social insurance programs such as employment insurance and public pensions in protecting or including vulnerable labor market participants. This analysis demonstrates that merely expanding or strengthening existing social assistance cannot be the solution, highlighting the need to gradually replace social assistance with NIT-type basic income. Furthermore, it notes that although Korea's income tax system is highly progressive, various regressive income deductions weaken this progressivity and reduce tax revenue, making a reform toward universal refundable tax credits necessary.

Chapter 6 presents our proposal, which includes Common Wealth Dividend basic income, NIT-type basic income, and universal EITC. It provides detailed discussions of each program's benefit levels, funding mechanisms, and net benefits. Key topics include guaranteed income levels, threshold income and clawback rates, the introduction of a basic income tax and its relationship with existing income taxes, and alternative funding options. The chapter also addresses practical issues, such as defining comprehensive income, measuring income, calculating benefits, payment cycles, and gradual implementation strategies.

Chapter 7 examines the fiscal and administrative feasibility of our proposed basic income system. Using household survey data and income tax administrative data, we conduct a microsimulation to analyze gross and net benefits, gross and net tax increase, and net fiscal cost. Although the gross benefits reach approximately 10% of the Gross National Income (GNI), the net benefits and the net tax increase can be reduced to about 4.3% and 4% of GNI, respectively, through the refundable tax credit mechanism.

Consequently, the net fiscal cost—the difference between the two—is only about 0.3% of GNI. Amidst the rapidly aging trend, we also examine the mid- to long-term fiscal outlook. The long-term fiscal impact of aging is projected to maintain the current level of net fiscal requirement, indicating fiscal sustainability. While the gross benefits will increase over time, both the net benefits and net tax increase amount will slightly decline over time due to increasing replacement of existing social assistance benefits.

Chapter 8 estimates expected effects of the basic income system, including the income redistribution effects and changes in the participation rates and effective marginal tax rates. Significant inequality and poverty reduction effects are evident, with income inequality expected to fall to the levels of Nordic welfare states. The study demonstrates that changes to the participation tax rate and effective marginal tax rate promote substantive freedom while also pursuing sustainable efficiency without negatively impacting labor supply and economic growth. In addition, the proposed system will eliminate the unfairness of income reversal, marriage penalty, and incentives for household dissolution, and instead provide incentives for household formation, thereby increasing marriage and birth rates.

Chapter 9 discusses the political feasibility of the proposed basic income policies. Drawing on theories such as the median voter theorem, elite domination, path dependence, loss aversion, and framing effects, the chapter examines the political context of basic income in Korea, changes in public opinion, and the positions of major political parties and politicians. In particular, we analyze the reasons for the decline in public support for basic income prior to the 2022 presidential election and discuss its implications. We also examine the political landscape under President Lee Jae-myung, known as a proponent of basic income, as well as his plan for experimental introduction and potential expansion of rural basic income. Finally, we review strategic considerations for achieving a more comprehensive implementation of basic income.

The concluding chapter will summarize the main findings of the study and suggest topics for further research. In particular, we discuss the significance of implementing basic income in the historical context of Korea's economic growth and welfare state development, considering rising inequality, sociopolitical conflicts, the climate crisis, and demographic challenges. We also discuss universal basic services and universal basic capital (or minimum inheritance) proposals in relation to universal basic income, and consider the extent to which our proposals and analyses may apply to other countries.

CHAPTER 2

# NIT-Type Basic Income

During the 2022 South Korean presidential election, the debate over basic income centered on allocative efficiency: whether a limited budget should be concentrated exclusively on the poor or distributed universally. Furthermore, the prospect of tax increases sparked significant anxiety not only among the wealthy but also within the middle class and the younger generation.

This chapter evaluates the effectiveness and efficiency of basic income in mitigating inequality and poverty. We highlight the inherent inadequacies of traditional welfare state models and demonstrate why an NIT-type basic income offers a superior alternative. Here, effectiveness refers to the degree of poverty and inequality reduction, while efficiency denotes long-term systemic sustainability rather than mere short-term target efficiency. We also examine the fiscal impact on the middle class to determine whether they emerge as net beneficiaries or net contributors under an NIT-type scheme.

The fact that income inequality in most OECD countries is higher today than in the 1980s underscores the declining effectiveness of the postwar welfare state. While William Beveridge envisioned social insurance as the cornerstone of the welfare state—providing benefits "as a right" without means-testing—the coverage of these programs has steadily shriveled. Consequently, the share of means-tested social assistance in total social spending has risen. In the UK, for instance, social insurance


J. S. You et al., *UBI from Idea to Reality*, Exploring the Basic Income Guarantee,
https://doi.org/10.1007/978-3-032-26200-4_2

plummeted from over 70% to less than 50% of social spending between the 1960s and 2010s, while social assistance doubled from 20% to 40%. Unemployment benefit coverage has similarly fallen below 50% in most countries (Atkinson, 2015), with even Sweden experiencing a drop from 70% to approximately 40% (You, 2018).

The erosion of social insurance coverage is particularly problematic because it leaves the most vulnerable unprotected. Deindustrialization and the Fourth Industrial Revolution have bifurcated the labor market, creating a dualism in social protection. Labor market insiders with stable, high-paying jobs remain shielded by traditional social insurance. In contrast, outsiders—freelancers, gig workers, and those in precarious employment—are often excluded despite facing greater risks. These "precarious workers" (or the precariat) are forced to rely on stigmatized, means-tested social assistance when they lose earned income (Lee, 2023; Standing, 2011).

We contend that social insurance for consumption smoothing should not be replaced by basic income but reformed to encompass all working people. Social insurance can help individuals maintain their previous level of income to a certain extent to smooth consumption over the life course. On the other hand, basic income serves as a universal floor—a "minimal level of universal social insurance" that rational actors would agree upon from the original position under a veil of ignorance (You, 2021).

The global trend toward increased means-testing to improve "target efficiency" has paradoxically contributed to rising inequality (Atkinson, 2015: 205–206). While intended to focus resources, these systems often fail to reach those in need due to low take-up rates. In every country, take-up rates of means-tested social assistance benefits are not very high (Bargain et al., 2012; Eurofound, 2015; Fuchs et al., 2020; Goedeme and Janssens, 2020). Japan's take-up rate for social assistance is estimated at only 20–30% of the eligible poor (Kobayashi, 2014), and France sees only a 50% take-up for its minimum income guarantee(France Strategie 2014: 85, Van Parjis and Vanderborght 2017: 254). Even In the U.S., while the EITC performs better (78%), programs like TANF (28%) and Housing Assistance (22%) suffer from chronic under-utilization (Macartney and Ghertner, 2021).

Beyond non-take-up, targeted programs create prohibitive Participation Tax Rates (PTR) and Effective Marginal Tax Rates (EMTR). While appearing efficient under tight budgets, these structures generate profound economic deadweight losses by discouraging labor supply. They also create income reversals between recipients and non-recipients or when recipients lose eligibility by earning more.

In the following sections, we first analyze why short-term target efficiency leads to long-term economic inefficiency and fiscal strain. We demonstrate the possibility of designing Pareto-superior NIT schemes that outperform current social assistance. We then discuss the merits of a "basic income with a flat tax" model, address the trade-offs in setting income floors, and explain our preference for individual-based (rather than household-based) NIT-type basic income, including the advantages of age-differentiated payments.

## 2.1 The Inefficiency of Social Assistance

Income security systems in the modern welfare state primarily consist of social assistance and social insurance.[1] Social assistance entails providing cash or in-kind benefits to individuals or households unable to maintain a minimum standard of living. In contrast, social insurance is a contributory system—funded by employees and employers—designed to mitigate social risks such as sickness, unemployment, childbirth, and retirement. Additionally, many states provide categorical allowances based on demographic criteria (e.g., child benefits or basic pensions), which can be conceptualized as categorical basic income.

Social assistance is broadly classified into two mechanisms: fixed-amount and supplemental (gap-filling). Fixed-amount assistance provides a predetermined benefit to those below a specific income threshold, regardless of their exact income level within that bracket. Supplemental assistance, on the other hand, provides the exact amount necessary to bridge the gap between an individual's current income and a defined minimum threshold. Both are typically administered on a household basis and are subject to rigorous means testing.

### *Fixed-amount Social Assistance*

Figure 2.1 illustrates the relationship between market income (X) and disposable income (Y) under a fixed-amount system that provides a benefit

[1] This section is largely based on Kang (2019a).

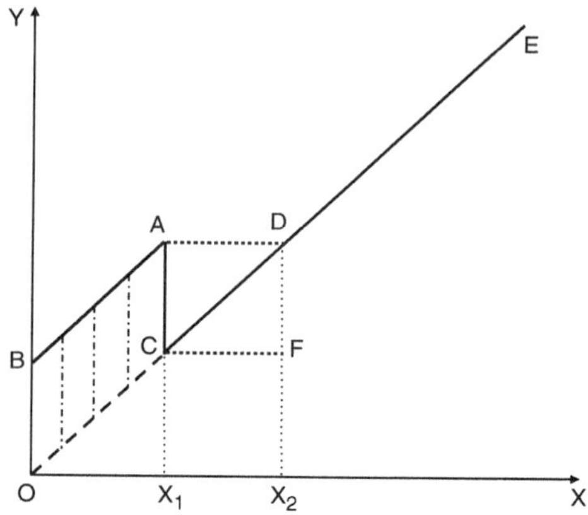


**Fig. 2.1** Fixed-Amount Social Assistance

(OB) to those whose market income is below the eligibility threshold ($X_1$). For analytical simplicity, we assume no income tax or social security contributions apply within this range.

Since all individuals with market income between 0 and $X_1$ receive the same benefit, the segments OB and AC are equal in length. While market income follows the line OCDE, disposable income is represented by the segments BA and CDE. A critical flaw emerges here: individuals with market income slightly above $X_1$ do not qualify for benefits, causing their disposable income to remain equal to their market income. Consequently, those earning between $X_1$ and $X_2$ end up with lower disposable income than those earning exactly $X_1$. In other words, the problem of income reversal occurs.

The primary issues with this selective support system are the "cliff effect" and the resulting unfairness of income reversal near the threshold $X_1$. As the benefit amount increases (the length of AC), the range of income reversal ($X_1X_2$) expands proportionally.

This problem is best understood through the Effective Marginal Tax Rate (EMTR), defined as:

$$\text{EMTR} = 1 - \frac{\text{increase in disposable income}}{\text{increase in market income}}$$

In Fig. 2.1, if an individual's market income increases slightly beyond $X_1$, their disposable income drops abruptly from $AX_1$ to $CX_1$. Since the change in disposable income is negative, the EMTR exceeds 100%. Within the range of $X_1$ to $X_2$, any additional effort to increase earned income results in a net loss of disposable income.

As shown in Fig. 2.2, rational actors within the $X_1$ to $X_2$ bracket are incentivized to reduce their labor supply to reach the $X_1$ threshold. When individuals choose to work less to qualify for benefits, GDP declines by the triangle CFD, while the social assistance budget swells by the rectangle ACFD. Furthermore, if one considers the secondary costs of working—such as commuting and opportunity costs—even those with market income significantly higher than $X_2$ may opt to reduce their earnings to $X_1$. In such cases, the deadweight loss to the economy and the fiscal burden on the state are even more substantial.

This highlights the inherent inefficiency of fixed-amount social assistance. While individuals who lower their income to qualify for benefits are acting rationally from a personal utility-maximizing perspective, their behavior manifests as opportunistic moral hazard from a societal standpoint. Ultimately, a focus on short-term target efficiency (concentrating resources on the poor) inadvertently fosters long-term economic inefficiency.

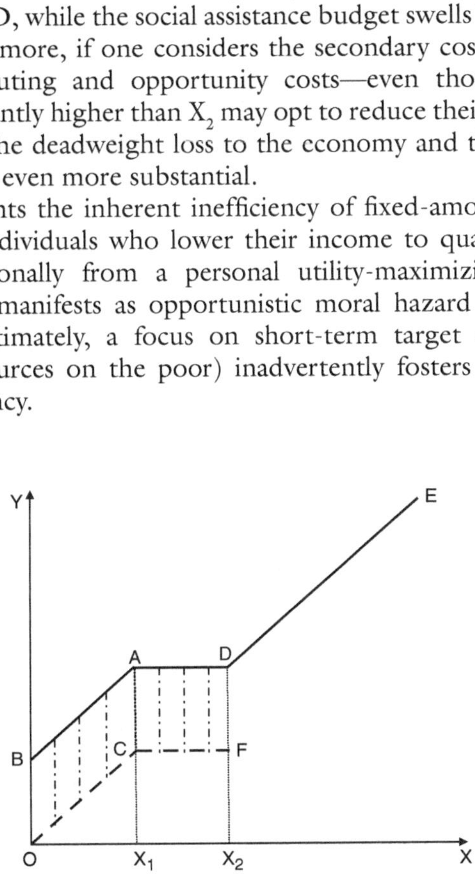


**Fig. 2.2** Results of Fixed-Amount Social Assistance Due to Moral Hazard

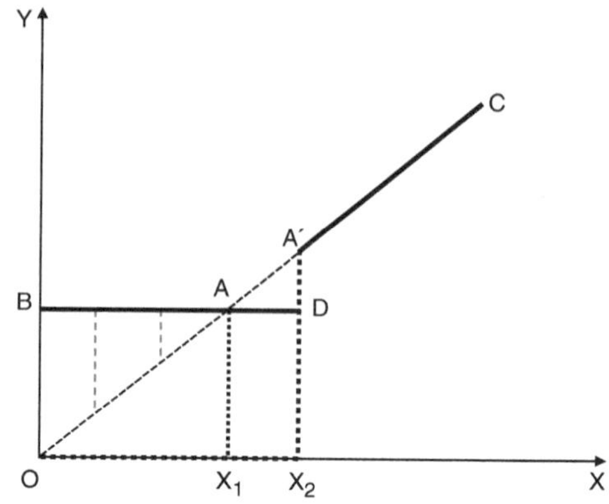


**Fig. 2.3** Results of Gap-Filling Social Assistance

### *Gap-Filling Social Assistance (Minimum Income Guarantee)*

To mitigate the "cliff effect" and the resulting income reversals inherent in fixed-amount systems, many welfare states employ a supplemental (gap-filling) approach. This mechanism ensures that if an individual's market income falls below a defined threshold, the state provides a benefit exactly equal to the difference. Theoretically, this eliminates the problem of disposable income reversal by creating a continuous income floor.

Figure 2.3 illustrates the relationship between market income (X) and disposable income (Y) under this supplemental model. The 45-degree line OAC represents market income, while the line BAC represents disposable income. $X_1$ serves as the guaranteed minimum income threshold.

**The Trap of 100% Effective Marginal Tax Rates**: Within the income range of 0 to $X_1$, the Effective Marginal Tax Rate (EMTR) is exactly 100%. For every additional unit of currency earned through labor, the benefit is reduced by an equivalent amount, leaving disposable income (OB) unchanged. When work-related expenses—such as commuting and childcare—are factored in, the EMTR often exceeds 100%. Furthermore, because an individual receives the same disposable income whether they earn $X_1$ or 0, the Participation Tax Rate (PTR) also reaches 100%. This creates a powerful structural incentive to abstain from the labor market entirely.

**The Reality of "Hidden" Income Reversals**: While theoretical models suggest that gap-filling systems eliminate income reversals, the reality is often different. Recipients of social assistance typically qualify for a "bundle" of auxiliary benefits (e.g., energy subsidies, housing support, or medical exemptions). Upon crossing the $X_1$ threshold, the abrupt loss of these secondary transfers—often referred to as "categorical leaching"—can cause the EMTR to spike well above 100%, reintroducing the very income reversals the system was designed to avoid.

**High Participation Tax Rates (PTR) and Labor Supply**: For households with market income slightly above $X_1$, the PTR remains prohibitively high. In Fig. 2.3, the PTR at market income $X_2$ can be expressed as:

$$\text{PTR} = 1 - \frac{\text{increase in disposable income when working}}{\text{market income when working}} = 1 - \frac{(X_2 - X_1)}{X_2} = \frac{X_1}{X_2}$$

If $X_2$ is 1.25 times $X_1$, the PTR is 80%. Once auxiliary benefit losses and opportunity costs are included, the PTR may exceed 100%, meaning a household is financially worse off by working than by remaining entirely dependent on the state. Unless a "high-quality" job offering income significantly above $X_1$ is available, rational actors will remain in the welfare trap.

**Economic Inefficiency and Deadweight Loss**: As depicted in Fig. 2.3, the labor supply distortions lead to significant economic losses. Individuals between 0 and $X_1$ are incentivized to reduce their labor to zero (point O), resulting in a deadweight loss represented by the triangle $OAX_1$. This shifts the fiscal burden from the anticipated triangle OBA to the larger rectangle $OBAX_1$. If the "trap" extends to individuals earning up to $X_2$, the deadweight loss expands to triangle $OA'X_2$, and the required budget swells to the rectangle $OBDX_2$.

**The Structural Failures of Social Assistance**: In conclusion, both fixed-amount and gap-filling social assistance create profound work disincentives and economic inefficiencies. They lead to a diminished labor supply, reduced GDP, and bloated fiscal requirements. Furthermore, they cause an unfair reversal of disposable income. This phenomenon can occur not only between recipients and non-recipients who slightly exceed the eligibility criteria but also between actual recipients and those who remain in a state of non-receipt despite being eligible. As previously noted, the take-up rate for means-tested selective social assistance is not high in most countries. Beyond the economic costs, these systems produce social stigma and restrict an individual's capacity to achieve real freedom through self-sufficiency. Consequently, many are trapped in a cycle of poverty, while others—driven by self-esteem—may refuse even necessary aid to avoid the psychological toll of means-tested assistance.

## 2.2 Basic Income and Negative Income Tax with Pareto Superiority[2]

As analyzed in the previous section, both fixed-amount and gap-filling social assistance systems inadvertently suppress labor supply, resulting in significant deadweight losses and a contraction of GDP. Moreover, these systems suffer from fiscal slippage, where the actual budget required far exceeds the initial design due to the endogenous increase in recipients. Is there a mechanism to eliminate this economic inefficiency?

We contend that it is possible to design an income security policy that is Pareto superior to traditional social assistance. A Pareto improvement occurs when the well-being of at least one individual is enhanced without diminishing the well-being of any other. The key to this transition lies in mitigating the prohibitively high Participation Tax Rates (PTR) and Effective Marginal Tax Rates (EMTR) inherent in selective welfare. This is achieved through a Negative Income Tax (NIT) or Basic Income (BI) approach, funded by recapturing the "lost" GDP from recovered deadweight losses and the avoided fiscal overruns of the current system.

### *Surpassing Fixed-Amount Social Assistance*

Figure 2.4 illustrates an NIT scheme that is Pareto superior to fixed-amount social assistance. Under the fixed-amount model, individuals earning between $X_1$ and $X_2$ are incentivized to reduce their labor, shifting the market income line to OCFDGE and the disposable income line to BADGE. This creates a deadweight loss (triangle CFD) and inflates the budget by the area of rectangle ACFD.

To prevent such inefficiencies, an NIT approach can be adopted. In this model, benefit payments do not cease at the threshold income of $X_1$ but continue up to the market income level of $X_3$, with the benefit amount gradually reduced at a fixed rate for income exceeding the threshold. The budget required to provide benefits to those with market incomes between $X_1$ and $X_3$ can be secured from the additional budget generated under the fixed-benefit social assistance scheme (rectangle ACFD), while also

[2] This section is largely based on Kang (2019a).

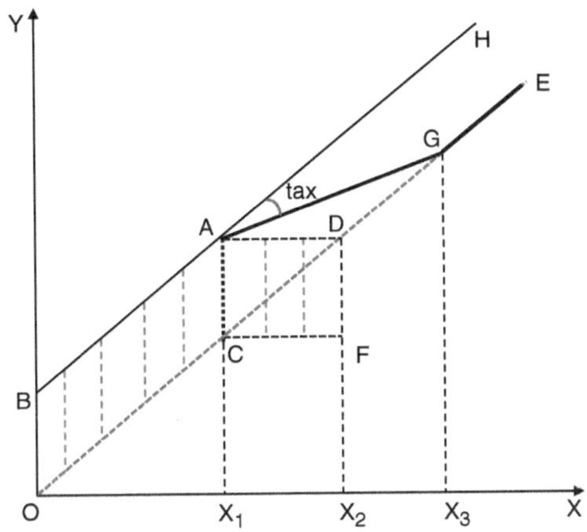


**Fig. 2.4** Pareto Superior Negative Income Tax and Basic Income Schemes Compared to Fixed-Amount Social Assistance

utilizing the recovery of the deadweight loss from triangle CFD. Adopting this method ensures that no individual's disposable income decreases. For individuals between $X_1$ and $X_3$, income increases as the disposable income line changes from ADG to AG.

Furthermore, Fig. 2.4 shows that the Pareto-superior NIT system can be replaced by a Basic Income (BI) system. This implies that everyone receives a basic income of OB, though income exceeding $X_1$ is taxed as shown in the figure. Specifically, a fixed tax rate can be applied to income between $X_1$ and $X_3$. For income exceeding $X_3$, a lump-sum tax equivalent to OB can be levied, effectively clawing back the entire basic income amount.

Finally, let us compare the effective tax rate and effective marginal tax rate of Pareto-superior NIT or BI with those of fixed-amount social assistance. In the Pareto-superior NIT or BI systems, the negative effective tax rate results in an expanded income range where disposable income exceeds market income. While the negative effective tax rate range under fixed-amount social assistance was limited to 0 to $X_1$, it extends from 0 to $X_3$ under the Pareto-superior NIT or BI models. In fixed-amount social assistance, the effective marginal tax rate at $X_1$ exceeded 100%, causing an income reversal and a subsequent decline in labor supply. However, in the Pareto-superior NIT or BI systems, the effective marginal tax rate is lowered to $t = AC/X_1X_3$, thereby maintaining work incentives.

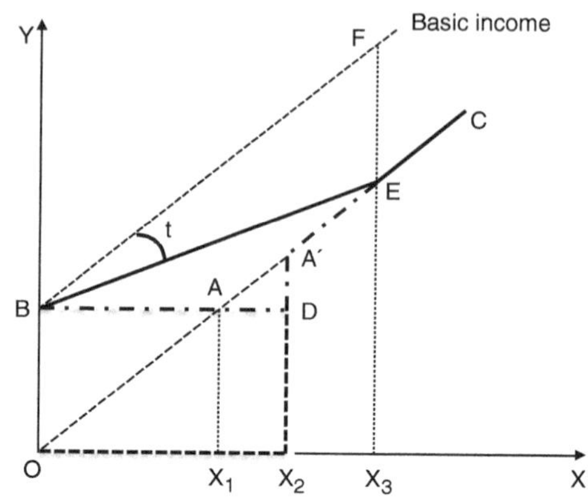


**Fig. 2.5** Pareto Superior Negative Income Tax and Basic Income Compared to Filling-the-Gap Social Assistance

### *Surpassing Gap-Filling Social Assistance*

Similarly, Fig. 2.5 compares NIT/BI schemes with gap-filling (minimum income guarantee) assistance. Under the gap-filling model, the 100% PTR for market income up to $X_2$ causes a widespread withdrawal from the labor market, resulting in a massive deadweight loss (triangle $OX_2A$') and an expanded budget (rectangle $OX_2DB$).

By utilizing the realized budget and the recovered GDP, we can implement a Pareto-superior NIT. This system provides a base payment of OB at zero income, which gradually decreases as market income rises toward $X_3$. The resulting disposable income line (BE) remains consistently higher than the social assistance counterpart (BDA'E) .

By reallocating the social assistance budget (rectangle $OX_2DB$) and the efficiency gains from eliminating the deadweight loss (triangle $OX_2A$'), it becomes possible to implement a Pareto-superior NIT system. In this model, a benefit of OB is provided when an individual's market income is zero, and the benefit amount is phased out at a constant rate until market income reaches $X_3$. For incomes exceeding $X_3$, the benefit becomes zero.

In this scenario, the disposable income line for individuals with market incomes between 0 and $X_3$ is represented by BE, which is higher than the disposable income line BDA'E under the gap-filling social assistance scheme. Furthermore, if a basic income of OB is provided to all individuals, taxed at a specific rate until market income reaches $X_3$, and a tax equivalent to OB is levied on income exceeding $X_3$, the resulting disposable income becomes identical to that under the NIT system.

Under this superior scheme:

- **The Negative Effective Tax Range Expands**: The income range where disposable income exceeds market income extends from $0–X_1$ to $0–X_3$.
- **Labor Incentives are Restored**: The EMTR drops from 100%+ to a fixed rate (t), while the PTR—previously at or near 100%—diminishes significantly as income rises.
- **Fiscal Self-Sufficiency**: Although the NIT/BI scheme covers more individuals, its net fiscal requirement is neutralized by the elimination of the systemic inefficiencies inherent in the "welfare trap".

### *Practical Considerations and the Necessity of Going Beyond Pareto*

While we have theoretically demonstrated that NIT/BI can be Pareto superior without requiring extra financial resources, several practical challenges remain. Measuring precise deadweight losses is difficult, and the transition from household-based social assistance to individual-based basic income complicates the design of a perfect Pareto improvement. Furthermore, integrating these schemes with existing tax structures and social security contributions requires sophisticated administrative calibration.

Beyond these technicalities, we must consider whether Pareto superiority is the ultimate goal. Pareto superiority, by definition, avoids redistribution from the wealthy. However, in an era where the top 10% capture an ever-increasing share of national income while the bottom 50% remain stagnant, a purely Pareto-based approach may be insufficient. To achieve substantive equality and address growing structural imbalances, we must eventually look beyond Pareto improvements toward active redistribution.

## 2.3 Negative Income Tax and Basic Income with a Flat Tax Model

In this section, we examine the merits of a streamlined model of basic income (BI)—or its functional equivalent, the negative income tax (NIT)—integrated with a flat income tax. As introduced in Chapter 1, a fiscally neutral basic income paired with a flat tax is mathematically equivalent to an NIT that applies the same clawback rate for benefits as it does the tax rate for income exceeding the threshold (break-even point). In this framework, the threshold income is defined as the mean personal income, and the guaranteed basic income amount is calculated as "(Mean Income) × (Tax Rate)."

For example, a basic income set at 20% of the mean income, financed by a 20% flat tax, effectively redistributes 20% of the total personal income equally across the population. Under this mechanism, individuals with below-average incomes emerge as net beneficiaries, while those with above-average incomes become net contributors. This model carries significant egalitarian weight: it has been theoretically established that a basic income funded by a flat tax of *t* percent reduces the Gini coefficient—the standard metric for inequality—by exactly *t* percent (Miller, 2017: 245–246).

**The Progressivity of Effective Tax Rates:** Table 2.1 illustrates the transformation of effective tax rates (ETR) under a BI/NIT model based on a 20% flat tax. Assuming a mean income of $50,000 and a guaranteed basic income of $10,000, the resulting effective tax rates demonstrate a striking progressive schedule. At a market income of $1,000, the ETR is –980%. At $10,000, it is –80%. At $40,000, it is –5%. It reaches 0% precisely at the mean income of $50,000. Beyond this point, the ETR becomes positive, reaching 3.33% at $60,000, 10% at $100,000, and asymptotically approaching the 19% mark at $1,000,000.

While the nominal tax rate is flat, the effective tax rate is highly progressive, transitioning from deeply negative rates for low-income earners to zero at the average, and gradually approaching the flat rate for the highest earners. This progressive structure is theoretically robust yet avoids appearing confiscatory or overly burdensome to high-income individuals. Despite criticisms that universal payments lack redistributive power because the same amount is given to everyone, this simple model proves capable of a massive redistributive impact—lowering the Gini index of income inequality by a full 20%.

**Harmonizing Work Incentives and Real Freedom:** Furthermore, Table 2.1 demonstrates that both the effective marginal tax rates (EMTR) and the participation tax rates (PTR) are stabilized at 20%—identical to the flat tax rate—across all income levels. By replacing the current convoluted tax and transfer system with this flat-tax-based BI or NIT, the state can eliminate the prohibitive tax spikes (often exceeding 100%) inherent in

**Table 2.1** Effective Tax Rates, Marginal Effective Tax Rates, and Participation Tax Rates Under a Flat-Tax-Based Basic Income with the Mean Income of $50,000 and the Basic Income of $10,000

| *Person* | *Market income* | *Basic income* | *Tax* | *Disposable income* | *Effective tax rate* | *Effective marginal tax rate* | *Participation tax rate* |
|---|---|---|---|---|---|---|---|
| Person 0 | 1,000 | 10,000 | 200 | 10,800 | -980% | 20% | 20% |
| Person 1 | 10,000 | 10,000 | 2,000 | 18,000 | -80% | 20% | 20% |
| Person 2 | 20,000 | 10,000 | 4,000 | 26,000 | -30% | 20% | 20% |
| Person 3 | 30,000 | 10,000 | 6,000 | 34,000 | -13.3% | 20% | 20% |
| Person 4 | 40,000 | 10,000 | 8,000 | 42,000 | -5.0% | 20% | 20% |
| Person 5 | 50,000 | 10,000 | 10,000 | 50,000 | 0% | 20% | 20% |
| Person 6 | 60,000 | 10,000 | 12,000 | 58,000 | 3.3% | 20% | 20% |
| Person 7 | 70,000 | 10,000 | 14,000 | 66,000 | 5.7% | 20% | 20% |
| Person 8 | 80,000 | 10,000 | 16,000 | 74,000 | 7.5% | 20% | 20% |
| Person 9 | 90,000 | 10,000 | 18,000 | 82,000 | 8.9% | 20% | 20% |
| Person 10 | 100,000 | 10,000 | 20,000 | 90,000 | 10% | 20% | 20% |
| Person 11 | 1,000,000 | 10,000 | 200,000 | 810,000 | 19% | 20% | 20% |

traditional social assistance. Consequently, work disincentives cease to be a primary concern, as every unit of earned income yields a consistent net gain. By providing a guaranteed income floor, this system not only ensures material security but also empowers individuals to exercise real freedom.

**Considering a Full Basic Income:** A critical question arises: Is it financially feasible to implement a flat-tax-based "full" basic income capable of entirely replacing existing cash benefits? Figure 2.6 illustrates this scenario, comparing a full BI/NIT model against both gap-filling social assistance and the previously discussed Pareto-superiorscheme.

In this model, the line OB represents the basic guaranteed income—whether framed as a universal basic income, an NIT payment at zero income, or the minimum guarantee under social assistance. The bold line BGH depicts disposable income under a flat-tax-based BI/NIT system. While the line BF represents the sum of "market income plus basic income (OB)," the bold line BGH shows the actual disposable income after a flat tax (t) is applied. Under the NIT framework, benefits decrease at the tax rate (t) as market income rises toward the break-even point ($X_4$), or the mean personal income, positioning disposable income along the segment

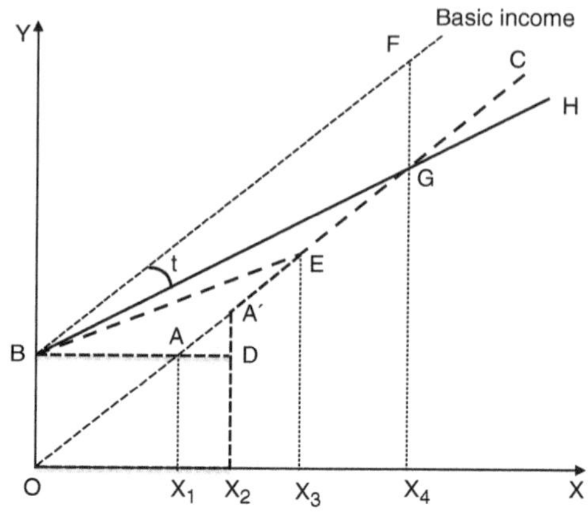


**Fig. 2.6** Full Basic Income and Negative Income Tax Schemes Based on a Flat Tax, with a Greater Redistributive Effect Than Both Gap-Filling Social Assistance and Pareto Superior Basic Income/Negative Income Tax Schemes

BG. Once market income exceeds $X_4$, individuals become net taxpayers, with their disposable income following the segment GH.

The scope of redistribution is substantially broadened. Until market income reaches the average income ($X_4$), the disposable income under our proposed model (the bold line BG) remains consistently higher than that of both gap-filling assistance (the dotted line BDA'G) and the Pareto-superior scheme (the dotted line BEC). Conversely, for market incomes exceeding $X_4$, disposable income (the bold line GH) falls below both the alternative schemes and the market income itself. This demonstrates that a flat-tax-based BI/NIT model achieves a greater redistributive effect than either traditional social assistance or a purely Pareto-superior reform. Similarly, a fiscally neutral BI/NIT can be designed to outperform fixed-amount social assistance in redistributive power by setting the basic income floor equal to or higher than the current fixed benefit level.

**The Practical Shift Toward a Partial Basic Income:** The theoretical elegance of a full basic income must be weighed against the practicalities of existing tax and benefit structures. When accounting for the minimum tax revenue required to finance public goods—such as healthcare and education—budgetary constraints impose a ceiling on the feasible level of basic income. While debates on the financial viability of a full BI continue, it is often deemed prohibitively costly for advanced welfare states. Atkinson (1995), for instance, advocated for a partial basic income, noting that a full BI in the UK would necessitate a daunting tax rate of 68% to 86%.

Van Parijs and Vanderborght (2017: 137) pointed out that in the United States, where government spending reaches 35% of GDP (consisting of 12% for education and healthcare, 10% for other social expenditures, and 13% for non-social spending), the introduction of a full basic income at 25% of GDP to replace half of existing public social spending would bring the total fiscal size to 55% of GDP. Similarly, introducing a full basic income at the same level in France would increase its total fiscal size to 65% of GDP. Given that household income accounts for approximately two-thirds of GDP, they recognized that a full basic income—representing 80% to 90% of household income—may be valid as a long-term vision but difficult to realize in the short term. Considering the uncertainty in predicting its impact on the labor market, they proposed starting with the introduction of a lower-level partial basic income.

Consider a scenario where the guaranteed income is set at 50% of the median income (to eradicate poverty) and the median income is roughly 80% of the mean. This would require a 40% flat tax on top of social security contributions and other necessary government expenditures. While such a universal 40% rate could technically eliminate poverty, it would do so by fully replacing existing social insurance. This would leave many current beneficiaries worse off, particularly those who rely on social insurance for consumption smoothing and maintaining their prior standard of living. Consequently, wholesale replacement of social insurance remains a suboptimal strategy.

Furthermore, we must account for work disincentives arising from both the income and substitution effects triggered by high tax rates. While the net impact of a full BI on GDP is subject to debate across different institutional contexts, the political and economic risks associated with high marginal tax rates suggest a more cautious approach.

**Designing a Fiscally Neutral Partial Basic Income:** Given these challenges, a partial basic income presents a more viable alternative. Figure 2.7 illustrates a fiscally neutral partial BI (or its equivalent NIT). In this model:

- The guaranteed income level ($OB_1$) is set lower than that of a full BI ($OB_0$), and the associated flat tax rate ($t_1$) is correspondingly reduced.
- The break-even point ($X_4$) remains at the mean personal income.

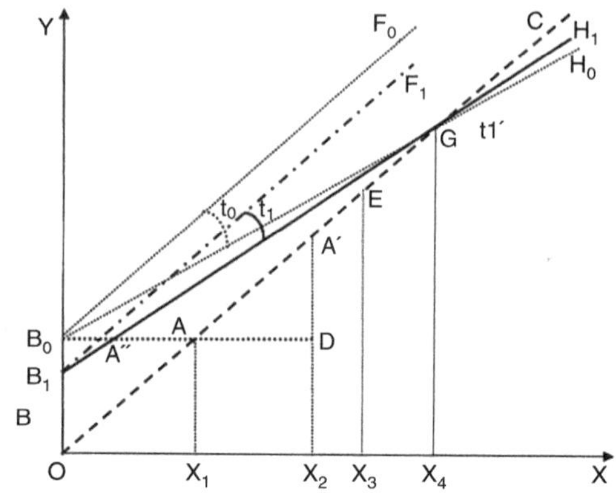


**Fig. 2.7** Partial Basic Income and Negative Income Tax Schemes Based on a Flat Tax

A critical concern with partial BI is that if it fully replaces existing social assistance, those with very low market income (below $X_5$) could experience a net loss. To prevent this, we propose a transitional hybrid model: current recipients with market income below $X_5$ maintain their existing benefits, while the partial BI fully replaces social assistance only for those earning above $X_5$.

Under this scheme, the disposable income line becomes $B_0$A''G. Those earning more than $X_5$ transition away from stigmatized, means-tested assistance to a system that provides them with higher disposable income. Simultaneously, the social assistance budget is optimized—shrinking from the large rectangle $OB_0DX_2$ to the smaller triangle $B_0B_1$A''.

While the income tax schedule may become slightly less progressive compared to a full BI, the overall tax burden on high-income earners remains higher than under current systems, and the redistributive impact is significantly stronger than that of traditional social assistance or the Pareto-superior scheme. Under this partial scheme,

1. Lowest earners (below $X_5$) are protected by maintaining their previous benefit levels.
2. The "Working Poor" and Middle Class (between $X_5$ and $X_4$) see a net improvement in their financial position.
3. Higher earners (above $X_4$) act as net contributors.

Ultimately, although a partial basic income involves less total redistribution than a full basic income, it remains a superior and more sustainable mechanism for enhancing real freedom than the existing social assistance framework.

Critics often contend that a low-level (partial) basic income could paradoxically transform existing social assistance recipients into net losers, thereby potentially increasing the poverty rate. For instance, an OECD (2017) policy briefing noted that while basic income may improve overall income distribution, it could be less effective than targeted systems in reducing poverty if it merely replaces existing benefits. However, as Philippe Van Parijs and Yannick Vanderborght (2017) as well as Guy Standing (2017) argue, it is not necessary—nor desirable—to fully liquidate existing social assistance to fund a partial BI. Instead, we propose a "top-up" approach: replacing only the portion of social assistance that falls below the BI level, while maintaining supplemental benefits to ensure that no recipient suffers a net loss. We adopt this integrated approach to guarantee a robust social safety net.

A pivotal question remains: What is the optimal level of a flat-tax based partial basic income, or an equivalent NIT, when balanced against the requisite tax rate? As the level of guaranteed income increases, the efficiency gains—derived from streamlining and partially replacing current social assistance—also grow. Conversely, a higher BI and its associated tax rate may induce economic inefficiencies via income and substitution effects on labor supply. While there is no single theoretical solution to this optimization problem, our policy proposal seeks to identify the "sweet spot" that maximizes poverty reduction while preserving economic dynamism and fiscal sustainability.

**The Multifaceted Advantages of a Partial Basic Income:** The flat-tax based partial basic income (BI), or NIT, approach, which strategically replaces a portion of existing cash benefits, offers significant advantages across several dimensions:

**1. Robust Vertical and Horizontal Redistribution**: Under this framework, everyone with a market income below the national average remains a net beneficiary or maintains their current benefit level, characterized by a negative effective tax rate. Conversely, those earning above the average become net contributors, with the magnitude of contribution increasing progressively with income.

Beyond vertical redistribution between income groups, this model facilitates horizontal redistribution across the life course. Individuals typically act as net beneficiaries during childhood and old age—periods of higher vulnerability—and transition into net contributors during their healthy, productive years. This ensures that redistribution occurs not only between the rich and poor but also between different stages of an individual's life.

**2. Preservation of Labor Incentives**: Compared to full basic income, this partial scheme significantly minimizes work disincentives. For non-recipients of social assistance, the marginal effective tax rate (EMTR) and participation tax rate (PTR) rise only by the modest tax rate associated with the partial BI. Consequently, both the income and substitution effects that might discourage labor are far less pronounced than under a high-tax, full BI model.

**3. Administrative Efficiency**: A partial BI approach radically streamlines administrative procedures. Traditional social assistance relies on intrusive means testing, involving a complex conversion of assets into "recognized income" and rigorous scrutiny of household compositions. This process often imposes a psychological burden on applicants, who must endure invasive interviews and provide exhaustive documentation, sometimes leading to underreporting of assets. For officials, the constant need to police fraudulent claims creates a climate of suspicion rather than support.

In contrast, NIT determines eligibility only through income data, and BI does not require even income test. Both can be managed via existing tax administrations. By removing asset tests and household-based criteria, the system reduces the administrative burden for both the state and the citizen, fostering a relationship of mutual trust.

**4. Mitigation of Selection Errors**: The shift toward individual-based, income-centered transfers drastically reduces selection errors—both the exclusion of eligible individuals (Type I error) and the inclusion of ineligible ones (Type II error).

**5. No Stigma**: Because basic income is provided universally or managed through the tax system, it eliminates the social stigma historically associated with welfare. This addresses the "non-take-up" problem where eligible individuals forgo necessary aid to preserve their self-esteem. By providing an unconditional floor, basic income fosters true freedom and protects the dignity of every recipient.

## 2.4 Household-Level Versus Individual-Level NIT: Pros and Cons

A pivotal design choice in income security is whether to transition from current household-based social assistance to a household-level NIT, or toward an individual-level NIT or Basic Income (BI).

**Fiscal Efficiency and Economies of Scale**: Traditionally, social assistance programs are administered on a household basis to account for economies of scale. This approach recognizes that the basic cost of living does not increase proportionally with the number of household members; shared resources like housing and utilities reduce the per-capita requirement. In contrast, universal basic income and individual-level NIT ignore these scale effects, providing the same amount to every person regardless of their living situation. Critics argue that this creates an unfair transfer of wealth from single-person households to larger families (Yang, 2020).

From a purely fiscal perspective, a household-level NIT can improve income distribution with a significantly lower budgetary requirement than an individual-level system. This is because poverty and inequality indicators are typically measured using "equivalized income," which adjusts household income for size. Therefore, a household-level NIT that sets its eligibility threshold based on the median equivalized income is theoretically more "efficient" in moving households above the statistical poverty line at a minimal cost.

The methodology for calculating equivalized income varies, but the OECD standard involves dividing the total household income by the square root of the number of household members. For example, if a single-person household earns $1,000, its equivalized income is $1,000. For a four-person household earning $4,000, the raw per-capita income is also $1,000. However, its equivalized income is calculated as: $4,000/ sqrt(4) = $4,000/2 = $2,000.

Since basic income provides a flat amount per individual, the equivalized benefit becomes progressively larger for multi-person households.

**The Short-term Efficiency of Household-level NIT**: A compelling model for a household-based NIT involves setting the guaranteed income at 50% of the median household income, with the median income itself serving as the break-even point. Under this scheme, the benefit clawback rate would be set at 50% and the tax rate on excess income would be set lower than 50%.

Because the poverty rate is officially defined relative to 50% of the equivalized median income, this household-based model could theoretically eliminate poverty at a relatively low fiscal cost. For instance, if the target is an equivalized income of $100 (with $50 as the poverty threshold), an individual-level BI would need to provide $50 to everyone, costing $200 for a four-person household. However, a household-level NIT could achieve the same poverty-reduction goal by providing that four-person household with only $100. Thus, in the short run, the household-level approach appears more "efficient" in terms of budgetary impact on redistribution indicators.

**The Long-term Pitfalls of Household-level NIT**: While a household-based NIT appears fiscally efficient in the short run, it faces severe structural and behavioral challenges. To maintain a 50% clawback rate while keeping the overall Effective Marginal Tax Rate (EMTR) and Participation Tax Rate (PTR) at that same 50% level, the state would essentially need to abolish existing income taxes and social insurance contributions. This raises a critical dilemma: can public goods and in-kind services—such as education and healthcare—be financed solely through non-income tax sources? Furthermore, is it socially acceptable to dissolve the social insurance systems that facilitate vital consumption smoothing?

If current income taxes and social insurance premiums were maintained alongside a 50% NIT clawback rate, the resulting EMTR would skyrocket, significantly suppressing labor supply and stifling economic growth. Moreover, such high rates create powerful incentives for income concealment. Workers may gravitate toward the informal sector to hide earnings, while employers exploit this to lower labor costs. Consequently, the redistributive effectiveness of a household-level NIT, though impressive in the short term, is likely to erode over time due to these systemic distortions.

**The "Marriage Penalty" and Household Dissolution**: A more profound concern is the perverse incentive for household breakup. Because household-level systems are tied to shared income thresholds, they inadvertently penalize cohabitation. For example, a sole breadwinner earning just above the threshold might find that a "strategic divorce" allows the remaining family members to qualify for substantial guaranteed income as a separate household. This disparity in per-capita payments between single and multi-person households acts as a significant deterrent to marriage.

To prevent such fraudulent behavior, the state would be forced to conduct intrusive surveillance of citizens' living arrangements—monitoring marital status, divorce history, and even adoption status. Such an administrative burden inevitably leads to a violation of privacy, mirroring the very "intrusive bureaucracy" that basic income seeks to eliminate.

**Demographic Sustainability and Individual-level Benefits**: In stark contrast, individual-level NIT and Basic Income exert a positive influence on family formation without requiring administrative overreach. Under an individual-based system, there is no marriage penalty. Instead, couples can fully enjoy the economies of scale from cohabitation while retaining their individual entitlements.

For a two-member household, the same per-capita basic income results in an equivalized income that is 1.41 times higher than for a single-person household; for a four-member household, it is twice as high. In societies like South Korea, currently facing an existential crisis due to extremely low birth rates, these structural supports for marriage and childbearing are indispensable. Therefore, when considering demographic sustainability, the individual-level model—which encourages family formation—is far superior to household-level assistance.

**Sustainable Efficiency**: In summary, while a household-level NIT may be favorable if the sole, narrow objective is to reduce the statistical poverty rate, it fails the test of long-term sustainable efficiency. If the goal is to promote freedom and equality while fostering a resilient and growing society, an individual-level system is vastly preferable.

We advocate for an individual-level NIT or Basic Income with the average income as the threshold, rather than a household-level system tied to the median. This choice prioritizes personal agency, protects privacy, and ensures the long-term survival of the social contract in a changing demographic landscape.

## 2.5 Differentiated Payments Based on Age and NIT-Type Basic Income

### *The Strategic Necessity of Age-Differentiated Payments*

In the initial stages of implementation, a relatively low-level partial basic income may be more realistic. Yet, a low-level BI faces criticism for its limited efficacy in alleviating deep-seated inequality and poverty compared to expanded targeted transfers or household-based NITs. To resolve this tension, many proponents advocate for differentiating basic income levels by age—typically providing higher support to the elderly and lower amounts to children relative to working-age adults.

Universality, a cornerstone of basic income, is not necessarily violated by age-based differentiation (Miller, 2017: 58). While Philippe Van Parijs and Yannick Vanderborght (2017) are skeptical of "categorical" basic incomes based on occupation (e.g., for artists or farmers), they embrace age-based categories as a pragmatic stepping stone toward a fully universal system. Scholars like Annie Miller (2017) and Malcolm Torry (2017; 2018) propose tiered models for children, working-age adults, and the elderly, generally prioritizing higher payments for seniors to address the lack of earned income in old age.

### *Resolving the Fairness Dilemma Through NIT*

Age-differentiation introduces a complex fairness issue: if differentiated payments are paired with a single proportional tax rate, the threshold income (break-even point) will vary by age. This could lead to a scenario where high-income elderly individuals remain net beneficiaries while younger generations act as net contributors—a situation unlikely to gain political acceptance. If we attempt to set a uniform threshold (e.g., the average income) while differentiating payment levels, the benefit clawback rates must vary by age.

As a viable solution, we propose a Negative Income Tax (NIT) scheme as illustrated in Fig. 2.8. In this model:

- The threshold income and the tax rate for income above the threshold remain uniform across all age groups to ensure horizontal equity.
- The guaranteed income floors and the clawback rates for those below the threshold are differentiated by age.

Under this framework, elderly net beneficiaries (those below the average income) receive higher guaranteed support, which is phased out at a steeper clawback rate. This ensures that the most vulnerable seniors are protected without creating an unfair windfall for high-income elderly individuals, thereby maintaining intergenerational solidarity.

As illustrated in Fig. 2.8, our proposed model achieves intergenerational equity by maintaining a uniform threshold income ($x_1$) and a single tax rate ($t_3$) for income above that threshold, while differentiating the

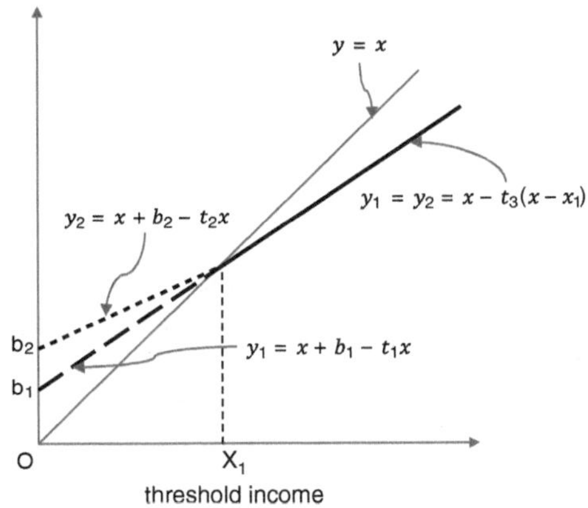


**Fig. 2.8** Negative Income Tax with Multiple Guaranteed Incomes and Claw-back Rates and a Single Threshold Income and Excess Income Tax Rate

support structure for those below it. The disposable income (y) for adults (subscript 1) and seniors (subscript 2) is defined as follows:

For market income below the threshold ($x < x_1$):

$$y_1 = x + b_1 - t_1x$$
$$y_2 = x + b_2 - t_2x$$

For market income above the threshold ($x > x_1$):

$$y_1 = y_2 = x - t_3(x - x_1)$$

Here, the relationships $t_1x_1 = b_1$ and $t_2x_1 = b_2$ hold. Since the guaranteed income for seniors ($b_2$) is set higher than that for adults ($b_1$), it follows that the clawback rate for seniors ($t_2$) must be steeper than the rate for adults ($t_1$).

This approach aligns with the theory of age-dependent taxation, which suggests that higher tax rates are more efficient for older cohorts due to their lower labor supply elasticity. In contrast, younger individuals typically exhibit higher labor supply elasticity, making lower tax rates ($t_1$) more conducive to economic participation (Weinzierl, 2011).

### *Demographic Imperatives: Children as a Priority*

While traditional literature (Miller, 2017; Torry, 2017) often suggests lower basic income levels for children, we contend that the South Korean context—characterized by a demographic collapse and extremely low birth rates—demands a different strategy. The prohibitive costs of child-rearing are a primary deterrent to family formation in Korea. Kang Nam-hoon (2019a: 171) and Basic Income Korean Network (2021: 103, 115) propose providing children with the same level of basic income as adults. We believe it is necessary to provide children with at least the same level of guaranteed income as adults, and preferably the same level as seniors.

In conclusion, we advocate for an NIT-type basic income that sets the threshold at the average national income while providing enhanced guaranteed floors for both children and seniors.[3] While critics often label NIT as administratively burdensome due to frequent income assessments, we argue that these challenges are overstated. By utilizing a refundable tax credit mechanism during the annual income tax filing process, this model can be implemented with minimal administrative friction. By integrating age-differentiated support within a unified tax framework, this approach offers a robust, sustainable, and politically viable path toward real freedom and social equality. A detailed analysis of this implementation strategy will be explored in Chapter 4.

[3] Almaz Zelleke suggested that we consider a higher basic guaranteed income for children than for adults, particularly given that low fertility is a pressing concern in South Korea. She pointed out that while working-age adults serve as primary revenue sources for families, children—much like the elderly—represent a source of family expense with limited earning potential. Zelleke (2007) previously explored the appropriate levels of basic income benefits within the U.S. context.

CHAPTER 3

# Common Wealth Dividend Basic Income

Basic income can be categorized into two types based on its funding source: tax-financed and common wealth-financed.[1] Tax-financed models rely on general tax revenue, whereas common wealth models are funded by income generated from common assets. For instance, a universal child allowance provided periodically as a flat cash payment from tax revenue is a tax-financed basic income. In contrast, the Alaska Permanent Fund dividend (PFD), distributed to all residents, is a prime example of a common wealth-financed basic income.

Even if a basic income is distributed through the tax system, it can be classified as common wealth-financed if the tax is levied on a specific common resource. Land is the most representative case. Since land is a natural heritage that should rightfully belong to everyone as common wealth, a basic income funded by a land value tax (LVT) is a form of common wealth dividend.

Can a carbon dividend based on a carbon tax also be viewed as a common wealth dividend? Traditionally, a carbon tax is a Pigouvian tax imposed on carbon emissions to address negative externalities. However, given that the atmosphere is clearly a common resource, we can shift our perspective as follows: The atmosphere, as a vital component of the ecosystem,

[1] In this chapter, the terms common wealth and the commons are used interchangeably. Similarly, common wealth basic income, common wealth dividend, and commons dividend refer to the same conceptual framework.

 
J. S. You et al., *UBI from Idea to Reality*, Exploring the Basic Income Guarantee,
https://doi.org/10.1007/978-3-032-26200-4_3

provides various services such as oxygen supply and rainfall regulation. Among these is the capacity to absorb carbon dioxide without raising the Earth's temperature. This service is a finite, exhaustible resource that is now reaching its limit. Thus, a carbon tax can be reinterpreted as a usage fee for those utilizing the atmosphere's dwindling absorption capacity. In this light, a carbon dividend also falls under the category of a common wealth dividend.

For a nation to implement a basic income based on common resources, there must be a social consensus that these resources indeed constitute common wealth. Therefore, the process of commoning—the transition where normative(potential) common wealth becomes recognized as positive(actualized) common wealth—is essential.

This chapter is organized as follows: Section 1 examines the characteristics of common wealth and the significance of commoning. Section 2 classifies natural common wealth and analyzes the generation of rent derived from it. Section 3 analyzes the circumstances under which common wealth dividends are necessary based on the type of common asset. Section 4 explores land dividends as a mechanism for land commoning, while Section 5 analyzes carbon dividends and sunlight income required during the energy transition.

## 3.1 Common Wealth and Commoning

Common wealth can be defined positively as assets or resources socially agreed upon as belonging to all members of a community, or normatively as assets or resources that ought to belong to all members of a community.

When adopting a normative definition, one must establish clear criteria or principles for what qualifies as common wealth. In this study, we assume that individuals behind a veil of ignorance would agree on a fundamental principle: *if an asset was not created by a specific individual's labor or unique contribution, it should not be exclusively owned by that person*. Applying this principle, common wealth can be categorized into two primary types:

First, natural common wealth: Resources provided by nature rather than human labor. This includes land, natural resources, the environment, and the ecosystem.

Second, social common wealth: Assets created collectively by countless individuals across present and past generations, such that exclusive private ownership lacks legitimacy. This includes language, institutions, common knowledge (excluding specific intellectual property currently protected by law), shared data such as administrative data or social media content (excluding data produced by private firms), social capital (as distinct from individual social capital), social infrastructure, and public institutions. It also encompasses inventions that have entered the public domain through donation or patent expiration.

Those who define common wealth positively often refer to it as the commons. The commons is defined as the totality of a resource, the community that manages it, and the rules governing that management (Bollier, 2025, p.16). In this context, commoning refers to the active process of establishing, complying with, monitoring, and enforcing these management rules. For these scholars, common wealth is a resource that has been successfully commoned.

In this study, we adopt the normative definition and use the terms the commons and common wealth interchangeably.[2] Our choice of a normative framework is driven by the fact that even if a resource currently exists as private property, transitioning it to common wealth is often desirable from the perspectives of legitimacy, efficiency, and sustainability.

Successful commoning requires overcoming the dilemma of the commons, a phenomenon where a community fails to maintain a resource as common wealth despite it being collectively beneficial to do so. Elinor Ostrom (1990), in her study of non-excludable but rivalrous common-pool resources (CPR), explained this dilemma using models such as the Tragedy of the Commons (Hardin, 1968), the Prisoner's Dilemma, and the Logic of Collective Action (Olson, 1965). At the core of these models lies the free-rider problem (Ostrom, 1990, p.6). Since individuals attempt to become free-riders based on a boundedly rational self-interest, this can be characterized as a problem of rational egoism.

The dilemma of the commons is driven not only by rational egoism but also by irrational egoism. Irrational egoism includes cognitive biases such as the mismeasurement of future benefits and costs, hyperbolic discounting (where future benefits are undervalued relative to immediate costs), and loss aversion—the tendency to perceive losses as psychologically more significant than equivalent gains (Kahneman, 2013).

[2] Brent Ranalli also adopts a normative definition: There are certain objects in this world, such as land and natural resources, that should be regarded as the common heritage of mankind. Those who own or control these common heritage resources have an obligation to provide corresponding compensation to the rest of the members who are excluded from their use (Ranalli, 2021, p. 1).

In the case of exhaustible or conditionally sustainable resources, it is imperative to preserve a portion for future generations. However, intergenerational egoism, where the current generation ignores the long-term costs of their actions, remains a formidable barrier. Carbon emissions represent the most prominent example of this failure.

Furthermore, dominant-group egoism—where a small elite leverages political, economic, and judicial power to monopolize the benefits of common wealth—can lead to the resource curse, potentially triggering civil unrest or international conflict.

In summary, the dilemma of the commons is precipitated by various forms of egoism: rational, irrational, intergenerational, and dominant-group. Commoning, therefore, is the multifaceted process of transcending these egoistic barriers. In many cases, a single mechanism is insufficient, necessitating overlapping or nested commoning processes.

Elinor Ostrom's eight design principles for long-enduring CPR (common-pool resource) management incorporate essential elements for overcoming egoism. Her eighth principle emphasizes the necessity of nested management:

> For CPRs that are parts of larger systems, appropriation, provision, monitoring, enforcement, conflict resolution, and governance activities are organized in multiple layers of nested enterprises (Ostrom, 1990, p.90).

Taxation is often the most effective way to reclaim privatized common wealth for the public. However, individuals may rationally or irrationally perceive a new tax as a personal loss, even if the collective benefit is demonstrably higher. In such instances, a secondary commoning process must be introduced to distribute the collective gains and mitigate perceived losses. This follows a logic similar to medical treatment: when a toxic but necessary drug is prescribed to a patient, a secondary medication is provided to counteract the toxicity.

A representative case is the implementation of a carbon tax to combat the climate crisis. While a carbon tax is a powerful tool for preserving the climatic commons for posterity, it reduces the real income of the current generation through price increases. If people undervalue future benefits and overvalue short-term losses, social consensus for the tax becomes impossible. However, if the carbon tax revenue is distributed back to the citizens as a carbon dividend (Basic income), the future benefit is effectively presented, alleviating the immediate burden and facilitating social agreement.

Ostrom noted that the very process of establishing rules to manage common wealth faces its own dilemma. Formulating new rules requires significant sacrifice and collective effort, leading to a secondary free-rider problem where individuals avoid the costs of rule-making. Ostrom termed this the "second-order dilemma" (Ostrom, 1990, p.42). To overcome the primary dilemma, rules must be established; to overcome the second-order dilemma arising from rule-making itself, additional layers of institutional rules are required.

Ultimately, commoning is a social consensus forged by successfully navigating these overlapping dilemmas. Nations that achieve such consensus are better positioned to ensure a higher quality of life for all their citizens.

## 3.2 Classification of Natural Common Wealth and the Emergence of Rent

Economists traditionally classify goods into four categories—public goods, private goods, common-pool resources (CPRs), and club goods—based on two criteria: rivalry and excludability.

It is crucial to note that common wealth is a distinct concept from public goods. common wealth can intersect with all four categories in Table 3.1. Take land, a form of common wealth, as an example: A vast national park managed by the government is non-rivalrous and non-excludable (public goods). Land for a private residence is excludable and rivalrous (private goods). A large mountain owned by a village where outsiders are barred is non-rivalrous but excludable (club goods). A small village forest where access is open but resources are limited is rivalrous and non-excludable (CPR). For these reasons, establishing an alternative classification for common wealth requires the following three considerations:

**Table 3.1** Classification of Goods Based on Rivalry and Excludability

| | *Non-rivalrous* | *Rivalrous* |
|---|---|---|
| Non-excludable | Public goods | common-pool resources (CPRs) |
| Excludable | Club goods | Private goods |

First, excludability is not an inherent physical trait of common wealth but an institutional feature determined by policy. Common wealth is excludable when privatized, non-excludable in a state of no-ownership (*res nullius*), and selectively excludable under public ownership based on state decisions. Making common wealth excludable through privatization is the process of enclosure, while bringing privatized common wealth under public control—to ensure non-excludability or to share its generated returns—is the process of commoning.

Second, the traditional concept of rivalry—where one person's consumption limits another's—does not fully capture the nature of common wealth services. Consider fish in a large lake. While a specific fish eaten by one person cannot be consumed by another, if the lake is abundant, one person's catch does not limit another's ability to enjoy the same type of resource. From this perspective, individuals do not consume a specific unit, but rather the service of resource provision offered by the common wealth.

Consequently, we propose to substitute the traditional concept of rivalry with that of relative scarcity. Under this framework, relatively scarce commons are characterized by an increasing marginal cost to access the same level of service, whereas relatively abundant commons are characterized by a constant marginal cost. Applying this to the previous example of the large lake, if the second consumer incurs the same fishing cost as the first, the fish stock serves as a relatively abundant common wealth.

Relative scarcity is influenced not only by the magnitude of the service but also by its geographic scope. A resource easily accessible to locals but costly for outsiders is relatively scarce. For a group completely barred from access, the marginal cost can be viewed as increasing to infinity.

Finally, it is essential to distinguish between renewable and non-renewable common wealth. Renewable common wealth replenishes itself within an economically meaningful timeframe (e.g., ecosystems), whereas non-renewable wealth does not (e.g., minerals). Some renewable resources may become non-renewable if extraction exceeds their natural regeneration threshold.

Based on these considerations, Table 3.2 classifies natural common wealth using the criteria of renewability and relative scarcity.

Residential land is scarce but fixed, meaning it does not disappear. Water is renewable, but its scarcity depends on regional abundance. Petroleum and lithium are both scarce and non-renewable. category (D), such as asbestos, represents exhaustible minerals that lack economic value due to a lack of demand. In category (B), where demand exists, minerals follow Hotelling's Rule (Hotelling, 1931), which posits that the price of an exhaustible resource will rise over time at the rate of interest due to its relative scarcity.

Figure 3.1 illustrates the supply curve for scarce common wealth in categories (A) and (B). In a competitive market, the price is determined by the marginal cost of the last unit traded. Since these resources are relatively scarce, the marginal cost of the final unit is higher than that of the preceding units. Consequently, the sellers of the earlier units obtain a surplus exceeding their marginal costs. This surplus constitutes economic rent (Kang, 2019a), which arises fundamentally from the relative scarcity of common wealth.

Generally, rent does not occur in category (C) abundant and renewable common wealth. However, if property rights are established and access is restricted, the supply can be artificially constrained so that the resource is

**Table 3.2** Classification of Natural Common Wealth Based on Scarcity and Renewability

| | *Relatively scarce* | *Relatively abundant* |
|---|---|---|
| Renewable | (A) Residential/Industrial land; Water in arid regions (demand cannot be met at constant marginal cost) | (C) Oxygen, sunlight; Water in water-abundant regions (demand met at constant marginal cost) |
| Non-renewable (exhaustible) | (B) Gold, lithium (minerals with active demand) | (D) Asbestos (minerals with no demand) |

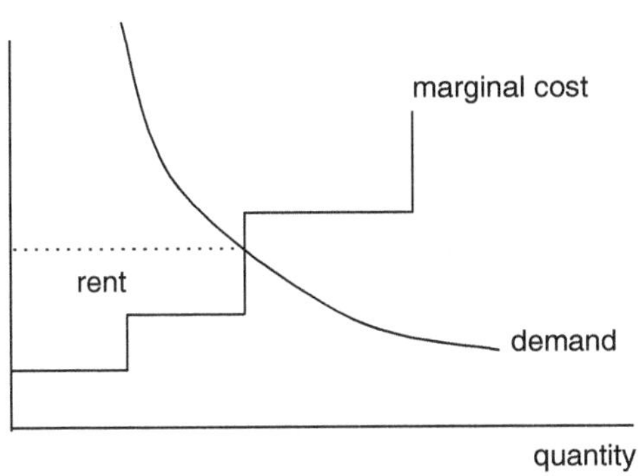


**Fig. 3.1** The Emergence of Rent from Relatively Scarce Common Wealth

sold at a price above the marginal cost. This results in monopoly rent. This monopoly rent differs from the rent generated by scarce common wealth (categories A and B) in three key aspects:

First, market structure. Rents associated with (A) and (B) are generated in competitive markets, while the rent in (C) is a product of a monopolistic market.

Second, the efficiency of rent. While the rents arising from the commons in (A) and (B) are efficient, the rent in (C) is deemed inefficient. In the former cases, artificially lowering prices to curb rent prevents the supply of commons where the marginal cost exceeds the price, leading to excess demand and market inefficiency. Conversely, in the latter case (C), price suppression can stimulate both consumption and supply, ultimately enhancing efficiency.

Third, the causes of rent. In commons (A) and (B), rent is attributed to natural scarcity, whereas in (C), it is the result of artificial scarcity created by monopoly.

The ultimate source of common wealth rent is the superior use-value (when consumed directly) or productivity (when used as a means of production) of the resource. For example, a factory located in a water-abundant area will be more productive than one in a water-scarce region. Since common wealth rent is generated independently of the labor or individual contribution of the producer, its private monopolization constitutes plunder of the commons (Standing, 2019) and is inherently unjust.

Technological shifts are constantly giving rise to new forms of common wealth, most notably the accumulation of data and knowledge on the internet. As these new resources often begin in a state of no-ownership, the process of common wealth enclosure is actively unfolding today. To transform these commons into private property, developers innovate technologies that enhance excludability, such as user surveillance, encryption, and location tracking.

Another method of enclosing common wealth that is physically difficult to privatize is by controlling access to the essential resources coupled with it. Some common wealth is accessible only through other common or private assets. For instance, data generated by users on the internet is stored in the clouds of platform corporations. Accessing messages or photos shared on Facebook is nearly impossible without passing through the platform's private infrastructure. Platform firms leverage this monopolized data to attract advertising or develop artificial intelligence, thereby capturing immense digital rents.

A further significant example is the sunlight required for solar power generation. While sunlight itself is a non-excludable common wealth, it requires land to be utilized for energy. Sunlight provides the service of power generation only when coupled with land. Although land ought to be treated as common wealth, much of it is currently privatized. If land owners privatize the sunlight commons and capture a substantial share of solar power returns, the transition to renewable energy will paradoxically exacerbate social inequality.

## 3.3 The Commoning of Privatized Common Wealth

The process of commoning privatized resources primarily involves eliminating or reclaiming the rents generated from them. This section evaluates various methods of commoning through the lenses of fairness, efficiency, and sustainability.

In this context, sustainability is defined as a state in which the welfare of future generations is not diminished relative to that of the current generation (Goodstein and Polasky, 2020, p.120). While renewability is a physical metric, sustainability serves as an economic one. Even for exhaustible (non-renewable) resources, sustainability can be maintained if financial capital equivalent to the value of the depleted resource is bequeathed to subsequent generations.[3]

### *Prohibition of Private Ownership and Guaranteed Free Access*

For category (C) common wealth (relatively abundant/renewable), prohibiting private ownership and allowing free (open) access tends to improve both fairness and efficiency by meeting broader demand without artificial barriers.

However, for categories (A) and (B) (Relatively Scarce), free access tends to deteriorate both fairness and efficiency. Due to relative scarcity, open access allows some individuals to capture disproportionate benefits while others are left with diminished gains or no access at all.

Regarding sustainability, free access generally reduces sustainability for category (B) by accelerating the depletion of exhaustible resources.

[3] Sustainability that recognizes the substitutability between natural (physical) capital and financial capital is referred to as "weak sustainability," whereas "strong sustainability" rejects such substitutability (Goodstein and Polasky, 2020, p.143).

Furthermore, certain renewable resources in categories (A) and (C) are sustainable only within specific extraction thresholds. For instance, if fish are harvested beyond the maximum sustainable yield (MSY), the population will crash and eventually face extinction. This scenario epitomizes the tragedy of the commons (Hardin, 1968). Rendering renewable common wealth non-renewable by over-extraction violates the principle of sustainability as it erodes the welfare of future generations.

#### *Recognition of Private Ownership with Rent Reclamation*

**Price Regulation**: For category (C), price regulation can modestly improve fairness and efficiency if it reduces rents and allows more people access at a lower cost. However, the improvement is far less significant compared to a total prohibition of private ownership.

For categories (A) and (B), price regulation creates market distortions: supply ceases for units where the marginal cost exceeds the price cap, while demand increases, leading to chronic excess demand. Thus, while price regulation may slightly enhance fairness, it significantly reduces economic efficiency.

For exhaustible resources (B) and threshold-dependent renewable resources (A, C), price regulation encourages higher consumption, thereby decreasing long-term sustainability.

**State Sale of Usage Rights at Market Price**: The state can reclaim 100% of the rent by maintaining formal ownership and selling usage rights through auctions at market prices. Selling these rights at competitive prices is functionally similar to reclaiming rent through taxation. However, in a state where resources are already privatized, this requires the prior step of de-privatization, which often faces immense political resistance.

**Rent Reclamation through Taxation**: Generally, reclaiming rent through taxation improves fairness, though it may occasionally decrease efficiency depending on the tax structure. However, for resources like land, where supply is perfectly inelastic and does not decrease due to taxation, there is no loss of efficiency. For category (C), the degree of rent reclamation via tax is smaller than under a ban on private ownership but larger than under price regulation, leading to a moderate improvement in fairness. Crucially, for exhaustible (B) and threshold-dependent renewable resources (A, C), taxation increases the cost of use, thereby curbing consumption and increasing sustainability.

## 3.4 The Significance and Principles of Common Wealth Dividends

Policies that dismantle enclosures or reclaim rents while recognizing private ownership are fundamental acts of commoning. By preventing a specific group from monopolizing the returns from shared resources, these policies restore the collective nature of the commons.

Based on the preceding analysis, for category (C) common wealth (Relatively Abundant/Renewable), the most desirable approach is to prohibit private ownership and ensure free, open access. Such policies are politically highly feasible because they directly increase the welfare of the vast majority of residents.

However, for categories (A) and (B) (Relatively Scarce), a balanced consideration of fairness, efficiency, and sustainability suggests that reclaiming rent through taxation or the sale of usage rights is superior to a simple ban on private ownership. Yet, this approach often faces a political dilemma: if a significant portion of the population currently enjoys even a small benefit from the privatized state, they may resist the transition, turning a substantial number of citizens into net contributors.

As discussed in Section 1, this political dilemma can be resolved through nested commoning processes. The most effective strategy is the introduction of a common wealth dividend, whereby the entirety of the reclaimed rent is distributed to every citizen as a basic income. Since this is a policy of income distribution rather than price manipulation, it upholds fairness without compromising economic efficiency or sustainability. By layering the reclamation of rent with the distribution of dividends, a society can successfully transform potential common wealth into practical, realized common wealth.

Regarding the allocation of common wealth dividends, (A) and (B) require divergent approaches. Given the renewable nature of (A), it is permissible to distribute the full amount of appropriated rent income each year. Conversely, for the exhaustible commons (B), dissipating the rent annually would compromise the welfare of post-exhaustion generations. Consequently, one must observe the Hartwick Rule (Hartwick, 1977): all rents accruing from non-renewable resources should be reinvested into capital to establish a permanent fund, allowing only the interest generated from this capital to be consumed. The Alaska Permanent Fund serves as a paradigmatic instance of strict compliance with this rule.

**Table 3.3** Principles of Common Wealth Dividends

| | *Relatively Scarce* | *Relatively Abundant* |
|---|---|---|
| Renewable | (A) Reclaim rent and distribute as common wealth dividend | (C) De-marketize, ensure open access, and manage for sustainability |
| Non-renewable (Exhaustible) | (B) Reclaim rent to establish a Permanent Fund; distribute fund returns as dividend | (D) No economic value |

Common wealth dividends offer two distinct advantages over general basic income regarding financing (Table 3.3). First, the source of revenue is inherent to the system itself. Consequently, it circumvents the objection frequently raised against tax-based basic income models—specifically, the question of where the money comes from (Ranalli, 2021).

Second, the validity of the common wealth dividend is not contingent upon the size of the payout. For general basic income, the issue of sufficiency is a critical constraint; if the objective is to guarantee real freedom, a nominal amount would fail to achieve this goal. In contrast, since the common wealth dividend represents the restitution of collective assets to the public, its distribution is justified as a matter of right, regardless of whether the amount is sufficient for subsistence (Standing, 2019).

## 3.5 Land Dividend

### *Characteristics of Land as Common Wealth*

In this study, land refers to residential and industrial (agricultural, industrial, and commercial) land. With rare exceptions, land is a renewable common wealth with a fixed supply. While land is inherently a natural common wealth, it also possesses the attributes of social common wealth, as its value shifts significantly due to public investment and industrial evolution.

Land exhibits strong rivalry: if one unit of land is occupied by an individual or firm, it cannot be used by others. It also possesses intense relative scarcity, with distinct variations in benefits and costs depending on the specific plot. For instance, urban land values differ starkly based on their distance from the city center. This scarcity generates pronounced economic rents for individual units. As cities develop and populations concentrate, the gap between prime land and marginal land widens, leading to a general rise in rents.

The escalation of rents drives up land prices, which in turn fuels real estate speculation, creating a feedback loop of further price hikes. Rising property prices not only exacerbate asset inequality but also increase income inequality through higher rents. In a rent-seeking economy, the incentive for innovation among individuals and firms diminishes. When the expected returns from real estate speculation far exceed those from self-development or skill acquisition, people naturally gravitate toward speculation. Similarly, firms prioritize real estate over technological innovation if it offers higher profitability. This leads to a misallocation of resources, where capital that should flow into entrepreneurship and R&D is locked in real estate. Furthermore, high land prices raise the cost of starting a business, stifling the formation of new ventures.

Since land rents are generated by the services provided by natural and social commons—such as roads, transportation, and education—it is fundamentally unjust for land owners to monopolize these returns.

### *Commoning Through Land Value Tax (LVT)*

As a means of commoning land, prohibiting private ownership and distributing land equally is not a viable or fair policy. For example, if a state provided one house per household for free, those assigned to city centers would gain immense unearned advantages through saved time and transportation costs. A policy of free distribution for a resource with such high relative scarcity creates severe fairness issues. Most importantly, abolishing the private ownership of already privatized land faces overwhelming political resistance, making it practically unfeasible.

Henry George (1879) identified private land ownership as the root cause of poverty. While making land a common wealth is the solution, confiscating privatized land is realistically difficult. George proposed a mechanism to achieve the same results as common ownership without formal confiscation: reclaiming the entirety of the rent by imposing an LVT.

LVT has garnered support from a diverse array of scholars. Milton Friedman (1978) famously referred to it as the least bad tax. James Mirrlees and his colleagues evaluated LVT as efficient because it does not discourage desirable economic activity, reclaims benefits generated by external factors like public development, and creates no incentive for the inefficient use of land (Mirrlees et al., 2011).

The efficiency of LVT stems from the fixed supply of land. According to standard economic theory, a tax on a good with a fixed supply cannot be shifted. As Varian (2014) notes, in the case of perfectly inelastic supply, no part of the tax is shifted. Since land supply is fixed, the tax burden falls entirely on the landowner and cannot be passed on to tenants. Thus, LVT is an efficient tax with zero deadweight loss.

LVT also enhances the dynamic efficiency of the economy. Land speculation yields unearned income—it is not the result of labor or innovation. In countries dominated by unearned income from land, the incentive for innovation declines, eroding long-term growth. LVT discourages speculation by reducing these unearned gains. Stabilizing land prices not only ensures affordable housing but also encourages productive investment. Joseph Stiglitz (2015) pointed out that LVT not only reduces inequality but also stimulates economic growth by encouraging investment in physical capital rather than land.

LVT exerts a commoning effect not only at the income level by reclaiming rent but also at the asset level by reducing land prices and curbing speculation. The theoretical model for the price-suppression effect of LVT is as follows:

In equilibrium, land value ($V_0$) represents the capitalized flow of its annual returns ($R$) Assuming a constant annual rent ($R$) generated in perpetuity, the initial land value ($V_0$) is determined by the discount rate ($r$).

$$\mathrm{V}_0 = \mathrm{R} + \frac{\mathrm{R}}{1+\mathrm{r}} + \frac{\mathrm{R}}{(1+\mathrm{r})^2} + \ldots = \frac{\mathrm{R}}{\mathrm{r}} \tag{1}$$

If an annual land tax ($T$) is imposed, the net annual income decreases to $R-T$. Consequently, the new land value $V_1$ is expressed as:

$$V_1 = \frac{R-T}{r} = \frac{R}{r} - \frac{T}{r} \tag{2}$$

This indicates that land value decreases by the capitalized amount of the tax. If the tax is proportional to the land value($T = V_1 \times \mathrm{t}$), where t is the tax rate, Equation (2) can be rewritten as:

$$V_1 = \frac{R}{r+t} \tag{3}$$

Comparing Equations (1) and (3), it is evident that LVT effectively lowers land value by increasing the denominator (the effective discount rate) used to capitalize rent (Buettner, 2003).

### *Nested Commoning Through Land Dividends*

While a universal LVT is an efficient tool for commoning land—promoting equity, suppressing speculation, and enhancing both static and dynamic efficiency—it faces a second-order dilemma. In many countries, home-owning households constitute a majority. Even though LVT is socially optimal, these households often exhibit political resistance, fearing the increased tax burden.

Much of this resistance stems from irrational egoism or bounded rationality. In reality, most households would benefit: LVT stabilizes housing costs, increasing the real income of non-homeowners; it stimulates the economy and job growth; and for those seeking to upgrade to better housing, the price drop of the prospective home would far exceed the tax paid. However, these macro-level benefits are long-term and abstract, whereas the annual tax bill is immediate and visible.

To overcome this, a secondary policy mechanism is required: the land dividend, which distributes LVT revenue back to all citizens as a basic income. By coupling LVT with dividends, the majority of households become net beneficiaries (Jeon & Kang, 2017). This overlapping structure can effectively neutralize political opposition based on tax increases.

However, resistance is not solely about the tax payment; it is also about the decline in asset value. Even a net beneficiary (one whose dividend exceeds their LVT) might oppose the policy if their property value drops significantly. The perceived loss from asset depreciation often outweighs the annual net gain in income. Consider the following example:

Assume a landowner receives an annual rent of $10,000. At a 5% interest rate, the land is valued at $200,000. Suppose this person pays $1,000 in LVT but receives $1,500 in land dividends, making them a net beneficiary of $500 per year. Table 3.4 illustrates the resulting change in their economic position.

In this scenario, the individual's annual income increases by $500. However, because the $1,000 tax is capitalized (Equation 2), it acts as a $20,000 liability, reducing the asset value to $180,000. The asset depreciation is 40 times the annual income gain. Faced with a 10% drop in their primary asset, would even a net beneficiary support the LVT/land dividend policy?

The political resistance arising from asset depreciation can be overcome by shifting people's perspective. If an LVT is capitalized as a negative asset (a liability), it is only logical that the annual land dividend be capitalized as a positive asset. While the tax reduces the value of one's private property, the dividend represents the creation of a new form of wealth: common property.

Every citizen receives a land dividend because they are the collective owners of the land as a natural and social common wealth. Before the dividend, an individual's wealth consisted solely of private land; after the dividend, their total wealth is the sum of their private assets and their common assets.

As shown in the highlighted column of Table 3.5, the $1,500 annual dividend is capitalized into a $30,000 asset—this represents the individual's rightful stake in the land commons. When this collective equity is included, the individual's total net wealth actually increases from $200,000 to $210,000. Thus, a net beneficiary experiences an increase not just in income flow, but in their total asset portfolio.

**Table 3.4** Asset Value for a Net Beneficiary of LVT/Land Dividend

| | *Before LVT/Dividend* | *After LVT/Dividend* |
|---|---|---|
| Income ($) | Rent: 10,000 | Rent: 10,000<br>LVT: –1,000<br>Dividend: +1,500 |
| Total income | 10,000 | 10,500 |
| Land Value ($) | Capitalized rent: 200,000 | Capitalized rent: 200,000<br>Capitalized LVT: –20,000 |
| Total Land Value | 200,000 | 180,000 |

**Table 3.5** Total Value of Private and Common Assets for a Net Beneficiary

| | *Before LVT/dividend* | *After LVT/dividend* |
|---|---|---|
| Annual income ($) | Rent: 10,000 | Rent: 10,000<br>LVT: –1,000<br>Dividend: +1,500 |
| Total income | 10,000 | 10,500 |
| Asset value ($) | Capitalized rent: 200,000 | Capitalized rent: 200,000<br>Capitalized LVT: –20,000<br>Capitalized dividend: +30,000 |
| Total net wealth | 200,000 | 210,000 |

The capitalization of the LVT into a liability is a phenomenon that occurs within the market mechanism. When an LVT is levied, the trading price of the land declines immediately, as privately owned land is an asset traded in the open market. However, the reconversion of land dividends into common assets is not a market-mediated phenomenon. Consequently, pedagogical efforts are required to foster the recognition that land dividends are grounded in common assets. Only when individuals realize that they receive dividends by virtue of the existence of common assets can they conclude that the land holding tax and dividend policy enhances their total asset value.

To facilitate this, governments could establish formal funds—such as the Citizens' Capital Accounts proposed by Widerquist and Howard (2012)—and issue official documents affirming each citizen's right to the common wealth. Guy Standing (2023) envisions a Commons Capital Fund financed by levies on users rather than traditional taxes. For example, what is paid is not a tax, but a land value levy (p. 316). The resulting dividend is then distributed as a common property right granted to all (p. 315). Issuing Common Land Equity Certificates to every citizen could be a powerful tool for this realization.

In countries like South Korea, where property taxes are levied on buildings and land together, the transition can be managed to minimize market hybrid . For non-homeowners, land dividends are provided as direct cash. For homeowners, instead of direct cash, the dividend can be applied to offset the property tax on the building structure, with any surplus paid in cash.

Under this scheme, non-homeowners have no reason to object, as they receive a pure gain. Meanwhile, the majority of middle-class homeowners would see their total property tax burden decrease, effectively neutralizing political resistance.

In 1990, 30 prominent economists—including William Vickrey, James Tobin, William Baumol, and Robert Solow—sent an open letter to Mikhail Gorbachev, urging him to maintain public ownership of land and reclaim its full rental value. They argued that land value increases due to three factors: natural productivity, community growth, and the expansion of public services. It is only just that the government reclaims these rents, distributing the natural increment equally to all citizens and using the increment from public services to finance those very services (Tideman et al., 1991).

## 3.6 Carbon Dividend and Sunlight Income

A carbon dividend is a policy that imposes a tax on carbon emissions and returns the entirety of the resulting revenue to residents in the form of a basic income. This model has been implemented in various forms in Switzerland and Canada and is consistently proposed in the U.S. Congress through the *Energy Innovation and Carbon Dividend Act*.[4]

In 2025, the Lee Jae-myung administration in South Korea announced plans for a Rural Basic Income Pilot Project and the Sunlight Income Village initiative. The Rural Basic Income is a universal payment provided to all residents of a county (Gun), regardless of wealth, with no strings attached—amounting to 150,000 KRW monthly per individual. This policy meets the core criteria of basic income at the local government level. The pilot will be implemented in 10 counties in 2026 and 2027, with plans to expand to all 69 counties currently facing regional extinction due to population decline.

Sunlight income[5] is an attempt to scale up the solar-power-based basic income model successfully pioneered in Shinan-Gun to the national level. Under this scheme, village residents take equity stakes in local solar power plants and receive dividends as a form of basic income. Starting in 2026, the government plans to establish 500 sunlight income villages annually. While Rural Basic income and sunlight income are distinct initiatives, they are deeply interconnected, as sunlight income is expected to serve as a vital funding source for the broader basic income framework.

This section theoretically examines the necessity, characteristics, and relationship between carbon dividends and sunlight income within the context of the global energy transition.

### *Carbon Dividend*

Carbon pricing implemented through carbon taxes or emissions trading systems (ETS) aims to raise the cost of carbon above its market price. While carbon pricing alone is insufficient to halt climate change, it is undeniably a centerpiece of global climate strategy (Boyce, 2018; 2019). As of 2023, 73 carbon pricing schemes are in operation worldwide,

[4] The Energy Innovation and carbon dividend Act was introduced in 2018, 2019, 2021, and 2023. See: https://www.congress.gov/bill/118th-congress/house-bill/5744

[5] While this could be called sunlight and Wind income to include wind power, this study uses sunlight income as the umbrella term.

covering 23% of global greenhouse gas emissions (World Bank Group, 2023). Furthermore, the European Union's carbon border adjustment mechanism (CBAM), currently in its pilot phase, is set for full implementation in 2026, signaling that carbon pricing will soon evolve into a universal trade norm.

An alternative method for energy transition is command and control policies, such as the renewable portfolio standard (RPS), which mandates a certain percentage of renewable energy generation. However, as long as renewable energy remains more expensive than fossil fuels, any transition—whether via carbon taxes[6] or administrative mandates—inevitably leads to higher electricity prices. This price hike disproportionately burdens low-income households, thereby exacerbating inequality (Andersson, 2009).

Compared to command-and-control mandates, a carbon tax has the advantage of generating revenue that can be used to mitigate this rising inequality. There are several conventional proposals for utilizing carbon tax revenue:

First, tax swaps: Using carbon revenue to reduce existing income or corporate taxes. While this may correct certain economic inefficiencies, it tends to increase inequality. Corporate tax cuts primarily benefit high-income shareholders, and income tax exemptions offer no relief to the elderly or low-income earners who fall below the taxable threshold.

Second, green investment: Allocating revenue toward energy transition technologies. While this enjoys public support, the scale of carbon tax revenue is often insufficient for the massive investment required for a full transition. Funding for such infrastructure should instead be secured through instruments like Climate Bonds. The primary flaw in this approach is that it fails to compensate low- and middle-income households for the loss of real income due to energy price hikes. Without broad public support, it becomes politically impossible to raise carbon taxes to the necessary levels.

Third, targeted transfers: Distributing revenue only to low-income households. Providing energy vouchers (in-kind transfers) can actually hinder the transition by removing incentives for energy conservation within the voucher limit. While targeted cash transfers are better, they do

[6] For simplicity, this study analyzes the carbon tax as the representative form of carbon pricing. The effects on revenue, rent, and inequality are similarly applicable to Emissions Trading Systems (ETS).

nothing to address the real income decline of the middle class, making the sustained escalation of carbon prices politically unviable.

To achieve carbon neutrality, nations must not only implement carbon pricing but also eliminate fossil fuel subsidies (Standing, 2017: 40). In a country like South Korea, which provides significant implicit subsidies for fossil fuels,[7] raising carbon taxes to European levels would cause a drastic spike in electricity prices, which currently remain among the lowest in the OECD.[8]

In this scenario, distributing carbon tax revenues exclusively to low-income households would inevitably lead to a significant decline in the real income of the middle class. Without the political support of the middle class, it becomes difficult to sustain or increase carbon taxes, thereby creating a barrier to achieving carbon neutrality (Dixson-Declève et al., 2022).

Fourth, revenue can be distributed to all residents in the form of equal carbon dividends. According to estimates by Ummel, assuming 85% of the carbon tax is passed on to consumers, a carbon tax-carbon dividend scheme would result in 61% of all households becoming net beneficiaries, while 39% would be net payers. Among the net payers, 85% of all households would face a net burden of less than 0.2% of their income (Ummel, 2020) .

By preventing an increase in inequality while securing political support for carbon tax hikes, carbon neutrality can be achieved more rapidly (Boyce, 2019; Howard, 2012). In 2019, over 3,000 American economists, including 28 Nobel laureates, issued a statement supporting carbon dividends. The fifth article of this statement succinctly captures these advantages:

> V. To maximize the fairness and political viability of a rising carbon tax, all the revenue should be returned directly to U.S. citizens through equal lump-sum rebates. The majority of American families, including the most vulnerable, will benefit financially by receiving more in 'carbon dividends' than they pay in increased energy costs.[9]

[7] KEPCO's cumulative deficit has reached 200 trillion KRW. Since most of the electricity supplied is generated from carbon-intensive sources, this deficit effectively serves as a fossil fuel subsidy.

[8] As of August 2023, South Korea's residential electricity rate was \$106.8/MWh, significantly lower than the US (\$151.2), Japan (\$240.2), Germany (\$348.9), and Denmark (\$518.3).

[9] Retrieved 2023. 11. 18 from https://www.econstatement.org/. This statement was first published in the Wall Street Journal on January 16, 2019.

Carbon taxes can be viewed as a tool for commoning the climate commons. If implemented effectively, they preserve the climate commons for future generations. However, in the current state where the majority benefits from carbon emissions, imposing a carbon tax raises prices and reduces everyone's real income. Consequently, political resistance is so potent that many nations continue to delay its introduction. Carbon dividends serve as an overlapping commoning mechanism that mitigates this political friction.

Despite these advantages, carbon dividends possess a significant limitation: as the energy transition progresses, carbon tax revenues will inevitably decrease (Andersson, 2009; Howard and Pinto, 2019). If net-zero emissions are achieved by 2050, carbon emissions will equal the amount absorbed by forests or oceans. No matter how high the tax rate, the total revenue will dwindle to a negligible scale. Ultimately, while carbon dividends play a crucial role in reducing inequality in the early stages, their impact will diminish over time as the revenue pool shrinks. This process is examined in detail in the following section.

### *Carbon Rents and Renewable Energy Rents*

Economic rent is defined as the amount paid to a factor of production in excess of the cost required to supply it. Carbon rent refers to the economic rent captured by fossil fuel corporations. Such rents are generated not only by carbon pricing but also by carbon regulations. This section analyzes the emergence of carbon rents within the electricity industry, a representative energy sector.

Figure 3.2 is based on several simplifying assumptions. The total electricity demand for the economy is assumed to be fixed at $O_CO_R$. The vertical axis represents price. Fossil fuel power generation starts from origin $O_C$ and increases to the right, while renewable power generation starts from origin $O_R$ and increases to the left. The supply curve (marginal cost curve) for fossil fuel is $C_0D_0$, and for renewable energy is $R_0S_0$. Both are assumed to be upward-sloping (from their respective origins). The steeper slope of the renewable energy supply curve reflects the reality that costs vary significantly by source (hydro, solar, wind, etc.) and location (land prices).[10]

[10]In 2022, the construction cost per 1GW of renewable energy was 1.3 trillion KRW for onshore solar, 2.7 trillion KRW for onshore wind, and 5.5 trillion KRW for offshore wind—a difference of more than fourfold between onshore solar and offshore wind (Lee & Lim, 2022).

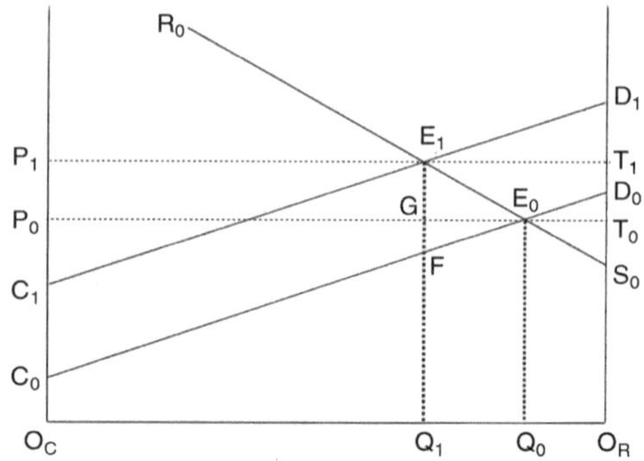


**Fig. 3.2** Carbon Rents and Renewable Energy Rents (Initial Stage)

Under these assumptions, the initial equilibrium is reached at point $E_0$, with the equilibrium price at $P_0$. Fossil fuel generation is $O_CQ_0$, and renewable generation is $O_RQ_0$. As illustrated, it is cheaper to produce $O_RQ_0$ of power via renewables, while the remainder is more cost-effective via fossil fuels. The producer surplus (rent) for fossil fuel firms is $\Delta P_0C_0E_0$, and for renewable firms, it is $\Delta E_0S_0T_0$.

If the government limits fossil fuel generation to $O_CQ_1$ through mandates and regulations, the deficit must be covered by renewable power ($O_RQ_1$). To produce $O_RQ_1$, the price must increase to $P_1$. Consequently, fossil fuel firms capture a rent of $\square P_1C_0FE_1$. Government regulations reduce their rent by $\Delta GFE_0$ but increase it by $\square P_1P_0GE_1$. In the early stages depicted in Fig. 3.2, total rents for fossil fuel industries can actually increase. Meanwhile, consumer energy expenditure increases by $\square P_1P_0T_0T_1$.

Now, let us analyze the case where the government imposes a carbon tax of $C_0C_1$ on fossil fuel power generation instead of relying on command-and-control mandates. The carbon tax shifts the fossil fuel supply curve upward to $C_1D_1$. The new equilibrium is reached at $E_1$, with the price increasing from $P_0$ to $P_1$. Consequently, fossil fuel generation decreases to $O_CQ_1$, while renewable generation increases to $O_RQ_1$. Consumer energy expenditure rises by $\square P_1P_0T_0T_1$. Notably, the generation volume, price, and consumer expenditure under the carbon tax are identical to those under the command-and-control regime.

Under the carbon tax, the rent captured by fossil fuel firms is $\Delta P_1C_1E_1$, and the carbon tax revenue is $\square C_1C_0FE_1$. The sum of these two equals $\square P_1C_0FE_1$, which is the total rent fossil fuel firms would have captured

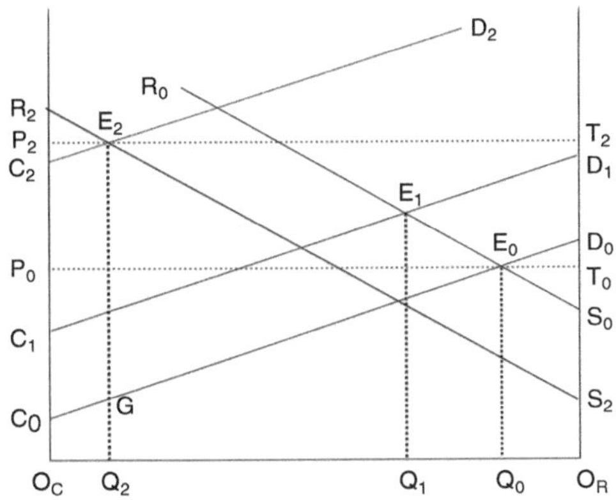


**Fig. 3.3** Carbon Rents and Renewable Energy Rents (Late Stage)

under mandates. Therefore, the carbon tax can be interpreted as a policy that generates the same level of rent as regulations while simultaneously reclaiming a portion of that rent equivalent to the tax revenue. As shown in Fig. 3.2, the total carbon tax revenue can cover most of the increase in consumer expenditure if distributed as carbon dividends. Thus, in the early stages, the carbon tax facilitates an energy transition that reduces inequality without diminishing the real income of consumers. Since rent represents a transfer of value rather than its creation, this reclamation and distribution are economically justified (Boyce, 2020). From another perspective, the carbon tax is a usage fee for the exhaustible common wealth of the atmosphere's carbon absorption capacity; thus, it is only just to distribute it equally to all community members as a basic income (Boyce, 2019). Under this tax, renewable energy rent becomes $\Delta E_1S_0T_1$, which remains with renewable firms as profit and is relatively small in the initial stage.

As the government further increases the carbon tax to $C_0C_2$, the fossil fuel supply curve shifts to $C_2D_2$, as shown in Fig. 3.3. Simultaneously, we assume the renewable supply curve shifts downward from $R_0S_0$ to $R_2W_2$, reflecting the ongoing trend of falling generation costs. The new equilibrium is $E_2$ at price $P_2$. Fossil fuel generation shrinks to $O_CQ_2$, and renewable generation expands to $O_RQ_2$. At this stage, while the increase in energy expenditure is $\square P_2P_0T_0T_2$, the carbon tax revenue is only $\square C_2C_0GE_2$. Even if all tax revenue is distributed as dividends, it can only cover a small fraction of the increased costs. Therefore, carbon dividends alone cannot achieve an energy transition that prevents rising inequality.

Meanwhile, the renewable energy rent increases substantially to $\Delta E_2S_2T_2$. This rent is driven by both natural conditions (reflected in the slope of the cost curve) and public policy (carbon taxes or mandates). If public policy is viewed as a social common wealth, then both natural and social commons are generating this rent. To mitigate inequality, it is necessary to reclaim and distribute not only carbon rents but also renewable energy rents. As the transition progresses, carbon rents shrink while renewable rents grow; thus, a new method to reclaim the latter—explored in Section 4—is required.

Does rent still occur when renewable marginal costs fall enough to reach grid parity (where the new equilibrium price is below the original $P_0$)? First, it must be noted that due to the intermittency of renewables, this is difficult to achieve without significant investment. In South Korea, where existing grids are saturated, investments in new HVDC lines and large-scale storage are required, and these costs must be reflected in the levelized full system cost of energy (LFSCOE). Idel (2022) estimated that while gas CCGT costs were $35–40/MWh in Germany and Texas, solar costs reached $1,548 and $413 respectively when accounting for full system integration.

Furthermore, even if equilibrium prices fall, high carbon taxes remain necessary. As fossil fuel demand drops, its market price may fall toward the marginal extraction cost.[11] According to environmental economics, the marginal cost of an exhaustible resource equals the sum of marginal extraction cost and marginal user cost. When use is low enough that exhaustion is not imminent, the marginal user cost becomes zero (Tietenberg and Lewis, 2024). Let us analyze this scenario in Fig. 3.4.

The original equilibrium is $E_0$ at price $P_0$. We assume the renewable marginal cost curve drops significantly to $R_2S_2$. Without a carbon tax, the equilibrium would be $E_1$ at price $P_1$. However, this is short-lived; as fossil fuel demand falls, its cost curve also shifts down to $C_2D_2$. The resulting equilibrium $E_2$ would actually lead to higher fossil fuel generation ($O_CQ_2$) than before the cost drop. To restrict fossil fuel generation to $O_CQ_3$, a carbon tax of $C_2C_3$ (or equivalent mandate) is essential. The final equilibrium $E_3$ results in a price $P_3$, lower than the original $P_0$. Even at this lower

[11] In 2016, the marginal extraction costs in Saudi Arabia, Iran, and Iraq were less than $10 per barrel, and less than $20 in Russia (California Energy Commission, 2021).

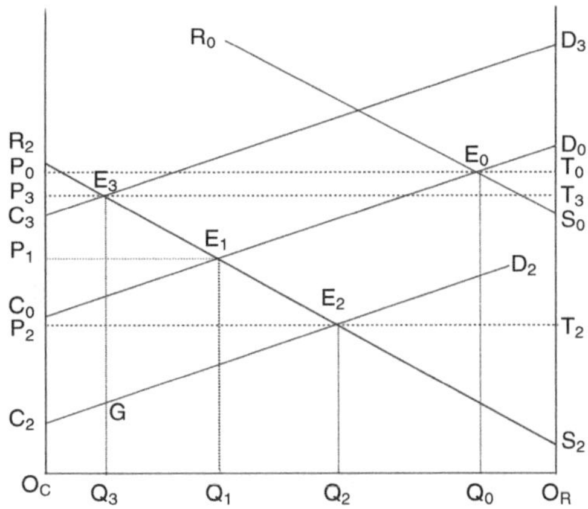


**Fig. 3.4** Case of Significant Decline in Renewable Marginal Cost Curve

price, renewable firms capture a massive rent of $\Delta E_3S_2T_3$. A significant portion of this $\square E_3E_2T_2T_3$ is a form of unearned income generated by public policy. Since carbon taxes can only reclaim carbon-related rents, a different mechanism—sunlight dividends—is needed to reclaim and distribute this growing renewable energy rent.

### *Sunlight Dividend: Mechanisms for Reclaiming Renewable Rents*

There are three potential methods for reclaiming renewable energy rents generated from the commons.

First, profit regulation: Governments can regulate renewable energy firms by setting prices based on average costs rather than marginal costs. However, the information costs for oversight are prohibitive. In private monopolies, this often leads to the Averch-Johnson effect (1962), where firms have incentives to inflate costs or over-invest in unnecessary equipment. Most importantly, suppressing profit rates can deter and delay the transition to renewable energy.

Second, taxation: Since renewable rents stem from natural and social commons rather than corporate innovation, there is a clear justification for taxation. However, this often triggers political conflict over legitimacy and risks moral hazard, such as cost-padding to evade taxes. Like profit regulation, it may weaken private incentives for green investment.

Third, equity participation and dividends: This method involves the government or local residents taking equity stakes in renewable energy projects. Based on the principles of a joint-stock company, this approach allows for the efficient reclamation of rents through dividends without the typical friction associated with taxation. Since it does not lower the return on equity for private capital, its deterrent effect on private investment is minimal. Moreover, as the public sector and residents become active investors, overall renewable investment can be catalyzed.

Denmark has pioneered this model. Its Renewable Energy Act of 2008 mandated that all renewable power plants offer at least a 20% equity stake to local residents.[12] Recently, while the mandatory sale to residents was removed, it was replaced by a requirement to provide a 20% stake to the state free of charge as a condition for bidding (Reuters, 2023).

In South Korea, the sunlight dividend (Sunlight Pension/Income)[13] in Shinan-gun serves as a model case. By allowing residents to hold a 30% equity stake in the power plant corporations (representing 4% of total capital), 30% of profits are distributed as sunlight income. Shinan-gun plans to install 1.8 GW of solar and 8.2 GW of offshore wind by 2030. Upon completion, the county intends to provide a monthly Wind dividend of 500,000 KRW per resident (Kwon et al., 2023). The program is notable for its universal participation, sharing benefits in a form closely resembling a basic income. President Lee Jae-myung is currently seeking to scale this sunlight income model nationwide.

### *Just Energy Transition and Common Wealth Dividends*

The energy transition process generates both carbon rents and renewable energy rents. As the transition advances, carbon rents diminish while renewable rents grow—even after achieving grid parity. Because the source of these rents lies in the natural and social commons, reclaiming and distributing them as a basic income is not only just but also essential for preventing rising inequality during the transition.

As climate-related damages escalate, carbon pricing (carbon taxes and ETS) will become a global trade standard. While carbon pricing is an

[12] See: https://www.elov.dk/energifremmeloven/#%C2%A71-stk1

[13] In Korea, the terms "Sunlight Dividend", "Sunlight Income", and "Sunlight Pension" are used interchangeably. In Shinan-gun, it is called a pension, but as it is a universal payment regardless of age, it is more accurately described as a dividend or basic income. The Ministry of Agriculture uses the term sunlight income.

efficient tool for transition, it risks exacerbating inequality and sparking political resistance. To mitigate this, carbon dividends have been proposed and implemented in countries like Canada.

However, the fundamental weakness of carbon dividends is that in the late stages of transition, tax revenues will fall far short of the increase in energy expenditures, weakening their inequality-reducing effect. To ensure an equitable transition through its final stages, sunlight dividends are required alongside carbon dividends. The most effective way to reclaim renewable rents is for the state and residents to actively invest in renewable projects and share the resulting dividends. By combining carbon dividends with common wealth equity dividends, a society can achieve a net-zero transition that remains equitable from start to finish.

A carbon tax is a means of commoning the climate commons to ensure a livable planet for posterity. The carbon dividend acts as a nested commoning tool that overcomes political resistance to the tax. Sunlight income, in turn, serves as another nested commoning mechanism that overcomes the limitations of carbon dividends, sustaining the drive toward carbon neutrality until the ultimate goal is reached.

CHAPTER 4

# Universal Refundable Tax Credits

In the preceding chapters, we established the necessity and validity of both NIT-type (Negative Income Tax) and Common Wealth-financed basic income. This chapter explores the "Refundable Tax Credit"—based on an integrated approach to taxation and benefits—as an administrative framework for implementing such a system. Furthermore, we demonstrate that the refundable tax credit mechanism serves as an effective tool for the progressive reform of regressive tax expenditures. Specifically, we examine the transformation *of personal income tax allowances* into a universal basic income and the universalization of the Earned Income Tax Credit (EITC)—often referred to as the "Work Incentive Payment(근로장려금)" in South Korea—into a universal support system for all working individuals.

## 4.1 An Integrated Approach to Taxation and Benefits

As previously discussed, when taxation and public transfers are integrated into a single framework, a universal basic income and an individual-level Negative Income Tax (NIT) can be functionally equivalent. This integrated perspective underscores the inherent advantages of the NIT-type model and introduces critical analytical metrics, such as the effective tax rate (ETR), effective marginal tax rate (EMTR), and participation tax rate (PTR). Specifically, the ETR is negative when benefits exceed



J. S. You et al., *UBI from Idea to Reality*, Exploring the Basic Income Guarantee,
https://doi.org/10.1007/978-3-032-26200-4_4

tax liabilities, and conversely, it becomes positive when taxes exceed benefits. The EMTR and PTR quantify the combined impact of increased taxes and reduced benefits relative to a marginal unit of additional earnings and total earnings, respectively. While the EMTR influences the incentive to increase work effort (the intensive margin), the PTR determines the decision of whether to participate in the labor market (the extensive margin).

An integrated approach is also instrumental in explaining that the right to a basic income is fundamentally linked to the duty of taxation. It allows for a clearer understanding of income redistribution, moving beyond simple transfers from the rich to the poor to include inter-temporal transfers across an individual's life cycle—shifting income from productive adulthood to childhood and old age. The NIT-type basic income makes these principles transparent by explicitly showing whether an individual is a net beneficiary or a net contributor in any given year.

Furthermore, this integrated view allows us to interpret various tax exemptions and deductions as "tax expenditures" that function essentially as social benefits. Common methods of tax relief include non-taxable income, income deductions, and tax credits. These are termed tax expenditures because they are functionally equivalent to the state collecting taxes on all income and then redistributing the exempted amounts as benefits. Historically, tax expenditure budgets have faced less public scrutiny than cash outlays, leading scholars to refer to them as the "Hidden Welfare State" (Howard, 1997).

Many current tax expenditures are regressive, providing greater benefits to high-income earners than to those with low incomes. For instance, non-taxable capital gains and various income deductions tend to be regressive. Fixed-amount income deductions are meaningless for low-income earners below the tax threshold and offer larger tax savings to high-income earners subject to higher marginal tax rates. Fixed-amount tax credits provide a uniform reduction in tax liability regardless of income, but their benefit is limited for those whose tax liability is smaller than the credit amount or who fall below the tax threshold entirely.

During the COVID-19 pandemic, the argument that universal emergency grants are more effective than tax cuts gained significant traction (De Wispelaere and Morales, 2021; Torry, 2020), leading to global discussions on Disaster Basic Income.

Unlike traditional tax expenditures, a Refundable Tax Credit ensures that benefits reach individuals even if they fall below the tax threshold or have a tax liability smaller than the credit. If the credit amount exceeds the tax owed, the difference is paid out as a cash refund. Under this scheme, a basic income can be administered seamlessly: if the basic income amount is greater than the tax owed, the individual receives a refund; if the tax owed is greater, they simply pay the net difference. While standard basic income models often assume a monthly cash payment followed by separate tax filings, an NIT-type model streamlines this through the tax system.

A common critique of NIT is the administrative difficulty of reconciling taxes and benefits without a real-time income monitoring system. For example, the Finnish basic income experiment initially excluded the NIT model due to the lack of such a system at the time (Kangas, 2016). While many assume that NIT requires real-time reporting to calculate monthly payments, a more viable approach may be to keep the income assessment cycle annual while maintaining monthly or quarterly cycles for disbursements and tax payments (Green, 1967; Tobin et al., 1967). We will explore the merits of this decoupled timing later in this chapter.

Ultimately, converting income deductions into refundable tax credits is a highly effective means of enhancing the progressivity of the income tax system and expanding redistribution.

## 4.2 Practical Considerations in Implementing NIT-Type Basic Income

### *A Comprehensive Definition of Income and Dual-Track Operation with Existing Income Tax*

In an NIT-type basic income system, it is necessary to employ a broader definition of income than the narrow scope used in conventional income tax systems. Existing income tax regimes permit various non-taxable incomes and allow for numerous deductions, such as personal allowances and earned income deductions. Consequently, the taxable base (taxable income) is significantly lower than actual gross income. If an NIT-type basic income is introduced, it should naturally include all forms of cash income, including currently non-taxable items, while excluding all types of income deductions (Green, 1967: 84). Ideally, it should utilize a "comprehensive income" concept that encompasses not only capital income (interest, dividends, rental income, etc.) but also, to the extent possible, realized capital gains from assets like real estate, stocks, and cryptocurrencies (Friedman, 1966; Green, 1967; Tobin et al., 1967).

James Tobin and his colleagues suggested that while exceptions might be made for unavoidable high medical expenses, it would be more transparent to provide direct grants for medical costs exceeding a certain threshold rather than allowing deductions (Tobin et al., 1967). Abolishing all tax expenditures, such as income deductions, and replacing them with direct fiscal outlays or refundable tax credits would be both more transparent and progressive.

While it is theoretically possible to completely convert various policy-driven tax expenditures into fiscal budgets or refundable tax credits within the current tax framework, achieving this in the short term is challenging. Therefore, while efforts should be made to simplify the tax system and enhance progressivity by redefining income more comprehensively, it is more realistic for an NIT-type basic income to operate on a "dual-track" basis—using a maximally comprehensive definition of income while maintaining a separate operation from the traditional income tax system.

For instance, many countries either exempt capital gains and income or tax them at lower rates than earned income. Favoring capital gains, often regarded as unearned income, over income derived from labor is fundamentally unfair. Excluding capital income and gains from the definition of income under an NIT system would further highlight this inequity. Furthermore, it would be unjust if high-income earners were classified as low-income recipients of NIT benefits because of non-taxable items or deductions within their labor income. Even when certain deductions enjoy broad policy support, it is hard to justify their inclusion in an NIT-type basic income. However, even a comprehensive definition of income faces certain constraints. For example, unrealized capital gains—which are non-taxable in current systems—are difficult to include in an NIT framework.

One crucial item excluded from conventional tax definitions but essential for an NIT-type basic income is imputed rental income. This represents the estimated value of the housing services consumed by owner-occupiers—essentially the rent one would have to pay if they did not own the home. The following cases illustrate the necessity of including imputed rent:

- Suppose A and B have the same cash income. A lives in an owned apartment, while B lives in an identical rented apartment, paying half of their salary in rent. If their NIT benefits or taxes are identical because their cash incomes are equal, it would be unfair. Since A's effective income is higher by the amount of rent B pays, it is fairer for B to receive more NIT benefits or for A to pay more tax on their excess income.

- C receives the same salary as A and B but rents out an owned apartment and uses that rental income to pay for a separate rented residence. C's total income is salary plus rental income. Since C essentially enjoys the same income and housing consumption as A, it is illogical to include rental income for C while excluding imputed rent for A.

Given these cases, while including imputed rent in conventional taxable income might be difficult, it must be considered within the NIT framework. Tobin et al. (1967) proposed a specific method: applying a 5% interest rate to the market value of the home and deducting mortgage interest.

Let us compare this to social assistance (welfare) programs that typically consider both income and assets for eligibility: some programs use "recognized income" (which converts assets into an income equivalent), while others set a hard asset ceiling. The latter creates extremely high marginal effective tax rates near the asset threshold, causing unfairness and disincentivizing savings or encouraging asset concealment. The former, if the conversion rate is high, imposes what is effectively a very high property tax, which may lead to the intentional depletion of assets.

While there is a rationale for considering assets in social assistance, high conversion rates often disqualify low-income individuals with modest assets or lead to insufficient benefits. Considering that these individuals already pay property and income taxes on their assets, imposing an excessively high effective property tax only on welfare recipients is unfair. However, since owner-occupied housing does not generate cash rental income and is excluded from imputed rent taxation, it is reasonable to include imputed rental income in the definition of income for NIT, as cash rental income is already subject to income tax.

Since NIT-type basic income can replace all or part of social assistance but is not intended to replace social insurance, it is rational to include social insurance benefits—such as unemployment insurance and public pensions—within the definition of income. In contrast, social assistance benefits, which serve as a residual social safety net and a complementary mechanism to NIT, should be excluded from the income definition (Tobin et al., 1967). However, by including NIT payments in the means-testing for social assistance, NIT can effectively substitute for social assistance within the scope of the amount paid.

As discussed, while NIT-type basic income requires a dual-track operation due to its distinct definition of income, it should remain integrated with the existing tax administration. By leveraging the tax authorities' income-monitoring systems, individuals can report non-taxable income, social insurance benefits, and the information necessary for calculating imputed rent (such as property values) alongside their annual income tax returns. This allows the tax authorities to reconcile NIT benefits or taxes on excess income separately from conventional income tax. In fact, tax authorities can collect such data pre-emptively from relevant authorities. This dual-track approach can eventually evolve toward a unified system as the definition of taxable income in the conventional tax code expands.

### *Cycles of Income Assessment, Benefit Disbursement, and Tax Payment*

When implementing an NIT-type basic income, determining the frequency and timing of income assessment and disbursements is critical. Importantly, the cycle of income assessment does not need to coincide with the cycle of payment or tax collection; in fact, a longer assessment cycle coupled with shorter payment intervals may be superior. To prevent hardship for those with limited capital or credit, James Tobin suggested an annual assessment cycle with bi-weekly or bi-monthly disbursements (Tobin et al., 1967), while Green proposed quarterly or monthly intervals (Green, 1967).

Setting the income assessment period to one year is necessary not only for administrative convenience but also to ensure fairness for individuals with volatile incomes. Even with real-time monitoring systems, determining monthly benefits based on monthly fluctuations can be irrational—particularly for the self-employed, whose monthly income is difficult to track accurately. If benefits or taxes are determined monthly, individuals with fluctuating incomes may be advantaged or disadvantaged compared to those with steady incomes unless the benefit reduction rate and the tax rate on excess income are identical.

For example, consider individuals A and B, whose annual incomes both equal the "break-even" threshold. A earns a steady monthly income, while B earns nothing for six months and twice the threshold for the remaining six months. If the benefit reduction rate (clawback rate) is higher than the tax rate on excess income, B (the volatile earner) ends up as a net beneficiary. Conversely, if the tax rate is higher, B becomes a net contributor. A, having a steady income at the threshold, neither receives benefits nor pays additional taxes in either scenario.

To resolve this, it is ideal to align the reduction rate with the tax rate or, at the very least, utilize a longer (annual) assessment cycle. Even if payments are made monthly, an annual assessment ensures that individuals with the same annual income are treated equally. While applying a uniform tax rate across all income levels is difficult when overlaying NIT onto an existing tax system, an annual reconciliation remains the most practical solution.

Administratively, this is straightforward as it aligns with the annual tax filing cycle. During the year-end settlement, individuals can reconcile the previous year's benefits and taxes, choosing to receive refunds or pay balances in monthly, quarterly, or lump-sum installments. Those for whom NIT is a primary income source would likely prefer shorter intervals, while those with higher incomes might opt for a single settlement.

A potential issue is that benefits are determined based on the previous year's income rather than current circumstances. While negligible for those with stable incomes, this can pose a challenge for those facing sudden income drops. In such cases, individuals should be allowed to report recent fluctuations (e.g., quarterly) to request adjusted advance payments, with a final reconciliation occurring the following year. During the COVID-19 pandemic, the United States successfully operated a similar system for the expanded refundable Child Tax Credit, allowing for advance payments based on the most recent data with a subsequent reconciliation (Lee, forthcoming).

While a monthly "pay-as-you-go" universal basic income might be administratively simpler in a vacuum, the NIT approach offers distinct advantages: it reduces the total fiscal size (gross cost), is more palatable to the general public, and allows for age-adjusted guaranteed income levels. Despite being slightly more complex than a purely universal model, NIT remains significantly simpler and more efficient than existing fragmented tax and welfare administrations.

## 4.3 Transforming Basic Personal Allowances Into Universal Basic Income

As previously analyzed, income deductions in the personal income tax system possess inherently regressive characteristics. A fixed-amount income deduction provides no benefit to low-income earners below the tax threshold, while offering larger tax savings to high-income earners in higher tax brackets. While converting these into fixed-amount tax credits can mitigate this regressivity, they remain ineffective for those whose tax liability is zero. This section explores a strategy to transform personal allowances into refundable tax credits and expand their eligibility to the entire population.

In many countries, a certain amount of income is exempted from taxation for the taxpayer and their dependents under the name of "Personal Allowance," "Basic Deduction," or "Standard Deduction." This practice diminishes the progressivity of the income tax and reduces tax revenue, as high-income earners in higher tax brackets receive a larger effective tax reduction. Some countries, such as Canada, provide a fixed-amount tax credit instead of a deduction. While this ensures that the tax reduction amount is equal between high and low-income earners, it still fails to provide benefits to those below the tax threshold or those whose tax liability is less than the credit amount. Therefore, converting personal allowances or standard deductions into Universal Refundable Tax Credits is an excellent means of enhancing income redistribution.

The primary rationale for personal allowances is to ensure that a minimum level of income remains untaxed. However, the fundamental spirit of NIT-type basic income extends beyond mere tax exemption; it entails applying negative taxation to incomes falling below this minimum threshold. Therefore, the benefits inherent in personal allowances should be extended to low-income earners whose earnings do not reach this level. Furthermore, in most nations, even low-income earners who do not file income tax returns are subject to taxation through withholding systems, and tax authorities generally track this administrative data. Consequently, if all adults are mandated to file tax returns regardless of their income level—or are registered as dependents of a filer—and are subsequently provided with a refundable tax credit, the system effectively functions as a Universal Basic Income (UBI) distributed on an annual basis.

The transition to a universal refundable tax credit is relatively straightforward: it requires ensuring that individuals who are currently neither tax filers nor dependents are integrated into the system, and then making the existing credits refundable. This could be achieved with modest fiscal input while maintaining current credit levels. To achieve fiscal neutrality—implementing the change without additional fiscal resources—the total tax revenue gained from abolishing existing deductions would be divided by the total population to determine the universal refundable credit amount. Adding further fiscal resources to this base would allow for a more substantial UBI amount.

The proposal to transform personal allowances into refundable credits as a path to UBI has been advocated by various scholars. Al Sheahen and Karl Widerquist (2004), co-founders of the U.S. Basic Income Guarantee Network, proposed a "Partial Basic Income" by converting personal exemptions (then $4,750 for singles, $9,500 for couples, and $3,050 for dependents) into refundable credits ($2,000 for adults, $1,000 for children), funded by rolling back the Bush-era tax cuts. Similarly, Stevens and Simpson (2017) of the University of Manitoba argued that converting several non-refundable credits, including the basic personal amount, into refundable ones could introduce a meaningful National Universal Guaranteed Basic Income without increasing tax rates.

In South Korea, basic personal allowances are relatively low (1.5 million KRW for the taxpayer, spouse, and dependents), suggesting that a UBI implemented solely through this conversion would be modest in scale. Nonetheless, such a policy would be significant as a form of "Broad Common Wealth Basic Income," representing an equal distribution of a portion of the social commons—a concept wider than natural commons alone.

In addition to personal allowances, many countries like the U.S. have introduced refundable Child Tax Credits (CTC). While non-filers might miss out on these benefits, mandating tax filings for all adults would effectively turn child tax credits into a Basic Income for Children.

## 4.4 The Introduction of a Universal EITC as a Form of Participation Income

### *A Proposal for the Universalization of the Earned Income Tax Credit (EITC)*

The EITC was first introduced in the U.S. in the 1970s and has since spread globally. South Korea benchmarked the U.S. model to introduce its own "Work Incentive Payment" (근로장려금) in 2008.

In the current U.S. EITC system, benefit amounts depend not only on earned income but also on marital status and the number of children. If earned income is zero, the EITC is zero. As income rises up to a certain level, the credit increases; this is known as the "phase-in" range. This is the opposite of a Negative Income Tax (NIT), where the maximum guaranteed income is paid at zero income and is then clawed back. The phase-in is designed specifically to incentivize labor. Following this is the "plateau" range, where benefits remain constant, and finally the "phase-out" (taper) range, where benefits are reduced as income increases until they reach zero.

Recently, scholars such as Benjamin Leff and Leonard Burman have proposed transforming the U.S. Earned Income Tax Credit (EITC) into a "Universal EITC" (Burman, 2019, 2020; Leff, 2020). Their proposal entails eliminating the "phase-out" (taper) range of the credit to cover all earners and transitioning from a household-based to an individual-based disbursement system. This model moves the EITC closer to a basic income while addressing public concerns regarding "free-riding" by workless individuals, thereby aiming to secure broader political support.

Leff (2020) acknowledges the advantages of the EITC: it provides cash similarly to a basic income, is administratively efficient, lacks the stigma associated with traditional welfare, and has a relatively moderate clawback rate compared to other means-tested programs. However, he identifies four critical flaws in the existing EITC:

1. The phase-out range begins at a relatively low income level, creating a work disincentive for those near the poverty line.
2. Its dependence on family structure is unfair, intrusive to privacy, and creates distortions in incentives regarding marriage, divorce, and cohabitation.
3. Integration into the tax system means benefits are based on previous year's income, leading to a time-lag that fails to meet immediate needs while imposing administrative burdens.
4. Benefit levels are insufficient as a safeguard against underemployment and deep poverty.

The work disincentive in the phase-out range is a challenge shared by the NIT. Its impact depends on the clawback rate and the Effective Marginal Tax Rate (EMTR) when combined with other taxes and benefits. Leff's primary critique is that the EITC reduces benefits just as low-income earners begin to see modest income gains, thereby discouraging labor.

Furthermore, Leff points out that the U.S. EITC provides negligible benefits to childless workers and imposes a "marriage penalty." Because the credit for a married couple is often less than the sum of what two individuals would receive separately, it can act as a deterrent to marriage. Additionally, because it is claimed during annual tax filings, the refund arrives too late to address the recipients' immediate financial crises.

To remedy these, Leff proposes reforming the EITC to function more like a basic income by eliminating the phase-out range, shifting to an individual basis, providing monthly cash disbursements, and expanding the overall benefit level.

Burman (2019, 2020) also advocates for a universal, individual-based EITC with specific policy parameters. He proposed two options:

- Option A: An EITC equal to 100% of earned income up to a $10,000 cap, combined with a $2,500 refundable Child Tax Credit.
- Option B: An EITC at a 50% rate up to a $14,000 cap, plus a $2,000 basic income per person (including children and adults) .

He suggests funding these through an 11% Value-Added Tax (VAT) or a 12% surtax on taxable income. Under this proposal, 80% of the population (excluding the top 20%) would become net beneficiaries, providing relief not only to the poor but also to middle-class workers. Burman estimates that the bottom 20% would see a 25% increase in after-tax income, while the top 1% would face a 7–14% tax increase.

Burman highlights two main reasons for preferring a Universal EITC over a pure UBI. First, by targeting only the working population (including employees and the self-employed), it can garner bipartisan support and broader public legitimacy. He cites recent polls showing 87% support for work requirements in welfare programs. Second, he argues that unlike UBI, a Universal EITC encourages low-skilled workers to maintain a connection to the labor market and develop job skills. He also notes that a Universal EITC removes the disadvantage current models impose on dual-income couples.

### *Universal EITC as a Form of Participation Income*

The "Universal EITC" recently proposed by U.S. policy researchers differs from conventional EITC in its universal coverage of all working individuals. However, unlike Universal Basic Income (UBI) , it remains conditional on participation in paid labor, thereby diverging from the core principles of universality and unconditionality. In this sense, it can be categorized as a form of Participation Income (PI). Yet, it is distinct from the traditional concept of PI, which typically recognizes unpaid labor—such as domestic work and caregiving—as valid forms of participation, making it functionally nearly identical to UBI.

The concept of Participation Income was first introduced by the British economist Anthony Atkinson, who dedicated his life to studying income inequality (Atkinson, 1996; 2015). Unlike UBI, PI is provided to working-age adults on the condition of participation, with exceptions for illness or disability. Atkinson defined "participation" broadly as social contribution, encompassing not only paid employment and self-employment but also care work, recognized volunteer activities, education, training, and job-seeking efforts.

Before proposing PI, Atkinson had theoretically defended a UBI model based on a flat rate tax (Atkinson, 1995). He cited John Rawls' objection to UBI as a primary reason for pivoting toward PI. Although Rawls mentioned the Negative Income Tax as a means of guaranteeing a social minimum in *A Theory of Justice* (Rawls, 1971[1999]: 243), he later expressed opposition to UBI, famously stating that "those who surf all day off Malibu must find a way to support themselves and would not be entitled to public funds" (Rawls, 1988). It is worth noting, however, that under the NIT models advocated by Milton Friedman or James Tobin, a surfer at Malibu with no income would indeed receive guaranteed income, as no conditions other than income are considered.

Atkinson proposed PI as a complement to, rather than a total replacement for, existing public transfer payments. Addressing critiques that monitoring participation would be administratively burdensome (De Wispelaere and Stirton, 2007), he argued that verifying participation is far simpler than conventional means-testing. He also noted that even UBI is not truly unconditional, as it is predicated on citizenship; PI merely substitutes "citizenship" with "participation." Furthermore, because his definition of participation was so broad, Atkinson estimated that very few people would actually be excluded, allowing him to include the entire population in fiscal projections (Atkinson, 1996; 2015: 219–221) .

Recently, Finnish social policy scholar Heikki Hiilamo (2022) proposed PI as an alternative to UBI for poverty alleviation. Hiilamo argues that the future of social security lies in "individuality" rather than "universality," suggesting that PI be provided to all individuals with below-average incomes on the condition of a broad social contribution. While he rejects household-based means-testing, he views individual income assessment as inevitable. Hiilamo warns that unconditional UBI might lead long-term unemployed or low-skilled individuals to rely on benefits perpetually rather than realizing their potential. He proposes "Eco-social Participation," which extends care not only to humans but also to the environment. He emphasizes that community organizations must collaborate to create projects in local development, ecological care, and training to provide participation opportunities for those long marginalized from the labor market.

Beyond these broad definitions, PI can also manifest in sector-specific or thematic forms. For instance, what has been termed "Farmer's Allowance" or "Artist's Basic Income" in South Korea can be understood as occupational participation income. While often called a "basic income" for a specific vocation, it is more accurately described as PI since it is conditional on professional activity.

However, PI still faces criticisms regarding the administrative burden of eligibility screening and potential disputes over assessment results. Occupational PI is no exception; disputes frequently arise over the criteria for being recognized as a "farmer" or an "artist" (Van Parijs and Vanderborght, 2017: 161). In this context, the proposed Universal EITC is worth considering as a viable form of PI, as it offers broad coverage while entailing minimal administrative difficulty or eligibility disputes. Since it encompasses all those earning broad labor income, including the self-employed, it can naturally include farmers and artists. Nevertheless, it has limitations: it offers meager benefits to those with very low earned income and, by focusing on formal paid labor, fails to cover unpaid family workers, the informal sector, domestic labor, and care work.

### *Universal EITC as a Complement to NIT-Type Basic Income*

Both the current EITC and the proposed "Universal EITC" inherently conflict with the principle of unconditionality, as they require participation in paid labor. Those who oppose participation income (PI) on the grounds of conditionality would likewise oppose a Universal EITC. Furthermore, since Universal EITC focuses exclusively on formal paid employment—excluding unpaid care work, volunteerism, and even informal sector labor—it may be seen as more restrictive than the broader PI models.

However, a comparative analysis of how Universal EITC and NIT-type basic income affect the effective tax rate, participation tax rate (PTR), and effective marginal tax rate (EMTR) reveals both similarities and differences. Both systems effectively turn the effective tax rate into a negative figure for low-income earners, thereby increasing disposable income relative to market income. However, their impacts on labor incentives are diametrically opposed. While an NIT-type basic income increases the PTR and EMTR for all workers (excluding those already on social assistance), a Universal EITC lowers these rates for low-income workers. Consequently, while NIT might unintentionally dampen the work incentives of low-income earners who were previously outside the welfare net, a Universal EITC actively encourages labor market participation.

Despite these advantages, a Universal EITC cannot assist those unable to work due to family care responsibilities, education, unemployment, illness, disability, or old age. It fails to provide the "real freedom" necessary for these individuals to escape poverty. Therefore, treating Universal EITC as a total *alternative* to basic income is not advisable.

Instead, Universal EITC can serve as a highly useful *complement* to NIT-type basic income for the following reasons:

1. **Supplementary Income Support**: As earned income increases, NIT benefits decrease (clawback), whereas Universal EITC benefits increase or remain stable. *This helps maintain a stable income floor for the working poor.*
2. **Mitigating High EMTR**: Coupling NIT with Universal EITC can effectively *lower the overall clawback rate.* This addresses the concern that combining NIT with existing income taxes and social insurance premiums could create punitively high EMTRs that discourage work.
3. **Enhancing Tax Equity**: Universal EITC helps rectify the unfairness of tax systems where *capital income and gains (interest, dividends, rental income)* are taxed more lightly than labor income. We believe that under no circumstances should labor income be taxed more heavily than unearned income.
4. **Poverty Alleviation**: For working-age populations where NIT might provide only modest support (due to age-graded guaranteed income levels), Universal EITC plays a crucial compensatory role in poverty alleviation.
5. **Closing Social Insurance Gaps**: Low-income, precarious workers often fall into social insurance blind spots because they cannot afford

premiums. Since premiums are proportional to earned income, a Universal EITC that also scales with earned income can function as an effective subsidy for social insurance participation.

6. **Political Viability and Local Integration**: Politically, a Universal EITC may be far more feasible than a pure UBI, given the existing bipartisan support for EITC programs. However, to address its exclusion of unpaid care and social labor, it can be integrated with the Participation Income model proposed by Hiilamo (2022). While the national government manages the Universal EITC based on formal labor income, local governments and community organizations can provide PI for various forms of unpaid social and ecological labor. This "active labor market" approach helps long-term job seekers and those with limited skills build the capacity for self-reliance.

In summary, a Universal EITC serves as a robust policy instrument to complement NIT-type and common wealth-financed basic incomes. In the Korean context, it offers the dual benefit of reforming the regressive employment income deduction system and closing the vast blind spots in social insurance.

Unlike the U.S., where a Universal EITC might primarily benefit middle-income earners by eliminating the phase-out range -if not carefully designed-, converting Korea's current regressive deductions into a Universal Refundable EITC would simultaneously increase benefits for low-income workers and reduce tax advantages for high-income earners. By integrating this with localized Participation Income programs, we can create a comprehensive social safety net that recognizes all forms of valuable social contribution.

CHAPTER 5

# The South Korean Social Security System at a Crossroads

South Korea, which was a poverty-stricken aid recipient in the latter half of the twentieth century, has achieved rapid economic growth and transformed into an advanced nation that now provides official development assistance (ODA) to developing countries. During this period of compressed growth, the nation was lauded as a model of "equitable growth" for maintaining relatively low levels of income inequality (World Bank, 1993).

During this era of rapid industrialization, South Korea's social security expenditure remained near zero. The low inequality without a welfare state was achieved by equal distribution of assets through land reform, expanding public education, and providing continuous job expansion through labor-intensive export-oriented industrialization (You, 2014; 2015). However, since the 1990s, income and asset inequality have surged. According to Kim (2018; 2023), the income share of the top 1% hovered around 20% during the colonial era but dropped sharply after liberation, remaining at approximately 7% from the 1970s to the mid-1990s. Since then, it has risen sharply, recently reaching about 15% (Fig. 5.1). Inequality in assets, such as real estate and financial holdings, is even more severe; the top 1% held 24% of the nation's net wealth as of 2016 (Kim, 2019).

The significant decline in the top 1%'s income share from 19% in 1942 to 7% by the mid-1970s is attributed largely to post-liberation land reform.



J. S. You et al., *UBI from Idea to Reality*, Exploring the Basic Income Guarantee,
https://doi.org/10.1007/978-3-032-26200-4_5

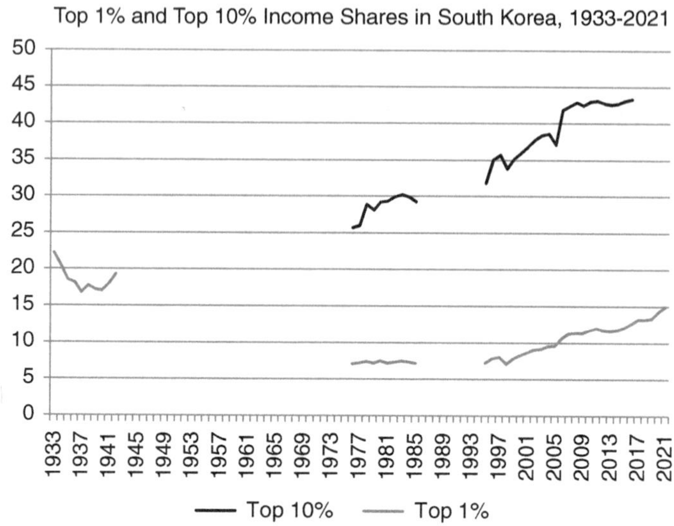


**Fig. 5.1** Income Share of the Top 1% and Top 10%, 1933–2016 (2021). Source: Kim (2018); The updates for the top 1% through 2021 follow Kim (2023)

Under the U.S. Army Military Government, the first phase addressed formerly Japanese-owned land, followed by a second phase in 1950 targeting Korean-owned farmland just before the outbreak of the Korean War. Based on the principle of "land to the tiller," the feudal landlord class was dismantled, and concentrated land ownership was redistributed to the peasantry. Consequently, the Gini coefficient for land ownership plummeted from 0.73 in 1945 to 0.38 by 1960 (You, 2015: 70–75, 89). Dani Rodrik (1995) noted that the success of industrialization in South Korea and Taiwan was underpinned by these initial conditions: specifically, high education levels and exceptionally low inequality in land ownership and income compared to other developing nations.

Throughout the industrialization era, the development of the welfare state was delayed by a "growth-first, distribution-later" policy. Substantial development of the welfare state began only after democratization in 1987, and demands for welfare expansion intensified following the 1997 Asian Financial Crisis. As shown in Fig. 5.2, South Korea's public social expenditure as a percentage of GDP rose rapidly from 2.5% in 1990 to 4.2% in 2000, 7.4% in 2010, and 10.2% in 2018. During the COVID-19

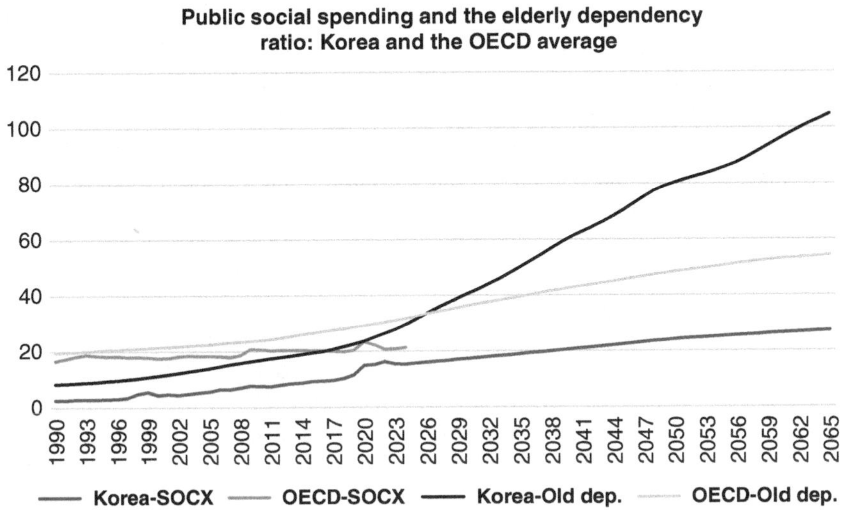


**Fig. 5.2** Trends in Public Social Expenditure (% of GDP) and Old-Age Dependency Ratio, 1990–2065. Source: OECD SOCX (2025), MOHW (2024), UN World Population Prospects (2025)

pandemic in 2020, it jumped to 14.9%, reaching 16.2% by 2022. Relative to the OECD average, South Korea's expenditure grew from 15% in 1990 to 79% by 2022, mirroring its history of "compressed growth" with a "compressed expansion" of the welfare state.

According to the 5th Social Security Financial Projections (Ministry of Health and Welfare, 2024), maintaining the current system amidst rapid population aging will cause social security expenditure to reach the OECD average of 20.5% of GDP by 2040 and surge to 27.1% by 2065. This would surpass the 2022 levels of Germany (26.7%) and Denmark (26.2%). While South Korea's old-age dependency ratio (the population aged 65+ relative to the working-age population aged 20–64) was historically lower than the OECD average, it is projected to overtake it in 2026. By 2063, it is expected to reach 101.3%, becoming the first country in the world to exceed 100% and nearly doubling the OECD average projection of 53.7% (UN, 2025; Fig. 5.2). Given this demographic shift, even 27% of GDP may be insufficient, yet the fiscal room for further expansion appears limited.

As social spending has expanded, the redistributive effect on market income inequality and poverty has also increased. The disposable income Gini coefficient fell from over 0.38 in 2011 to below 0.33 by 2024 (Ministry of Data and Statistics, 2025). Nevertheless, at 0.324 (as of 2022), it remains higher than the OECD average of 0.319. Furthermore, asset inequality—represented by the net wealth Gini coefficient—rose from 0.585 in 2016 to 0.625 in 2024. Most alarmingly, the relative poverty rate stands at 14.9% (vs. the OECD average of 11.1%), and the elderly poverty rate is 39.7%—the highest in the OECD and nearly triple the average of 14.8%. This persistent poverty and inequality stem from the low redistributive efficiency of the Korean tax and social security system. In 2022, while spending reached 79% of the OECD average, the reduction in the Gini coefficient (from market to disposable income) was only 18.2%, far below the OECD average of 31.8%, placing South Korea near the bottom, just above Mexico and Chile (Fig. 5.3).

Historically, the primary critique of the South Korean welfare state has focused on its "small" scale of expenditure (Yang, 2020). However, it is imperative to identify the structural reasons why redistributive efficiency remains weak despite the rapid increase in spending, particularly the persistent elderly poverty. While population aging will automatically expand the fiscal size of the welfare state under the current system, it is highly doubtful whether this expansion will naturally resolve high income inequality and elderly poverty.

The low redistributive function of the Korean welfare state stems from a structural imbalance: social security is heavily reliant on social insurance rather than general-tax-funded social assistance and social services. While the National Health Insurance (NHI) provides universal coverage through in-kind benefits, income-securing programs like public pensions and employment insurance fail to encompass the vast number of precarious workers and small-scale self-employed individuals.

This creates a dual social security system that mirrors the dual labor market. "Insiders," who enjoy stable employment and high income, are well-protected by social insurance against risks like unemployment or retirement. In contrast, "outsiders" in precarious and low-wage positions are largely excluded. In particular, the immaturity and broad blind spots of the public pension system are the primary driver of the staggering elderly poverty rate. Furthermore, the redistributive impact is limited because social assistance programs either have excessively narrow eligibility criteria or provide benefit levels too low to alleviate poverty effectively (You, 2020).

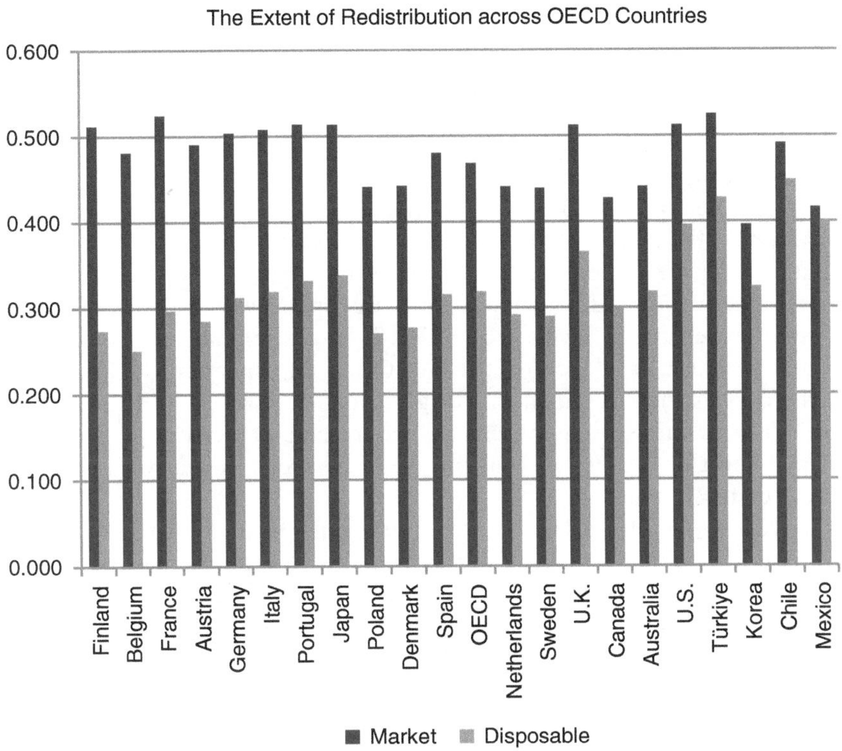


**Fig. 5.3** Gini Coefficients for Market and Disposable Income in OECD Countries, 2022. Note: Countries are ordered by the magnitude of the redistributive effect—the difference between market and disposable income Gini coefficients. Source: OECD (2025)

Without dismantling this dual structure, even a massive expansion in spending is unlikely to mitigate inequality. The 5th Social Security Financial Projections predict that by 2065, social insurance will account for 19.8% of the projected 27.1% GDP expenditure, while social assistance will stagnate at 7.3%. This is because spending on pensions and healthcare will automatically inflate due to aging, while social assistance spending remains flat as the decline in child-related outlays (due to low birth rates) offsets the increase in old-age support.

South Korea stands at a crossroads: it must choose between maintaining the status quo with minor incremental reforms or pursuing a fundamental structural overhaul to resolve the dualism of social security. Such reform is particularly urgent as the AI revolution threatens to decrease traditional jobs and exacerbate labor market polarization.

It is time to move beyond the discourse of a "small" welfare state (Yang, 2020) and provide a critical analysis of the structure and content of welfare expenditure. Scholars have noted significant differences between Nordic and Southern European welfare states despite similar expenditure levels. Kim (2013) suggests that South Korea's welfare system is closer to the Southern European model, characterized by severe dualism and high fiscal deficits. Yun (2019) *further* defines the Korean system as "Regressive Selectivism." To break away from this regressive dualism, we must seek alternatives rooted in Progressive Universalism.

A robust social security reform must look beyond cash and in-kind benefits to include tax expenditures and the very foundation of welfare financing: taxes and social insurance premiums. Effectiveness in reducing inequality and poverty must be weighed alongside fiscal sustainability, economic efficiency, and the promotion of real freedom, as well as ecological and demographic sustainability.

With this perspective, this chapter examines the current state and problems of major income security programs: public pensions, employment insurance, the National Basic Livelihood Security System, the Basic Pension, and the Work Incentive Payments (Korean-style EITC). We will analyze the broad blind spots of social insurance, the low take-up rates of social assistance, and the inherent unfairness caused by income reversals between recipients and non-recipients.

Crucially, we will investigate how the interplay of benefits (public transfers), income tax, and social insurance premiums results in prohibitively high Participation Tax Rates (PTR) and Effective Marginal Tax Rates (EMTR) for low-income workers. These high rates not only infringe upon the freedom to escape poverty through labor but also undermine economic efficiency by discouraging work. Finally, we will examine the "marriage penalty" and the incentives for household dissolution created by household-based social security programs.

## 5.1 Income Security Social Insurance: Public Pensions and Employment Insurance

### *Public Pensions*

The National Pension Service (NPS), the cornerstone of South Korea's public pension system, faces dual challenges: severe fiscal instability due to a disproportionately low contribution rate (13%) relative to the replacement rate (43% for an average earner with 40 years of contributions), and inadequate retirement income security caused by broad blind spots and short contribution periods.

The high elderly poverty rate in South Korea is partly due to the immaturity of the NPS, but it is more significantly driven by the regressivity inherent in its extensive blind spots. Since its inception in 1988 for employees in workplaces with ten or more people, the NPS has gradually expanded to include rural residents (1995), urban residents (1999), and eventually all workplaces with at least one employee and daily laborers (2003), nominally inaugurating an era of "universal pension." NPS benefits consist of an earnings-related component and a flat-rate (redistributive) component, both of which are contingent on the duration of coverage (contribution period). Achieving the full nominal replacement rate requires 40 years of contributions, a milestone that will only be reachable by 2028 for the earliest participants and 2043 for those who joined in 2003. Consequently, due to the system's immaturity, the effective replacement rate for current retirees remains far below the nominal rate. Furthermore, many low-income precarious workers and micro-business owners either fail to secure pension rights—due to non-enrollment or failing to meet the minimum 10-year requirement—or receive extremely low benefits based on barely ten years of contributions.

According to the 2023 Pension Statistics (Ministry of Data and Statistics, 2025b), the public pension coverage rate among those aged 65 and older was only 56.1% (50.1% for NPS and 6.0% for occupational pensions). The average contribution period for NPS recipients was a mere 13.6 years, with an average monthly benefit of only 452,000 KRW. The median value was even lower at 342,000 KRW—a level comparable to the non-contributory Basic Pension (average 292,000 KRW, median 323,000 KRW). This stands in stark contrast to occupational pensions for civil servants, teachers, and military personnel, where the average contribution period was

29.1 years, with an average monthly benefit of 2,662,000 KRW and a median of 2,676,000 KRW.

Such disparities—high benefits for occupational pensions versus broad blind spots and low benefit levels for the NPS—position the public pension system as a factor that reinforces income inequality in old age. Table 5.1 illustrates the market income and pension receipt status by disposable income deciles for the elderly. Higher income deciles show significantly higher receipt rates and benefit amounts for both market income and public pensions. While the Basic Pension plays a role in mitigating old-age income inequality, its impact is limited by its low benefit level. Factor decomposition of the Gini coefficient between 2011 and 2020 indicates that as the public pension system matures, its contribution to inequality has paradoxically increased (Choi & You, 2022).

While some expect the regressivity of public pensions to improve as the NPS matures, current data on enrollment rates and contribution periods among the working-age population suggest otherwise. Pension statistics

**Table 5.1** Market Income and Public/Basic Pension Receipt Status by Disposable Income Decile for the Elderly (2023) (Unit: 10,000 KRW per year)

| *Decile* | *Disposable income* | *Market income* | *Public pension* | *Basic pension* | *% recipients public pension* | *% recipients basic pension* | *% receiving neither* |
|---|---|---|---|---|---|---|---|
| 1 | 281 | 79 | 32 | 203 | 88% | 64.5% | 29.4% |
| 2 | 562 | 219 | 65 | 279 | 24.9% | 82.3% | 9.9% |
| 3 | 783 | 313 | 136 | 289 | 42.2% | 84.6% | 7.9% |
| 4 | 990 | 398 | 187 | 297 | 49.5% | 85.9% | 7.4% |
| 5 | 1,238 | 593 | 262 | 281 | 58.0% | 83.2% | 7.9% |
| 6 | 1,574 | 923 | 311 | 263 | 62.3% | 79.2% | 8.1% |
| 7 | 2,077 | 1,344 | 434 | 227 | 70.0% | 70.3% | 8.2% |
| 8 | 2,804 | 2,011 | 599 | 178 | 74.7% | 58.6% | 8.5% |
| 9 | 3,811 | 2,731 | 975 | 148 | 85.8% | 50.7% | 4.0% |
| 10 | 7,395 | 6,410 | 1,557 | 59 | 88.8% | 20.9% | 6.8% |
| Total | 2,151 | 1,502 | 456 | 222 | 56.5% | 68.0% | 9.8% |
| Decile ratio | 26.3 | 80.6 | 48.1 | 0.3 | 10.1 | 0.3 | 0.2 |

Note: Market and disposable income include imputed rent.
Source: Survey of Household Finances and Living Conditions, 2024.

for 2023 show that for those aged 18–59, the combined enrollment rate for NPS (73.6%) and occupational pensions (6.2%) was 79.8% or less. The effective enrollment rate is likely lower, as these figures include those exempted from premiums and those in arrears. One study by the National Pension Research Institute found that approximately 40% of the working-age population in 2019 were either non-enrolled or non-contributors (Yoo et al., 2022). Our analysis of the *Survey of Household Finances and Living Conditions* (Table 5.2) shows that only 65.3% of the 18–59 population paid NPS premiums for at least one month in 2023, while 6.0% paid into occupational pensions. The combined enrollment rate for at least one month was 71.1%. The monthly effective enrollment rate is estimated to be below 70%. This implies that even decades from now, when the NPS is "fully mature," roughly 30% of the elderly will still remain in the blind spots of the public pension system.

Table 5.2 reveals massive disparities in public pension enrollment rates based on labor income (sum of employment and business income) and employment status. Among adults aged 18–59, 15.5% had zero labor income in 2023, and only 15.7% of them were enrolled in public pensions. For those in the second and third labor income deciles, enrollment rates were 17.9% and 55.9%, respectively, indicating a high probability of old-age poverty. Disparities are also sharp by employment status: enrollment is 94.1% for regular employees and employers, but only 64.0% for precarious workers (temporary/daily workers, freelancers) and micro-entrepreneurs, and a mere 30.6% for others (unemployed, homemakers, students). Additionally, the enrollment rate for women (66.6%) is significantly lower than for men (75.6%).

Beyond enrollment rates, a critical issue is the overall short duration of contributions and the stark disparities in these periods based on income level and employment status. According to the National Pension Service, the average contribution period for new retirees in 2024 was 19.6 years. Even by 2050, when the system is expected to be fully mature, the average contribution period is projected to be only 26.2 years (Nam & Kim, 2023)—still shorter than the current 28.9 years for occupational pension recipients. This lags significantly behind the European Union, where the average contribution period was 35.7 years in 2019 and is projected to reach 37.1 years by 2050 (European Commission, 2021) .

Analysis of administrative social security data reveals a wide gender gap (11 years for men vs. 7 years and 8 months for women) and a twofold difference between the top and bottom income quintiles across all age

**Table 5.2** Public Pension Enrollment Rate by Earned Income Decile (Including Zero-Income Earners) and Employment Status, 18–59 Age Group (2023)

| *Income Decile* | *Earned Income* | *National Pension Enrollment* | *Occupational Pension Enrollment* | *Total Public Pension Enrollment* | *Male Ratio* |
|---|---|---|---|---|---|
| 1 | 0 | 15.5% | 0.1% | 15.7% | 34.9% |
| 2 | 69 | 17.9% | 0.1% | 17.9% | 36.3% |
| 3 | 610 | 55.2% | 0.8% | 55.9% | 34.6% |
| 4 | 1,581 | 73.8% | 2.8% | 76.2% | 37.0% |
| 5 | 2,479 | 86.3% | 1.7% | 87.4% | 38.1% |
| 6 | 3,237 | 82.9% | 3.2% | 85.9% | 46.0% |
| 7 | 4,053 | 83.8% | 6.7% | 90.3% | 58.7% |
| 8 | 5,108 | 82.1% | 12.2% | 94.2% | 69.0% |
| 9 | 6,762 | 76.0% | 18.8% | 94.8% | 72.7% |
| 10 | 12,147 | 81.1% | 14.1% | 95.0% | 78.9% |
| Total | 3,590 | 65.3% | 6.0% | 71.1% | 50.4% |
| *Employment Status** | *Earned Income* | *National Pension* | *Occupational Pension* | *Public Pension* | *Male Ratio* |
| 1 | 5,340 | 83.5% | 10.9% | 94.1% | 58.0% |
| 2 | 3,018 | 63.7% | 0.4% | 64.0% | 49.0% |
| 3 | 529 | 30.1% | 0.5% | 30.6% | 36.3% |
| Total | 3,590 | 65.3% | 6.0% | 71.1% | 50.4% |

Notes: Earned Income refers to the sum of wages for employees and business income for the self-employed (Unit: 10,000 KRW).
Income Deciles: The 1st decile consists of individuals with zero income (Income = 0), accounting for 15.5% of the population aged 18–59. The 2nd decile represents 4.5% of the same age group.
Employment Status Categories: Category 1 includes regular employees and self-employed individuals with employees. Category 2 includes temporary/daily workers, dependent self-employed (service contractors), self-employed individuals without employees, and unpaid family workers. Category 3 includes others (unemployed, homemakers, students, etc.).
Source: Statistics Korea (National Data Agency), *Survey of Household Finances and Living Conditions* (2024).

groups (Ku et al., 2021). Among those aged 55–59, *nearing the age limit for mandatory enrollment of 59*, 48.1% either lacked coverage or failed to meet the minimum 10-year requirement. For the first and second income quintiles, these figures soared to 78.4% and 63.3%, respectively. While some may reach the 10-year threshold through voluntary contributions before reaching the pensionable age (currently 63, rising to 65 by 2033), barely satisfying the minimum requirement will result in extremely meager benefit levels.

The National Pension system is designed with a strong redistributive function, consisting of an earnings-related component (B-value) and a flat-rate component- (A-value). Lower-income groups should receive a higher replacement rate for the same contribution period. In practice, however, this mechanism is broken: many low-income individuals fail to secure pension rights entirely, and those who do receive benefits often have such short contribution histories that the redistributive effect is minimized.

The high correlation between income level and contribution history stems from a system that distinguishes between "workplace-based enrollees" and "locally insured enrollees." For workplace-based enrollees (predominantly regular employees), employers cover half of the premiums, which facilitates longer contribution periods. Conversely, low-wage precarious workers often fall into the locally insured category or are excluded from the system entirely, as both employers and employees seek to avoid the financial burden of premiums. Similarly, micro-entrepreneurs, who must bear the full cost of premiums as local enrollees, frequently opt out of the system.

### *Employment Insurance*

Employment insurance also exhibits the "Dual Social Security" dilemma, failing to protect "outsiders" in the precarious labor market. According to the *Survey of Household Finances and Living Conditions* (Table 5.3), only 48.2% of those with labor income (employment income and business income) were enrolled in employment insurance as of 2023. While the enrollment rate for regular employees reached 80.4%, it plummeted to 31.9% for temporary/daily workers and 20.3% for individual service contractors (freelancers). Among the self-employed, enrollment rates were abysmal: 11.5% for employers and roughly 6% for those without employees or unpaid family workers. Paradoxically, those facing the highest job instability and lowest incomes who need insurance protection the most are excluded from protection.

Analysis of the distribution of employment insurance benefits such as job-seeking benefits (unemployment benefits) and maternity protection benefits (maternity and parental leave) shows a concentration of benefits in the middle- and high-income brackets. According to administrative data (Table 5.4), while the Work Incentive Payment (Korean-style EITC)

**Table 5.3** Employment Insurance Enrollment Rate by Earned Income Decile and Employment Status

| *Income Decile* | *Earned Income* | *Enrollment Rate* | *Employment Status* | *Enrollment Rate* | *Enrollment Rate* |
|---|---|---|---|---|---|
| 1 | 150 | 3.1% | Regular Employees | 5,123 | 80.4% |
| 2 | 617 | 15.9% | Temporary/ Daily Workers | 1,838 | 31.9% |
| 3 | 1,287 | 34.9% | Dependent Self-employed | 3,621 | 20.3% |
| 4 | 2,064 | 46.7% | Self-employed with Employees | 7,014 | 11.5% |
| 5 | 2,735 | 60.2% | Self-employed without Employees | 3,697 | 6.1% |
| 6 | 3,339 | 68.5% | Unpaid Family Workers | 1,604 | 5.4% |
| 7 | 4,049 | 64.4% | Others | 1,179 | 10.7% |
| 8 | 5,092 | 65.1% | Gender | Earned Income | Enrollment Rate |
| 9 | 6,757 | 60.2% | Male | 4,752 | 51.7% |
| 10 | 12,312 | 65.2% | Female | 2,725 | 44.0% |
| Total | 3,825 | 48.2% | Total | 3,825 | 48.2% |

Notes: Earned Income refers to the sum of wages for employees and business income for the self-employed (Unit: 10,000 KRW). Since individuals without earned income are ineligible for employment insurance, the earned income deciles in this table are restricted to those with positive earned income (Income > 0).
Source: Statistics Korea (National Data Agency), *Survey of Household Finances and Living Conditions* (2024).

as a social assistance benefit is concentrated among low-to-middle income households (2nd–5th deciles), job-seeking benefits are concentrated in the middle-income brackets (4th–6th deciles). Although low-income earners likely face higher unemployment rates due to precarious employment, their lack of insurance coverage results in lower benefit receipt rates.

Maternity protection coverage is even more regressive. For households with children aged 0–1, the combined usage rate of maternity and parental leave is only 25%. This rate scales sharply with income: from 6.9% in the 1st decile to 34.9% in the 10th decile. Even when including maternity

**Table 5.4** Receipt Rate and Average Benefit Amount for Work Incentive Payments, Unemployment Benefits, and Maternity Protection Benefits by Household Income Decile (2020) (Unit: 1,000 KRW)

| *Income decile* | *% WIP recipients* | *Avg.WIP amount* | *% UB recipients* | *Avg. UB amount* | *% MPB recipients* | *Avg. MPB amount* |
|---|---|---|---|---|---|---|
| 1 | 3.5% | 0 | 3.2% | 8,541 | 6.9% | 6,414 |
| 2 | 34.3% | 534 | 4.5% | 8,644 | 12.5% | 6,962 |
| 3 | 39.2% | 1,291 | 9.4% | 8,842 | 18.0% | 7,052 |
| 4 | 31.1% | 1,325 | 14.4% | 8,000 | 21.5% | 6,623 |
| 5 | 21.9% | 857 | 13.5% | 7,222 | 22.0% | 6,266 |
| 6 | 6.7% | 815 | 11.0% | 6,906 | 22.8% | 6,450 |
| 7 | 3.0% | 0 | 9.7% | 6,756 | 26.0% | 6,322 |
| 8 | 1.5% | 0 | 8.2% | 6,570 | 30.2% | 5,978 |
| 9 | 0.6% | 0 | 6.3% | 6,305 | 34.8% | 5,593 |
| 10 | 0.2% | 0 | 3.5% | 6,203 | 34.9% | 5,079 |
| Total | 11.5% | 1,084 | 8.5% | 7,261 | 25.0% | 6,100 |

Source: Lee et al. (2023: 126, 136, 139).

grants for those not covered by insurance, the receipt rate among low-income households remains staggeringly low.

Furthermore, the average benefit amounts for employment insurance (7.26 million KRW for unemployment benefits, 6.10 million KRW for maternity protection benefits) are significantly higher than the average *Work Incentive Payment* (1.08 million KRW). This illustrates a fundamental aspect of the "Dual Social Security" system: social insurance expenditures, which dwarf social assistance for the poor in both scale and individual benefit size, primarily protect "insiders" who enjoy relatively stable employment and higher incomes.

To address the extensive blind spots in employment insurance, the Moon Jae-in administration introduced the "Universal Employment Insurance" initiative, aiming to cover all employed persons, including the self-employed and individual service contractors (freelancers). As traditional social insurance based on formal employment relationships loses its alignment with the evolving labor market, reforms toward "Income-Based Employment Insurance" have been proposed. This model operates based on aggregated labor income, fundamentally resolving blind spots in cases where employers are not specified or multiple employers exist, making the boundaries between employment, unemployment, and non-economic activity increasingly blurred. To support this, the National Tax Service is establishing a real-time income monitoring system, which the government recently announced will be completed in 2026, with the phased implementation of income-based employment insurance set to begin in 2027.

South Korea's job-seeking benefits (unemployment benefits) currently face criticism for being too generous for low-wage workers due to a narrow gap between the lower limit (80% of the minimum wage) and the upper limit, while providing a replacement rate that is too low for high-wage earners. Eligibility is limited to involuntary unemployed persons who have been insured for at least 180 days, with the benefit duration ranging from 120 to 270 days depending on the contribution period.

Additionally, the government introduced the "Korean-style Unemployment Assistance" in 2021 for job seekers not covered by employment insurance. Those with a household income below 60% of the median and assets below 400 million KRW—who have worked at least 100 days in the past two years—or young job seekers (ages 18–34) below 120% of the median income, can receive a "Job Seeking Promotion Allowance" of 500,000 KRW monthly for up to six months. Unlike employment insurance, which does not require a means test, this assistance is characterized by very low benefit levels and highly restrictive eligibility due to means testing.

## 5.2 Social Assistance: NBLSS, Basic Pension, and Work/Child Incentive Payments

### *National Basic Livelihood Security System (NBLSS)*

The National Basic Livelihood Security Act, enacted in 2000, is regarded as a landmark piece of social security legislation following democratization. It recognizes the right of all citizens to lead a basic life with dignity and defines the state's obligation to guarantee it. Unlike its predecessor, the state is now mandated to provide supplementary livelihood benefits to households below the minimum cost of living—regardless of the members' capacity to work—to ensure basic survival and promote self-reliance. However, tragic incidents continue to occur, such as the "Songpa Mother and Two Daughters" case, where impoverished families committed suicide after falling through welfare blind spots. According to the Korean Society for Equity in Health (2018), there is a 6.6-year life expectancy gap between the top 20% and bottom 20% of earners, with suicide being the second leading cause of this disparity, following cerebrovascular disease.

Despite high poverty rates, the take-up rate for NBLSS remains remarkably low. In 2023, the overall receipt rate (for any benefit among livelihood, medical, housing, or education) was only 5.0%, representing only one-third of the population in poverty (14.9%). The receipt rate for Livelihood Benefits (targeted at those below 30% of the median income in 2023) was a mere 3.1%, and for Housing Benefits (below 47% of the median income in 2023), it was only 4.6% (MOHW, 2025).

The primary reason why two-thirds of the poor remain unprotected is that eligibility is determined by "Recognized Income"—the sum of assessed income and the income conversion of assets. The conversion rates applied to assets are punitively high.

The monthly income conversion rate for general assets is 4.17% (50.04% annually), for financial assets 6.26% (75.12% annually), and for automobiles, a staggering 100% per month (1,200% annually). Residential property is subject to a rate of 1.04% per month (12.48% annually) within certain limits (172 million KRW in Seoul), but the general conversion rate is applied for any excess. These represent effective property tax rates that are incomparably higher than standard residential property taxes (0.1% to 0.4%).

Eligibility for NBLSS is granted to households whose recognized income is below a certain percentage of the Standard Median Income, which is adjusted based on household size to account for economies of scale. Table 5.5 shows the 2026 eligibility criteria (32% and 48% of standard median income for livelihood and housing benefits, respectively) and benefit caps in KRW.

Livelihood Benefits are supplementary; the state pays the full difference between 32% of the standard median income and the household's recognized income. Housing Benefits vary by household size and region. For instance, the cap for a one-person household in Seoul (369,000 KRW) is nearly double that of a rural resident (212,000 KRW). While those whose recognized income is below the livelihood benefit criteria receive full benefits, those above the livelihood criteria receive 70% of full benefits.

Providing higher per-capita benefits to smaller households and residents of large cities follows the principle of "support according to need." However, this may inadvertently reinforce trends such as urban centralization and the rise of single-person households. Conversely, removing these differentials could potentially encourage regional decentralization

**Table 5.5** 2026 Standard Median Income, Livelihood and Housing Benefit Eligibility Criteria, and Housing Benefit Caps by Household Size (Unit: KRW/month)

| *Household Size* | *1-person* | *2-person* | *3-person* | *4-person* |
|---|---|---|---|---|
| Standard Median Income | 2,564,238 | 4,199,292 | 5,359,036 | 6,494,738 |
| Livelihood Benefit Criteria (32%) | 820,556 | 1,343,773 | 1,714,892 | 2,078,316 |
| Housing Benefit Criteria (48%) | 1,230,834 | 2,015,660 | 2,572,337 | 3,117,474 |
| Housing Benefit Cap (Tier 1) | 369,000 | 414,000 | 492,000 | 571,000 |
| Housing Benefit Cap (Tier 24) | 212,000 | 238,000 | 283,000 | 329,000 |
| Livelihood+Housing Benefits (Tier 1) | 1,189,556 | 1,757,773 | 2,206,892 | 2,649,316 |

Note: Classification of Housing Benefit Regional Tiers
- Tier 1: Seoul
- Tier 2: Gyeonggi Province and Incheon
- Tier 3: Metropolitan Cities, Sejong Special Self-Governing City, and Special Cases Cities outside the Seoul Metropolitan Area
- Tier 4: All other regions

and marriage/household formation. Notably, the share of single-person households among NBLSS recipients soared from around 50% in the early 2000s to 74.2% in 2024. For Livelihood Benefits, this share reached a staggering 81.4%, suggesting the system may be not just reflecting but potentially amplifying the general increase in one-person households.

Although Livelihood Benefits are designed as supplementary assistance covering the gap between the eligibility threshold and recognized income, the introduction of a 30% earned income deduction in 2020 theoretically lowered the marginal tax rate on labor from 100% to 70%. However, when factoring in conventional income tax (a minimum rate of 6.6%) and social insurance premiums (over 9% for employees and 18% for the self-employed), the Effective Marginal Tax Rate (EMTR) remains significantly higher. Consequently, the effect of this 30% deduction on enhancing "real freedom" or labor incentives is markedly limited.

For the two-level flat-rate Housing Benefits, a "benefit cliff" occurs at the eligibility threshold, leading to severe income reversals. When various overlapping public and private welfare benefits provided to NBLSS recipients are considered, the scale of this reversal is substantial—meaning the EMTR at the threshold far exceeds 100%. This restricts the individual's freedom to improve their circumstances through labor and creates incentives to avoid formal employment or hide income by working in the informal sector. Furthermore, the high income-conversion rate of assets near the threshold implies an extremely high effective property tax rate, discouraging savings and incentivizing the depletion or concealment of assets.

According to Lee et al. (2024), a significant number of households meet the "Recognized Income" criteria (including asset conversion) but do not receive benefits. Paradoxically, many recipients have recognized incomes that actually exceed the threshold (Table 5.6). Analysis of the Korea Welfare Panel Study (KOWPS) data shows that in 2022, 36% of individuals below the Livelihood Benefit threshold (30% of the median recognized income) did not receive Livelihood Benefits. Among recipients, only 70.5% were below the 30% threshold, while 14.4% exceeded 100% of the median recognized income, raising serious questions about the targeting accuracy of the selection process.

The high number of non-recipient households despite meeting recognized income criteria is largely due to the "Family Support Obligation" (support from first-degree relatives and their spouses). Although this requirement was significantly relaxed for Livelihood Benefits in 2021, it partially remains, and for Medical Benefits, it remains strictly enforced. It was abolished for Education Benefits in 2015 and Housing Benefits in 2018.

Data shows that among households that applied for NBLSS but were rejected for Livelihood Benefits, 43.5% exceeded the recognized income criteria, while 37.5% were disqualified due to the family support obligation. For Medical Benefits, only 19.8% of rejected households exceeded the income criteria, while a staggering 60.8% were disqualified because

**Table 5.6** Livelihood Benefit Receipt Rate and Composition of Recipients by Recognized Income Level, 2022 (Unit: %)

| *Recognized Income Relative to Median Income* | *Sample Share* | *Receipt Rate* | *Recipients in Sample* | *Composition of Recipients* |
|---|---|---|---|---|
| 30% or Less | 6.1 | 64 | 3.9 | 70.5 |
| Over 30% to 100% or Less | 9.9 | 8.5 | 0.84 | 15.1 |
| Over 100% | 84 | 0.9 | 0.76 | 14.4 |
| Total | 100 | 5.5 | 5.5 | 100 |

Source: Lee et al.(2024).

the income and assets of their "obligatory supporters" exceeded the limit (Lee et al., 2023).

Even when both recognized income and family support criteria are met, many forgo applying due to a lack of information, the complexity of the process, or the social stigma and shame associated with the application. According to the Seoul Welfare Survey (Seoul Institute, 2018), reasons for not applying despite economic need included: family support criteria (41.8%), lack of information on how to apply (26.6%), complex procedures and paperwork (13.0%), and stigma-related reasons such as not wanting others to know their situation or not wanting help (totaling 18%).

Low take-up rates for selective social assistance are not unique to Korea, but they inevitably lead to issues of horizontal inequity and unfair income reversals. Table 5.7 illustrates the income reversal between NBLSS recipients and non-recipients among applicants for the 2022 Seoul "Stepping Stone Income" experiment. Since this experiment targeted households below 85% of the median income, most non-recipients of NBLSS also belong to low-income groups. While the average earned income of non-recipients (530,000 KRW) was slightly higher than that of recipients (485,000 KRW), their total disposable income after public transfers (717,000 KRW) was significantly lower than that of recipients (1,061,000 KRW). Such a reversal, where the working poor end up with less than those on welfare, is fundamentally unjust.

**Table 5.7** Income Reversal Between NBLSS Recipients and Non-recipients Among Seoul Stepping Stone Income Applicants (Unit: 1,000 KRW/month)

| *Category* | *Earned Income* | *Total Disposable Income* |
|---|---|---|
| Total Applicants | 513 | 847 |
| Recipients | 485 | 1,061 |
| Non-recipients | 530 | 717 |
| Working Households | 956 | 1,209 |
| Recipients | 1,013 | 1,458 |
| Non-recipients | 927 | 1,074 |
| Non-working Households | 0 | 435 |
| Recipients | 0 | 696 |
| Non-recipients | 0 | 241 |

Source: Jeong (2022).

Beyond low take-up rates, social assistance forces recipients to constantly prove their "deservingness" and "pitiable state." Any attempt to earn a modest income or save results in reduced benefits or disqualification, trapping them in a "Poverty Trap."

### *Basic Pension*

The Basic Old-Age Pension, introduced in 2007 as part of a reform package for the National Pension Service (NPS), evolved into the current Basic Pension in 2014. Despite its modest benefit levels, it plays a pivotal role in alleviating elderly poverty and reducing old-age income inequality. Targeting the bottom 70% of those aged 65 and older based on "recognized income," the standard benefit began at 200,000 KRW per month, was raised to 300,000 KRW between 2019 and 2021, and reached 349,700 KRW in 2026 due to inflation indexing. When both spouses receive the pension, a 20% reduction is applied. Driven by both benefit hikes and rapid aging, the Basic Pension budget surged from 6.9 trillion KRW in 2014 to 26.2 trillion KRW in 2025 and is projected to rise continuously. While the system aims to cover 70% of the elderly, the actual take-up rate fluctuates around 66–67% annually.

As of 2020, the Basic Pension's effect on reducing the elderly poverty rate (based on 50% of median disposable income) was 6.9%, with a 13.8% reduction in the poverty gap. In the same year, although its impact on the poverty rate was smaller than that of public pensions (which reduced the rate by 12.7%), the Basic Pension was more effective in closing the poverty gap (13.8% vs. 9.8% for public pensions). Crucially, while public pensions tend to reinforce old-age income inequality, the Basic Pension serves to mitigate it (Choi & You, 2022).

The 70% coverage threshold represents a political compromise reached in 2007 between proponents of a universal basic pension and advocates for a selective social assistance model. During the 2014 transition, then-President Park Geun-hye initially pledged a universal basic pension but ultimately maintained the 70% target.

Eligibility is determined by "recognized income", the sum of assessed income and the income conversion of assets. In 2026, the eligibility threshold stands at 2.47 million KRW for single households and 3.95 million KRW for couples.

- Income Assessment: The system allows for more generous deductions than the National Basic Living Security System (NBLSS), deducting 1.12 million KRW from earned income followed by an additional 30% discount.
- Asset Conversion: An annual rate of 4% is applied. While significantly lower than the rate used in NBLSS, it remains very high compared to standard property tax rates (0.1%–0.4%). Consequently, elderly homeowners in the Seoul metropolitan area—where housing prices are high—are often excluded from the Basic Pension despite having very low cash incomes.

Since the Basic Pension is a selective flat-rate benefit, it is prone to income reversals near the eligibility threshold, potentially resulting in extremely high marginal tax rates on income and assets. To mitigate this, a "reversal prevention reduction" was introduced: if the sum of recognized income and the basic pension exceeds the threshold, the excess is deducted. Nevertheless, disparities between recipients and non-recipients often persist in terms of gross income or disposable income.

Furthermore, the Basic Pension faces institutional overlap and conflict with the "A-value benefit" (redistributive component) of the National Pension. To address this, a reduction is applied to those whose NPS benefit exceeds 150% of the standard Basic Pension amount. However, this rule is criticized for its complexity, making it difficult for the public to understand and disincentivizing long-term participation in the NPS for low-income earners. Additionally, the spousal reduction (couples' penalty) has been criticized for encouraging "twilight divorces" (divorce in old age). In response, President Lee Jae-myung pledged to lower this reduction to 10%. Despite these challenges, the Basic Pension remains a vital pillar in alleviating elderly poverty by compensating for the extensive blind spots of the public pension system.

### *Work Incentive Payment (WIP) and Child Incentive Payment (CIP)*

The Work Incentive Payment (Korean-style EITC) was introduced in 2008, benchmarking the U.S. EITC to incentivize labor among low-income households and provide real income support. Initially targeted at households with two or more children under 18, eligibility was gradually expanded to include childless and single-person households. In 2014, the system shifted from a child-based assessment to a household-type classification (Single, Single-earner, and Dual-earner households), and the Child Incentive Payment (CIP) was introduced in 2015. Consequently, the Korean model diverged from the U.S. EITC, where benefit amounts scale primarily with the number of qualifying children.

Since 2019, age restrictions for single-person households were abolished, income and asset thresholds were relaxed, and maximum benefit levels were significantly increased. In 2019 alone, a total of 5.26 trillion KRW (4.5 trillion in WIP and 750 billion in CIP) was distributed to 4.98 million households. This scale is now comparable to the combined expenditure of NBLSS Livelihood Benefits (4.65 trillion KRW) and Housing Benefits (1.99 trillion KRW).

As of 2025, eligibility for WIP requires a household to have earned or business income, with annual income thresholds set at 22 million KRW for single-person households, 32 million KRW for single-earner households, and 44 million KRW for dual-earner households. Additionally, total household assets must be below 240 million KRW; if assets are between 170 million and 240 million KRW, only 50% of the credit is paid.

The WIP structure consists of three phases based on income: the Phase-in range (benefits increase with income), the Plateau range (maximum benefits are maintained), and the Phase-out range (benefits decrease). As illustrated in Fig. 5.4, for a single-person household, the benefit is 42.5% of income up to 4 million KRW, stays at 1.65 million KRW up to 9 million KRW, and is then clawed back at a rate of approximately 12.7% for income exceeding 9 million KRW until it reaches zero at the 22 million KRW threshold.

Eligibility for the Child Incentive Payment (CIP) follows the same asset criteria as the EITC but applies to households with an annual income below 70 million KRW, regardless of household type. The benefit ranges from 500,000 to 1,000,000 KRW per child under 18. Single-earner households below 21 million KRW and dual-earner households below 25 million KRW receive the full 1 million KRW per child; above these levels, the amount decreases on a sliding scale to a minimum of 500,000 KRW.

Since the WIP is administered by the National Tax Service (NTS) in connection with the income tax system, its delivery—including application, verification, and payment—is simpler and less costly than the NBLSS. Research indicates that WIP-like programs improve income distribution, increase consumption, and enhance health and academic outcomes for children. Unlike other poverty policies criticized for discouraging labor,

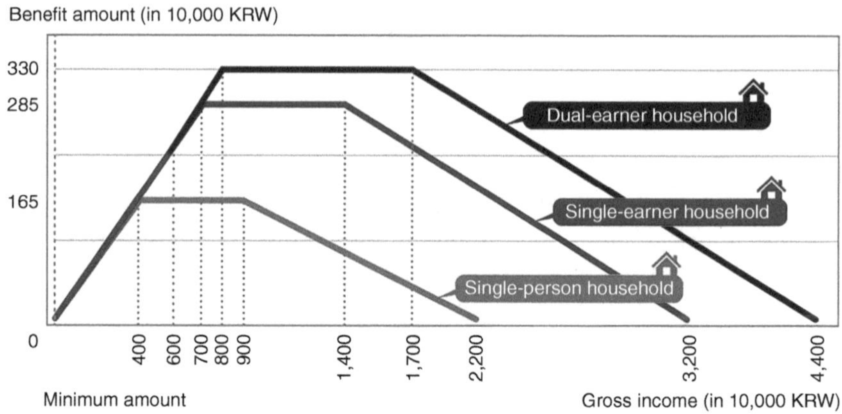


**Fig. 5.4** Work Incentive Payment (WIP) Schedule by Household Type and Income Level. Source: National Tax Service (2025). Notes: The X-axis represents annual gross income, and the Y-axis represents WIP benefit amounts (Unit: 10,000 KRW). The three lines depict the benefit structures for single-person households, single-earner households, and dual-earner households, respectively

the WIP incentivizes work because benefits are contingent upon and linked to earned income, particularly in the phase-in range (Cho et al., 2019).

However, the WIP exhibits structural distortions that favor single-person households over larger families (Kim, 2020). Table 5.8 compares the WIP income ceilings with the Standard Median Income by household type. For single-person households, the WIP ceiling (22 million KRW) reaches 76.6% of the median income. For dual-earner couples without children, it reaches 93.2%. In stark contrast, for a dual-earner four-person household, the ceiling is only 60.1% of the median income, and for a single-earner four-person household, it is a mere 43.7%—lower even than the eligibility threshold for NBLSS Housing Benefits.

Furthermore, because the plateau range ends at only 43% to 67% of the minimum wage, the system inadvertently incentivizes part-time or short-term labor (Kim, 2018). The work disincentive in the phase-out range is exacerbated when it coincides with the termination of Housing Benefits, creating a “benefit cliff” (Cho et al., 2019).

Another major issue is the low take-up rate. While the U.S. EITC reaches approximately 78% of the working poor (Macartney & Ghertner, 2021), WIP’s rate is estimated at around 40%. Analysis of the 2023 Survey

**Table 5.8** Standard Median Income vs. WIP Income Threshold by Household Type, 2023 (Unit: KRW)

| *Household Category* | *Family Size* | *Standard Median Income* | *WIP Income Threshold* | *Ratio to Median Income* |
|---|---|---|---|---|
| Single-person Household | 1-person | 28,704,156 | 22,000,000 | 76.6% |
| Single-earner Household | 2-person | 47,191,896 | 32,000,000 | 67.8% |
| | 3-person | 60,304,236 | | 53.1% |
| | 4-person | 73,173,276 | | 43.7% |
| | 5-person | 85,298,304 | | 37.5% |
| Dual-earner Household | 2-person | 47,191,896 | 44,000,000 | 93.2% |
| | 3-person | 60,304,236 | | 73.0% |
| | 4-person | 73,173,276 | | 60.1% |
| | 5-person | 85,298,304 | | 51.6% |

of Household Finances shows that only 40.6% of impoverished households with earned income received WIP and/or CIP. Even among those meeting the asset criteria, the take-up rate was only 50.6%. This is largely due to low awareness and administrative barriers. Unlike the U.S., where EITC is a simple part of the universal tax filing process, many low-income Korean workers (such as daily laborers and freelancers) do not file income taxes, requiring them to navigate a separate application process for the credits. Surveys indicate that nearly half of potential recipients are unaware of the details or even the existence of these programs (Lee et al., 2023).

## 5.3 The Redistributive Function of Income Tax

South Korea's income tax system appears highly progressive, featuring an eight-tier bracket structure with rates ranging from 6% to 45% (Table 5.9). However, the effective tax rate is considerably lower than the nominal rate due to regressive tax expenditures, such as non-taxable income and various deductions. This shrinks the overall tax base and significantly weakens the redistributive function of the system.

First, there is a disproportionately high amount of non-taxable income for capital income compared to labor income (Hong, 2021). Figure 5.5 illustrates the trends of National Income versus Fiscal Income (taxable income) attributed to the top 1% and 10%. The discrepancy between these two represents non-taxable capital income, which narrowed during the 1997–1998 Asian Financial Crisis but has since expanded (Hong et al., 2024).

Key items among income deductions include personal allowances: the basic allowance (1.5 million KRW per person for the taxpayer, spouse with income under 1 million KRW, and dependents) and additional allowances

**Table 5.9** Statutory Personal Income Tax Rates

| *Taxable Base (KRW)* | *Tax Rate* |
|---|---|
| Up to 14 million | 6% |
| 14 million–50 million | 15% |
| 50 million–88 million | 24% |
| 88 million–150 million | 35% |
| 150 million–300 million | 38% |
| 300 million–500 million | 40% |
| 500 million–1 billion | 42% |
| Over 1 billion | 45% |

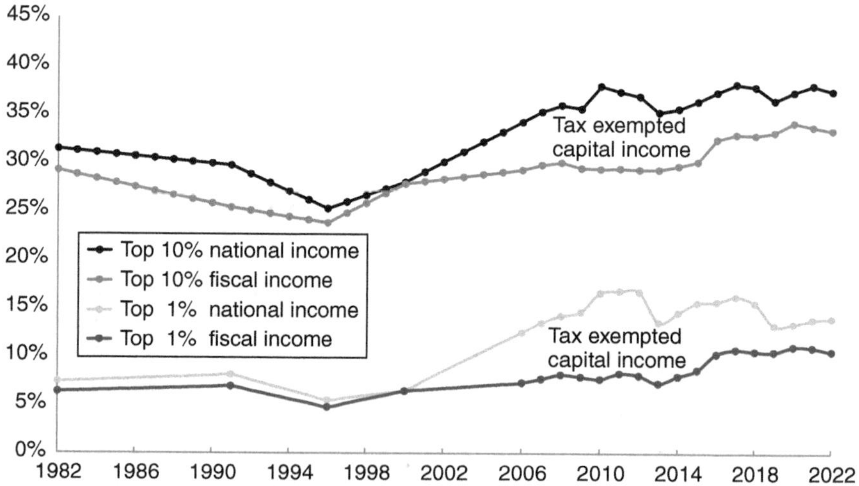


**Fig. 5.5** National Income vs. Fiscal Income for Top Earners, 1982–2022. Source: Hong et al. (2024)

(for those aged 70+, disabled, single parents, etc.). While the basic allowance is a fixed 1.5 million KRW regardless of income level, the actual tax-saving benefit increases with income. For a low-income earner subject to a 6.6% rate (including local income tax), the deduction saves only 99,000 KRW. In contrast, for a high-income earner in the top bracket (49.5% including local tax), it provides a tax saving of 742,500 KRW.

Furthermore, the system allows generous employment income deductions under the guise of "necessary expenses." Since an income deduction of the same amount provides greater tax savings to those in higher marginal tax brackets, the regressivity is inherent. Moreover, as shown in Table 5.10, the actual deduction amount increases as employment income rises, allowing high-income earners to reap even larger benefits.

Tax credits, such as the employment income tax credit and the child tax credit, are generally less regressive than deductions. The employment income tax credit phases in for low earners, plateaus for middle earners (capped at 700,000 KRW), and phases out for high earners (bottoming at 200,000 KRW). The child tax credit provides 150,000 KRW per year for qualifying children aged 8 and older (300,000 KRW starting from the third child), though it cannot be combined with the Child Incentive Payment (CIP).

Numerous studies have pointed out the regressive nature of personal and employment income deductions, noting that they drain tax revenue while primarily benefiting the wealthy. Table 5.11 shows the employment income deduction and its tax-saving effects compared to tax credits for 20.8 million regular employees in 2023. The total tax savings from employment income deductions reached 33 trillion KRW, while employment income tax credits totaled 8 trillion KRW. Combined, these 41 trillion KRW in tax expenditures represent nearly 70% of the 60 trillion KRW

**Table 5.10** Employment Income Deduction Schedule

| *Gross Employment Income* | *Deduction Amount* |
|---|---|
| Up to 5 million KRW | 70% of gross pay |
| 5 million–15 million KRW | 3.5 million + 40% of excess over 5 million |
| 15 million–45 million KRW | 7.5 million + 15% of excess over 15 million |
| 45 million–100 million KRW | 12 million + 5% of excess over 45 million |
| Over 100 million KRW | 14.75 million + 2% of excess over 100 million (Cap: 20 million) |

**Table 5.11** Tax-Saving Effects of Employment Income Deductions and Tax Credits by Income Bracket (Unit: 10 thousand KRW; 100 million KRW for Total Amount of Reduced Taxes only)

| *Income Bracket* | *# of Income Deduction Recipients* | *Income Deduction Amount* | *Tax Reduction due to Deduction* | *# of Tax Credit Recipients* | *Tax Credit Amount* | *Total Tax Reduction per Person* | *Total Amount of Reduced Taxes* |
|---|---|---|---|---|---|---|---|
| Employment income | 20,795,349 | 989 | 158 | 18,840,811 | 43 | 197 | 409,920 |
| Those with tax liability | 13,964,590 | 1,160 | 206 | 13,958,971 | 51 | 257 | 359,012 |
| up to 10 million KRW | 12 | - | - | 0 | 0 | 0 | 0 |
| up to 15 million KRW | 169,973 | 721 | 43 | 169,968 | 17 | 61 | 1,029 |
| up to 20 million KRW | 806,641 | 790 | 57 | 806,636 | 24 | 81 | 6,534 |
| up to 30 million KRW | 2,827,082 | 904 | 112 | 2,827,060 | 40 | 152 | 42,981 |
| up to 40 million KRW | 2,364,773 | 1,048 | 155 | 2,364,756 | 62 | 216 | 51,170 |
| up to 45 million KRW | 1,000,025 | 1,162 | 174 | 1,000,015 | 63 | 237 | 23,690 |
| up to 50 million KRW | 884,923 | 1,212 | 182 | 884,907 | 63 | 245 | 21,700 |
| up to 60 million KRW | 1,460,623 | 1,249 | 187 | 1,460,598 | 65 | 252 | 36,820 |
| up to 80 million KRW | 1,924,293 | 1,321 | 236 | 1,924,244 | 59 | 295 | 56,680 |
| up to 100 million KRW | 1,134,653 | 1,420 | 336 | 1,134,597 | 50 | 386 | 43,791 |
| up to 200 million KRW | 1,213,735 | 1,535 | 476 | 1,212,627 | 34 | 510 | 61,839 |
| up to 300 million KRW | 112,513 | 1,749 | 665 | 110,664 | 20 | 685 | 7,576 |
| up to 500 million KRW | 44,681 | 1,964 | 786 | 43,318 | 20 | 806 | 3,491 |
| up to 1 billion KRW | 15,863 | 2,000 | 840 | 15,031 | 20 | 860 | 1,293 |
| over 1 billion KRW | 4,800 | 2,000 | 900 | 4,550 | 20 | 920 | 419 |
| Those without tax liability | 6,830,759 | 640 | 61 | 4,881,840 | 20 | 75 | 50,908 |

| | | | | | | | |
|---|---|---|---|---|---|---|---|
| up to 10 million KRW | 2,811,731 | 306 | 18 | 1,039,861 | 4 | 23 | 5,621 |
| up to 15 million KRW | 1,105,635 | 639 | 38 | 1,000,737 | 10 | 49 | 5,277 |
| up to 20 million KRW | 481,709 | 785 | 47 | 440,652 | 11 | 58 | 2,762 |
| up to 30 million KRW | 1,192,204 | 906 | 89 | 1,165,194 | 23 | 112 | 13,272 |
| up to 40 million KRW | 881,590 | 1,040 | 144 | 878,110 | 36 | 180 | 15,828 |
| up to 45 million KRW | 180,262 | 1,158 | 169 | 180,000 | 46 | 215 | 3,879 |
| up to 50 million KRW | 92,007 | 1,211 | 179 | 91,904 | 52 | 231 | 2,121 |
| up to 60 million KRW | 63,849 | 1,244 | 185 | 63,758 | 58 | 243 | 1,553 |
| up to 80 million KRW | 18,524 | 1,304 | 195 | 18,439 | 61 | 256 | 473 |
| up to 100 million KRW | 1,752 | 1,411 | 274 | 1,716 | 49 | 323 | 56 |
| over 100 million KRW | 1,496 | 1,586 | 399 | 1,469 | 31 | 430 | 64 |

Source: National Tax Service (2024), and authors' calculations based on NTS statistics.

collected in employment income tax in 2023. Notably, the tax-saving effect of regressive deductions far outweighs tax credits and is seven times larger than the 4.6 trillion KRW spent on the EITC for the working poor.

In 2023, the average employment income deduction per person was 9.89 million KRW. Those with no tax liability received an average deduction of 6.4 million KRW, while those with tax liability received 11.6 million KRW (NTS, 2024). The average tax-saving benefit was 1.58 million KRW; however, the average for those with tax liability (2.06 million KRW) was more than triple that of those with no liability (0.61 million KRW). This suggests that without the deduction, many currently "exempt" earners would fall above the tax threshold. High earners benefited disproportionately: while those earning between 20 and 30 million KRW saved 1.12 million KRW, those earning over 100 million KRW saved 4.76 million KRW, and those earning over 1 billion KRW enjoyed a massive tax saving of 9 million KRW (9.9 million KRW including local tax).

When combining the tax-saving effects of both deductions and credits, earners with 10 million KRW or less received an average benefit of 230,000 KRW, significantly lower than the overall average of 1.97 million KRW. Conversely, the scale of tax benefits increases sharply alongside income, proving that the current system is profoundly regressive.

## 5.4 High PTRs and EMTRs: Obstacles to Freedom and Efficiency

We have examined the current status and limitations of social security benefits—such as social insurance and social assistance—as well as income taxation. Now, we turn to how these systems collectively impact the effective tax rate (ETR), participation tax rate (PTR), and effective marginal tax rate (EMTR) on earned income. High PTRs and EMTRs not only diminish work incentives but also substantively restrict an individual's "real freedom" to improve their circumstances through labor.

To analyze how these rates vary by household type according to earned income, we utilize the OECD Tax-Benefit Calculator (TaxBEN). TaxBEN contains major policy data for 40 countries, including OECD members, regarding the cash income and expenditures of low-income households. Based on this, TaxBEN simulates how gross earnings are converted into net income depending on the country, year, and household characteristics. Here, gross earnings refer to the sum of a household's labor and business income before the impact of taxes and benefits, while net income (equivalent to disposable income) is calculated as follows:

Net income = gross earnings + cash benefits - income tax - social security contributions

In this equation, cash benefits represent the sum of all cash-based welfare provided to the household, including unemployment benefits, NBLSS (livelihood and housing), child allowance, child incentive, and EITC. Income tax includes both central and local personal income taxes, factoring in standard deductions (personal, spouse, and dependents) but excluding deductions based on specific consumption expenditures. Social security contributions include only the employee's portion.

The impact of benefits and taxes on the ratio of net income to gross earnings is expressed as the Effective Tax Rate (ETR), which directly affects income redistribution. From a redistributive perspective, a progressive structure where the ETR is negative at low-income levels and increases as income rises is desirable.

Effective tax rate = (total income - net income) / total income

Furthermore, we measure the impact of these policies on work incentives using the Participation Tax Rate (PTR) and the Effective Marginal Tax Rate (EMTR). The PTR measures the extent to which net income increases when an inactive or unemployed person enters the labor market. A high PTR indicates that entering the labor market yields little to no increase in net income, thereby discouraging participation in formal labor. The EMTR indicates how much net income increases when gross earnings rise by one additional unit. A high EMTR means net income barely grows despite higher earnings; if it exceeds 100%, an income reversal occurs where net income actually decreases. While the PTR affects work incentives at the extensive margin (the decision to join the labor market), the EMTR affects the intensive margin (the decision to work more hours).

PTR = 1 - (net income when participating in labor - net income when not participating in labor)/ total income when participating in labor

EMTR = 1 - increase in net income / small increase in total income

### *Reversal of Income*

Figure 5.6 illustrates how the net income of a single-earner four-person household (head of household, spouse, and two children) changes based on gross earnings ranging from 1% to 200% of the average wage (4,337,964 KRW as of 2022). We present two net income lines: one including all eligible social assistance benefits (net w/SA) and one excluding NBLSS livelihood and housing benefits while including only child allowance and EITC (net w/o SA). While OECD TaxBEN typically assumes full take-up of all eligible benefits, we include both scenarios to better reflect the reality of low take-up rates.

Figure 5.6 starkly demonstrates an income reversal between recipient households (net w/PA) and non-recipient households (net w/o PA) across the range of 1% to 81% of the average wage. Furthermore, even if all assistance is received, reversals occur at various points—notably between 76% and 78% of the average wage, and most significantly between 81% and 97%. These reversals are caused by the termination of WIP eligibility after 76% of the average wage and the loss of the flat-rate NBLSS housing

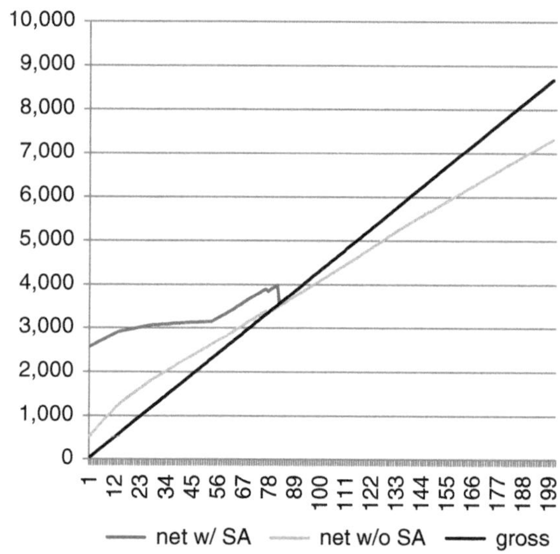


**Fig. 5.6** Net Income for Social Assistance Recipients and Non-Recipients by Gross Earnings (Four-person Single-earner Household). Notes: The X-axis represents gross earnings as a percentage of the average wage (Monthly average: 4,337,964 KRW = 100). The Y-axis represents the monetary value (in thousand KRW) of gross income (indicated by the 45-degree line), net income for social assistance recipients (net w/ SA), and net income for non-recipients (net w/ o SA). Source: Based on OECD Tax-Benefit Calculator (Tax-BEN) (2022, South Korea), with net income for non-recipients added by the author

benefit after 81%. Specifically, once a household "graduates" from housing benefits by exceeding 81% of the average wage, their disposable income does not return to its previous level until their gross earnings reach 97%. While the supplementary livelihood benefit (exited at 52% of the average wage) does not cause a reversal due to its phase-out design, the degree of income reversal between recipients and non-recipients remains largest at lower income levels where benefit amounts are highest.

### *Comparative Analysis of ETR, PTR, and EMTR*

A comparative analysis of the effective tax rate (ETR), participation tax rate (PTR), and effective marginal tax rate (EMTR) for a single-earner four-person household reveals stark disparities between NBLSS recipient households and non-recipient households. In both cases, the ETR is negative in the low-income range. For recipient households, the ETR remains below zero up to the 81st percentile of the average wage, while for non-recipients, this holds up to the 76th percentile. However, the magnitude of support differs vastly: the average ETR for recipient households between 1% and 81% of the average wage is −303%, compared to just −80% for non-recipients between 1% and 76% of the average wage.

The Participation Tax Rate (PTR) remains relatively low for non-recipient households but reaches prohibitively high levels for recipients. Specifically, across several income brackets (30–74%, 77–79%, and 82–111% of the average wage), the PTR exceeds 60%. Most alarmingly, in the 44–59% and 82–87% ranges, the PTR surpasses 70%, meaning that less than 30% of their earned income actually translates into increased net income compared to not working at all.[1] Such high PTRs significantly diminish the incentive to work.

The Effective Marginal Tax Rate (EMTR) likewise exhibits severe distortions. While remaining low for non-recipients, the EMTR for recipients exceeds 70% across a broad range (e.g., 14% to 52% of the average wage). In the 27–52% range, the EMTR exceeds 90%, meaning net income barely moves despite higher gross earnings. At critical thresholds, the EMTR reaches extreme peaks: 216% at 76% of the average wage and a staggering 1,189% at 81% of the average wage. These "benefit cliffs"

[1] Since OECD TaxBEN provides data starting from 1% of the average wage rather than 0%, the PTR was calculated based on net income at 1% of the gross average wage.

trigger the aforementioned income reversals between 76–78% and 81–96% of the average wage.

### *Incentives for Household Dissolution and the "Marriage Penalty"*

We further examine the incentives for household formation and dissolution. Suppose the four-person household undergoes a divorce (real or feigned) to split into a full-time working single-person household and a non-working single-parent three-person household. As shown in Fig. 5.6, the net income of the original single-earner household at the average wage is 4,108,892 KRW. After separation, the working single person's net income is 3,647,017 KRW, while the non-working single parent receives 1,909,000 KRW. Their combined net income increases to 5,556,017 KRW—a gain of 1,447,125 KRW per month. Clearly, the system provides a significant financial incentive for household dissolution.

Conversely, forming a household through marriage often results in a "Marriage Penalty." Consider two singles: one working full-time and the other part-time. While separate, the part-time worker receives livelihood benefits up to 40% of the full-time equivalent (FTE), housing benefits up to 61%, and EITC up to 84%. Their combined ETR remains negative until their total labor reaches 161% of an FTE (Fig. 5.7). However, upon marrying, they lose eligibility for most benefits once their combined labor exceeds 105% of an FTE (Fig. 5.7). Their combined net income can drop by more than 10% compared to remaining single.

For the part-time spouse, the PTR exceeds 100% until they work 17% of an FTE, meaning their net income actually *decreases* upon working. The EMTR reaches a peak of 1,707% at 4% of an FTE, leading to a persistent income reversal until they work 21% of an FTE.

The current system not only creates unfair income reversals between recipients and non-recipients but also actively encourages household dissolution and discourages labor. While the Yoon Suk-yeol administration's "Welfare for the Vulnerable" focused on raising the NBLSS threshold from 30% to 32% (with a goal of 35%), we must ask: which should take priority—simply increasing benefit amounts or resolving the structural flaws of low take-up rates, horizontal inequity, work disincentives, and household dissolution incentives? Our policy proposals in the next chapter are rooted in finding a comprehensive solution to these systemic failures.

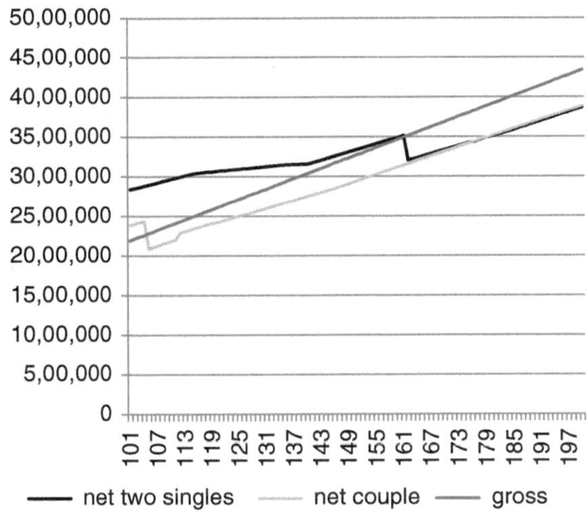


**Fig. 5.7** Change in Combined Net Income by Total Working Hours for Two Single Individuals with Average Wages Upon Marriage. Notes: The X-axis represents the combined working hours, ranging from 101% to 200%. This assumes one individual works full-time (100%) while the other increases their labor supply from 1% to 100% of a full-time equivalent. The Y-axis represents monetary values for "net two singles" (the sum of net incomes of two separate single-person households) and "net couple" (the net income of the combined two-person household). Source: Based on OECD TaxBEN (2022, South Korea)

CHAPTER 6

# Our Proposal: The Three-Pillar Integrated Model

In this chapter, we present concrete policy alternatives that integrate common wealth dividends, negative income tax (NIT) type basic income, and the universal earned income tax credit (Universal EITC).

Common Wealth basic income provides an equal amount to every citizen, funded by a portion of "broad" common wealth revenues and "narrow" natural common wealth revenues. Since it distributes actual common wealth gains, it does not incur fiscal deficits. On the other hand, NIT-type basic income applies a negative tax rate to everyone below the average income—providing graduated benefits based on income—while those exceeding the average income contribute a portion of their excess earnings through a fixed tax rate. Because the payments to those below the average are funded by those above it, this model also maintains fiscal neutrality.

Common wealth basic income is a fundamental right of all citizens, with the sole condition being the fulfillment of one's duty to pay taxes. Similarly, NIT-type basic income is a fundamental right; everyone has the right to receive graduated benefits when their income is absent or low—whether during childhood, retirement, or due to education, illness, accidents, caregiving responsibilities, or disability. However, this right is grounded in the obligation to contribute a certain percentage of one's earnings when they exceed the average income. This system functions as



J. S. You et al., *UBI from Idea to Reality*, Exploring the Basic Income Guarantee,
https://doi.org/10.1007/978-3-032-26200-4_6

a form of inter-temporal insurance, smoothing income and consumption over a lifetime, while simultaneously performing vertical redistribution from high-income to low-income earners. By explicitly linking the right to basic income with the duty of taxation, we ensure that "free-riding" is neither permitted nor encouraged.

The Universal EITC provides a specific percentage of labor income (earned and business income) to low-income earners, while providing a fixed amount to those above a certain income threshold. This can be fully funded by consolidating existing earned income deductions, earned income tax credits, and the current EITC, with the possibility of modest additional fiscal input. While the Universal EITC is also a right, it is exclusive to those participating in the labor market. For workers below a certain income level, it functions as an effective wage increase and covers all or most of their social insurance premiums. For high-income earners, the real benefit may decrease slightly compared to the current earned income deduction.

Our proposal does not aim to provide high levels of guaranteed income at the household level merely to achieve short-term efficiency in poverty reduction. Such an approach necessitates high participation tax rates (PTR) and high effective marginal tax rates (EMTR), which ultimately restrict the "real freedom" of recipients and increase the risk of trapping them in a poverty trap. To foster sustainable and efficient alleviation of inequality while enhancing individual freedom, we adhere to the principle of providing basic income on an individual basis rather than a household basis. By applying negative effective tax rates to low-income individuals, we provide a social minimum while ensuring that participation and marginal tax rates do not become prohibitively high.

Our proposal does not constitute a "Full Basic Income" capable of meeting all minimum needs solely through basic income, nor does it completely replace the existing social security system. Instead, we aim to design a meaningful Partial Basic Income that enhances real freedom and equality. We propose replacing existing social assistance only within the scope of NIT payments, while closing the blind spots of social insurance by supporting the premiums of precarious workers through the Universal EITC. Thus, basic income will serve as a vital pillar of social security—guaranteeing a minimum economic floor, contributing to the elimination of social insurance gaps, and enhancing real freedom by reducing dependency on selective social assistance. We now present our specific policy alternatives.

## 6.1 Universal Basic Income Based on Common Wealth Dividends

We propose three primary policies for a universal basic income (UBI) based on common wealth dividends. First, the transformation of personal income tax allowances into a UBI; second, the introduction of a Land Dividend based on a Land Value Tax (LVT) ; and third, Carbon and Renewable Energy Dividends based on carbon taxes and renewable energy revenues. In the initial stage, renewable energy dividends can serve as a vital funding source for Rural Basic Income, allowing for the prioritized implementation of basic income in rural areas before expanding to a nationwide universal system.

### *Transforming Basic Personal Allowances Into Universal Basic Income*

As discussed in Chapter 4, a modest level of UBI can be implemented by converting these allowances into universal refundable tax credits. This can be viewed as a form of Common Wealth basic income in a broad sense. As Herbert Simon argued, a significant portion of national income is based on the accumulation of common wealth inherited from the past rather than purely the individual efforts of the current generation. Thus, distributing a portion of national income equally to everyone is justified.

Applying this specifically to South Korea, the resulting basic income level would be relatively low due to the small size of current allowances. Nevertheless, this shift would enable the general public to grasp the relationship between taxation and basic income, serving as a catalyst for developing higher-level universal or NIT-type basic income models in the future.

Currently, the Basic Personal Allowance exempts a specific amount (1.5 million KRW per person) from the taxable income of the taxpayer, a spouse with no income, and dependents aged 20 or younger or 60 or older. Those who are neither taxpayers nor registered dependents are excluded.

Based on 2023 income data, approximately 26.74 million taxpayers received these allowances; including their dependents, the total beneficiaries reached 42.17 million, or 81.7% of the total population (Table 6.1). Crucially, the remaining 9.43 million, or 18.3% of the total population who are excluded, largely consist of the economically vulnerable: low-income daily laborers, unpaid family workers, and the economically inactive adult population. If the right to basic income is grounded in the duty

**Table 6.1** Reduced Tax Due to Basic Personal Allowances by Tax Base

| *Tax base (KRW)* | *Tax rate (%)* | *# Taxpayers (thousand)* | *# Dependents (thousand)* | *# Sum (thousand persons)* | *Reduced tax per person (KRW)* |
|---|---|---|---|---|---|
| up to 14 million | 6.6 | 13,570 | 3,231 | 16,801 | up to 99,000 |
| up to 50 million | 16.5 | 10,123 | 7,473 | 17,596 | 247,500 |
| up to 88 million | 26.4 | 1,990 | 2,947 | 4,937 | 396,000 |
| up to 150 million | 38.5 | 722 | 1,284 | 2,006 | 577,500 |
| up to 300 million | 41.8 | 240 | 373 | 614 | 627,000 |
| up to 500 million | 44.0 | 56 | 77 | 133 | 660,000 |
| up to 1 billion | 46.2 | 27 | 35 | 61 | 693,000 |
| over 1 billion | 49.5 | 9 | 10 | 20 | 742,500 |
| Not applicable | | | | 9,432 | 0 |
| Total population | | | | 51,600 | 183,000 |

Source: National Tax Service, Statistical Yearbook of National Tax (2024).

to pay taxes, then every citizen becomes a potential taxpayer. An individual may not be a taxpayer in a year without income, but they will contribute whenever they earn. Therefore, as potential taxpayers, they should receive the benefit of the Basic Personal Allowance even in years without income.

Furthermore, while the allowance amount is a uniform 1.5 million KRW per person, the tax-saving benefit is highly regressive. For a low-income earner in the 6% bracket (6.6% including local income tax), the deduction saves only 99,000 KRW or less. Conversely, for a high-income earner in the top bracket (over 1 billion KRW taxable base) subject to a 49.5% rate including local tax, the tax saving reaches 742,500 KRW.

Converting personal allowances into basic income involves covering the entire population—including the excluded 18.3%—and transitioning to a universal refundable tax credit to resolve the regressivity where the wealthy benefit more. As shown in Table 6.1, only 15.1% of the total population receives a tax-saving benefit exceeding 250,000 KRW per person (those with tax base of over 50 million KRW, which typically means earned income over 80 million KRW). The remaining 84.9% either receive no benefit or save less than 250,000 KRW.

Considering that the Lee Jae-myung administration distributed 150,000 to 250,000 KRW "Livelihood Recovery Coupons" to all citizens upon its inauguration, replacing the personal allowance with an annual

250,000 KRW Basic Income is a viable proposal. Of the 12.9 trillion KRW required, 9.4 trillion KRW can be funded by the revenue increase from abolishing current allowances, requiring only an additional 3.5 trillion KRW in fiscal input. Given recent legislative proposals to increase the personal allowance to 2 or 3 million KRW, implementing a universal basic income of 0.5% of GNI per capita (250,000 KRW in 2024; 300,000 KRW expected by 2030) is a far more equitable alternative.

### *Land Dividend Basic Income Based on Land Value Tax (LVT)*

In Chapter 3, we examined how a Land Value Tax (LVT) acts as a "good tax" (or the "least bad tax") by reclaiming a portion of land rent—a natural common wealth—from landowners to lower land prices and enhance land-use efficiency. Furthermore, we established that distributing the entire revenue from LVT as an equal Land Dividend Basic Income to all citizens can overcome tax resistance while mitigating inequality through income redistribution. We propose the following concrete plan to implement LVT and Land Dividends in South Korea.

First, the relationship with existing property and comprehensive real estate taxes must be addressed. While the tax on buildings within the current property tax should be maintained, the portion levied on land should be absorbed into the new LVT. We also propose that the Comprehensive Real Estate Tax (CRET) be subsumed under the LVT. The existing CRET has faced significant resistance because it heavily penalized housing over land, particularly under the Moon Jae-in administration, which applied punitive rates to owners of two homes in the Seoul metropolitan area.

Furthermore, the "fair market value ratio" (the ratio at which the taxable base reflects the officially announced price) is lower for detached houses than for apartments, and even lower for commercial land and buildings. Specifically, commercial building sites receive an exemption of up to 8 billion KRW. This structure inadvertently favors the ultra-wealthy in mansions and commercial landlords over the upper-middle class in apartments. Taxing housing more heavily than land contradicts the principle of efficient land use. Given that land ownership is highly concentrated at the top while housing is more broadly held by the middle and upper-middle classes, replacing CRET with a land-focused LVT is economically sound. We propose separating the valuation of residential land from the buildings and taxing the land more heavily.

Currently, the property tax on land is mostly levied at rates between 0.2% and 0.5% of the taxable base, with lower rates for farmland (0.07%) and higher rates for luxury land such as golf courses (4%). However, the taxable base is only 60% of the officially announced land price, which in turn is only about 65% of the market value, indicating that the effective tax rate is extremely low.

We propose applying a uniform flat rate of 1% on the officially announced land price for almost all land. While the higher rates for luxury properties like golf courses should be maintained, a slightly lower rate could be applied to farmland. To address concerns that this imposes an excessive burden on elderly homeowners with limited cash flow, we propose an "equity payment" option, allowing them to pay the tax in shares of land ownership instead of cash. With a 1% rate, paying the tax in equity for 100 years would result in the disposal of only about 65% of the total ownership. This is by no means a harsh tax. Moreover, the implementation of Land Dividends ensures that non-homeowners and landless citizens become net beneficiaries, and even many land-owning households will receive dividends that exceed their LVT liability due to the extreme concentration of land ownership.

According to the Bank of Korea's National Balance Sheet, as of 2024, the total value of privately held land assets in South Korea is 9,396 trillion KRW, with households and non-profit organizations accounting for 7,008 trillion KRW. Since the officially announced price is roughly 65% of the market value, a 1% tax on this base would generate approximately 61 trillion KRW in revenue. This represents an additional 49 trillion KRW compared to the 2024 land property tax (7.4 trillion KRW) and CRET (4.2 trillion KRW) .

Focusing solely on land owned by households and non-profits, the revenue would be 45.5 trillion KRW. Distributing this as a Land Dividend would provide approximately 880,000 KRW per person. Even with a conservative estimate accounting for lower rates on farmland, an annual Land Dividend Basic Income of about 1.5% of GNI per capita (750,000 KRW in 2024) could be fully funded.

### *Carbon and Renewable Energy Dividends Based on Carbon Taxes and Renewable Energy Revenues*

In Chapter 3, we examined how a carbon tax is one of the most efficient tools for achieving carbon neutrality and addressing the climate crisis.

By distributing the entire revenue from a carbon tax as an equal Carbon Dividend to all citizens, a majority of households—particularly those in the middle- and low-income brackets—become net beneficiaries. This mechanism helps overcome tax resistance and contributes to a Just Transition by mitigating inequality. Furthermore, we established that even if carbon dividends decrease as emissions fall, they can be sufficiently supplemented by Renewable Energy Dividends, which return a portion of profits from renewable energy to the public.

A carbon tax is justified because it is a fee for using the air's carbon-absorption capacity—a depletable common wealth. Therefore, it is only just to distribute the proceeds equally among all citizens, the co-owners of this common wealth. Similarly, renewable energy dividends are justified because the competitiveness of renewable firms often rests on public investments in infrastructure, such as energy storage systems (ESS) and transmission/distribution grids. It is only fair that the public reclaims and redistributes a portion of these returns.

South Korea's greenhouse gas emissions (the vast majority of which are carbon) stood at 780 million tons in 2018 and dropped to 690 million tons in 2024. The government aims to reduce emissions by 53% to 61% relative to 2018 levels by 2035. If achieved, per capita emissions will fall from the current 13 tons to approximately 6–7 tons. By starting the carbon tax at 40,000 KRW per ton and gradually increasing it to 80,000 KRW, a Carbon Dividend Basic Income of 1% of GNI per capita (500,000 KRW in 2024) can be implemented.

Under this system, any individual who consumes less energy than the per capita average becomes a net beneficiary, as their dividend will exceed the price increases triggered by the tax. This creates a powerful incentive for both individuals and corporations to adjust their energy consumption patterns toward lower emissions, while simultaneously enhancing the relative competitiveness of carbon-free renewable energy.

As the renewable energy industry matures, it will eventually generate sufficient revenue to offset any decline in carbon tax receipts. In the initial stages, it is pragmatic to begin with dividends for residents in rural and fishing communities where solar and wind farms are primarily located. Many local governments are already seeking to implement "Sunlight Income" and "Wind Income" models, inspired by the successful case of Sinan County in Jeollanam-do (Kwon et al., 2023).

Initially, restricting the dividend to residents living near these facilities is reasonable. This approach helps overcome the "NIMBY" (Not In

My Backyard) sentiment toward energy infrastructure and facilitates the smooth expansion of renewables. However, in the long run, a substantial portion of renewable energy profits must be expanded into a nationwide dividend. Determining the precise allocation between local community dividends and nationwide dividends will require social consensus and further research.

### *Rural Basic Income and Nationwide Universal Basic Income*

By integrating the three policies discussed above—the "basic income-ization" of the Basic Personal Allowance (0.5% of GNI per capita), Land Dividends (1.5% of GNI), and Carbon/Renewable Energy Dividends (1.0% of GNI)—a Universal Basic Income (UBI) equivalent to 3% of GNI per capita can be realized in a fiscally neutral manner. Based on 2024 figures, this amounts to 1.5 million KRW annually, and it is projected to reach approximately 1.8 million KRW by 2030.

We propose that the Lee Jae-myung administration implement this common wealth-based UBI during its term (from June 4, 2025 to June 3, 2030), by 2030 at the latest. Furthermore, as the government moves forward with the establishment of a "Korean Sovereign Wealth Fund" for long-term investment in national strategic sectors, a portion of the fund's future returns could eventually be distributed to the public as additional dividends.

While President Lee Jae-myung pledged a nationwide UBI including land and carbon dividends during his 2022 candidacy, and reportedly instructed his cabinet to review carbon dividends upon his inauguration in June 2025, he has yet to make a formal pronouncement on a nationwide rollout. Instead, the administration has launched a Rural Basic Income Pilot Project to be conducted in ten counties (*Gun*) throughout 2026 and 2027.

The pilot project provides all residents in selected areas with 150,000 KRW per month in local currency for two years. Out of 49 applicant counties facing population extinction crises, ten were selected. The budget is split between the central government (40%), provincial governments (30%), and the respective counties (30%). The objective is to analyze policy effectiveness and initiate public deliberation for a potential expansion to all high-risk regions.

To further promote "Sunlight Income," the government plans to expand Sunlight Villages to 2,500 in five years. These involve installing renewable energy facilities on public farmland or reservoirs in rural areas and sharing the proceeds with residents. These projects are categorized into Agrivoltaics (simultaneous crop cultivation and solar power generation) and Floating Photovoltaics (installing panels on water surfaces like reservoirs).

We recognize the necessity of prioritizing basic income in rural areas to address the population crisis and compensate for the "public interest functions" of agriculture, such as environmental preservation and food security. However, permanently limiting basic income to rural residents is undesirable and prone to complications.

The justification for Rural Basic Income rests on two pillars: first, compensating for the positive externalities (food security and conservation) that the market fails to reward; and second, preventing regional extinction due to urban centralization. As these projects expand, the demand for a nationwide UBI will inevitably grow.

Our principle—that the right to basic income is predicated on the duty to pay taxes—must apply equally to rural residents. This means gradually transitioning toward taxing crop cultivation and rural sideline income, even if at low initial rates.

As previously discussed, we propose a nationwide Common Wealth Basic Income equivalent to 3% of GNI per capita (1.5 million KRW as of 2024; projected at 1.8 million KRW by 2030). Given that the current Rural Basic Income pilot provides 1.8 million KRW annually, a full integration of the two systems would be difficult until the nationwide UBI reaches that same level—a milestone that would occur when South Korea's GNI per capita reaches approximately 60 million KRW.

Once the nationwide UBI meets or exceeds the 1.8 million KRW threshold, the Rural Basic Income can be fully absorbed into the national system. However, until the regional extinction crisis is fundamentally resolved, a small "Rural Resident Allowance" could be maintained as a supplementary top-up to the national UBI. This approach purposefully reverses the current "need-based" welfare principle, which provides higher housing benefits to residents of metropolitan areas like Seoul than to those in rural regions. Specifically, renewable energy dividends from solar and wind power could be channeled through "Sunlight Village" projects to provide slightly higher payouts to residents living in the immediate vicinity of these facilities.

The comprehensive structure of our proposed Common Wealth Basic Income is summarized in Table 6.2.

**Table 6.2** Proposed Structure of Common Wealth Basic Income

| | *% of GNI per capita* | *2024 Value (10k KRW)* | *2030 Projection (10k KRW)* |
|---|---|---|---|
| Basic income-ization of basic allowance | 0.5% | 25 | 30 |
| Land dividend | 1.5% | 75 | 90 |
| Carbon/renewable energy dividends | 1.0% | 50 | 60 |
| Nationwide Common Wealth UBI | 3.0% | 150 | 180 |
| Rural Common Wealth UBI | 3.0%+ α | 180 | 180+ α |

Note: Once GNI per capita reaches 60 million KRW, the nationwide UBI will equal the Rural Basic Income level, at which point they will be fully integrated with a potential minor supplementary allowance for rural residents. We assume that GNI per capita is projected to reach 60 million KRW by approximately 2030.

## 6.2 Negative Income Tax (NIT)-Type Basic Income

The design of a Negative Income Tax (NIT)-type basic income requires determining several critical variables: the break-even threshold (standard income level), the guaranteed income for those with zero market income, the clawback rate (benefit reduction rate) based on income, and the tax rate for income exceeding the break-even threshold.

We propose a fiscally neutral model that sets the national average income as the break-even threshold. To address specific demographic needs, we set higher guaranteed income levels for children and the elderly. Consequently, the clawback rates for these groups are also higher, ensuring that benefits reach zero exactly at the average income level. Existing social assistance programs will be replaced only within the scope of the NIT payments.

### *Definition of Income and the Break-even Threshold*

The national average income, which serves as the break-even threshold, varies depending on the definition of income. As discussed in previous chapters, we aim to use a comprehensive definition of income, encompassing not only taxable income but also non-taxable income and imputed rent. This definition includes earned income, business income, property income (including private pensions), realized capital gains, social insurance benefits (public pensions, employment insurance, and industrial accident compensation), and imputed rent. For capital gains on assets held for over two years, we allow for the deduction of consumer price inflation and the distribution of gains over the holding period.

Determining imputed rent requires an objective calculation method since it is not set by the market. Kim (2022) estimated the net output of housing services to be approximately 1.378% of housing asset value. While rental yields vary by region and housing type, applying such granular data administratively is challenging. Therefore, we propose applying an annual rate of 2% to the officially announced price (which reflects 60–65% of market value), resulting in an effective rate of roughly 1.2–1.3% of market value. This is significantly lower than the punitive income-conversion rates used in the National Basic Living Security System (50.04% annually; 12.48% for houses in Seoul under 172 million KRW). Unlike conventional social assistance, we do not convert other assets into income, as non-residential assets already generate cash income. Imputed rent is included because owner-occupied housing provides a valuable service equivalent to cash income without generating actual cash flow.

Since the NIT will replace existing social assistance within the scope of its payments, social assistance benefits are excluded from the definition of income. However, because the NIT does not replace social insurance, those benefits are included as income. Although job-seeking (unemployment) benefits, maternity benefits, and industrial accident compensation are currently non-taxable under income tax law, they are treated as income under our NIT model. Public pensions (NPS, civil service, military, and private school teachers' pensions) are also included. While current law allows for generous pension income deductions, our NIT model proposes either eliminating these deductions or reducing them to a minimum to ensure equity.

Using this comprehensive definition, the average individual income is expected to be approximately 60% of Gross National Income (GNI) per capita. In the national accounts, the share of households and non-profit organizations typically ranges from 60% to 62% (61.0% in 2024). This aligns with average income data derived from the Survey of Household Finances and Living Conditions (SHFLC).

While GNI and GDP (Gross Domestic Product) are nearly identical in South Korea—GNI being GDP plus negligible net primary income from abroad—we utilize GNI as the benchmark. As of 2024, GNI per capita stands at 50.12 million KRW, nearly equal to the GDP per capita of 49.41 million KRW (KOSIS, 2025). Since the NIT-type basic income involves the redistribution of national income within the household sector (excluding corporate and government sectors), GNI is the most appropriate metric. Although using NNI (Net National Income, which excludes fixed capital consumption) might be theoretically superior, fixed capital consumption is not a major factor in the household sector, and NNI data is less commonly published. Therefore, GNI remains a robust and practical baseline.

For the purpose of our analysis, we assume a GNI per capita of 50 million KRW in 2024 (projected at 60 million KRW by 2030). The national average income is set at 60% of GNI per capita, amounting to 30 million KRW in 2024 (projected at 36 million KRW by 2030). This average income is slightly higher than the 2024 median income for a single-person household (2.228 million KRW per month) or the minimum wage (2.06 million KRW per month). Since this average includes children, the elderly, and the economically inactive, most adults whose earnings exceed the average will contribute a 10% "Basic Income Tax" on their excess earnings rather than receiving NIT payments. However, when factoring in the common wealth dividends provided to all family members (including non-earning children), a significant majority of adults will still emerge as net beneficiaries.

### *Levels of Guaranteed Income and the Clawback Rate*

Defining the appropriate level of guaranteed income is the most critical decision in designing an NIT system. While a "Full Basic Income" sufficient for a dignified life is fiscally unrealistic at this stage, determining the ideal "Partial Basic Income" involves balancing social desirability with fiscal feasibility.

Surveys conducted in South Korea between 2019 and 2021 consistently showed that the most preferred monthly amount was between 200,000 and 300,000 KRW. For instance, a Hankook Research (2019) poll found that 34% of respondents favored a range of 100,000–300,000 KRW, followed by 300,000–500,000 KRW (29%). Support dropped significantly for any option exceeding 500,000 KRW. Similarly, Gyeonggi Research Institute surveys in 2019 and 2021 confirmed that more than two-thirds of respondents preferred a monthly benefit within the 100,000–500,000 KRW bracket. Interestingly, while 59.4% supported a 500,000 KRW benefit in principle, only 29.3% believed it was fiscally feasible, reflecting public concern over potential tax hikes (Yoo and Ma, 2020; Yoo et al., 2021).

Based on these findings, we believe a monthly basic income of 200,000 to 300,000 KRW (2.4 to 3.6 million KRW annually) is politically and socially viable. This represents approximately 6% to 9% of the 2020 GNI per capita, or 10% to 15% of the national average income. We previously proposed a Common Wealth Dividend of 3% of GNI (5% of average income). By adding an NIT Guaranteed Income of 6% of GNI (10% of average income), the total guaranteed floor reaches 9% of GNI, or 15% of the average income (4.5 million KRW annually or 375,000 KRW monthly in 2024).

While most surveys assume a flat amount for all citizens, we propose an age-graded NIT model (You, 2020b). We recommend setting the NIT guaranteed income at 10% of the average income for adults and 20% for children (0–18 years old) and the elderly (65 and older). In 2024 terms, this provides 6 million KRW annually (500,000 KRW monthly) to the elderly and children. When combined with the common wealth dividend, the total floor for these vulnerable groups rises to 25% of the average income (15% of GNI), amounting to 7.5 million KRW annually in 2024 (9 million KRW per year, expected by 2030).

For the elderly, this represents a substantial increase from the current Basic Pension (334,810 KRW per month in 2024), offering a robust solution to elderly poverty. For children, this ambitious guarantee aims to drastically reduce the financial burden of child-rearing in response to South Korea's record-low birth rate. Since the break-even threshold remains fixed at the average income regardless of age, the clawback rate is set at 10% for adults and 20% for children and the elderly.

The combined guaranteed income (for those with zero market income) from both common wealth and NIT components is summarized in Table 6.3.

### *The Introduction of a Basic Income Tax*

To fund the NIT-type basic income, it is necessary to levy a fixed-rate Basic Income Tax on income exceeding the break-even threshold, in addition to existing income taxes. In a fiscally neutral model—where total benefits equal total tax revenue—if the break-even threshold is set at the average income and the guaranteed income is 20% of that threshold, the tax rate on excess income must also be 20%.

In our model, we provide a guaranteed income of 10% for adults and 20% for children and the elderly. While this might suggest a tax rate

**Table 6.3** Combined Guaranteed Income: Common Wealth Dividend + NIT-Type Basic Income

| *Category* | *% of Avg. Income* | *% of GNI per capita* | *2024 Value (10k KRW)* | *2030 Projection (10k KRW)* |
|---|---|---|---|---|
| Nationwide Common Wealth UBI | 5% | 3% | 150 | 180 |
| Rural Common Wealth UBI | 5% + α | 3% + α | 180 | 180 + α |
| NIT Component (Adults) | 10% | 6% | 300 | 360 |
| NIT Component (Children/Elderly) | 20% | 12% | 600 | 720 |
| Total Guarantee (Adults) | 15% | 9% | 450 | 540 |
| Total Guarantee (Rural Adults) | 15% + α | 9% + α | 480 | 540 + α |
| Total Guarantee (Children/ Elderly) | 25% | 15% | 750 | 900 |
| Total Guarantee (Rural Children/Elderly) | 25% + α | 15% + α | 780 | 900 + α |

significantly higher than 10%, fiscal neutrality can still be achieved at a 10% Basic Income Tax rate. This is possible because the NIT will replace a substantial portion of existing social assistance, and the fiscal savings from these programs offset the additional costs of higher guarantees for children and the elderly. Our simulations using the SHFLC data confirm that a 10% tax rate indeed achieves fiscal neutrality.

Figure 6.1 illustrates the NIT-type basic income benefits and the corresponding Basic Income Tax (expressed as a proportion of the average income). For those with market income below the average, the payout is represented by two distinct lines based on age (adults vs. children/ elderly). For income exceeding the average, the 10% tax is represented by a single line regardless of age.

Furthermore, Fig. 6.2 displays the age-graded combination of Common Wealth Dividends and NIT-type Basic Income. While the Basic Income Tax is 10% on income exceeding the average, the inclusion of the Common Wealth Dividend means that, effectively, a 10% net tax burden is only realized for income exceeding 150% of the average income.

When this 10% Basic Income Tax is added to the existing personal income tax (which has a top marginal rate of 49.5% including local tax),

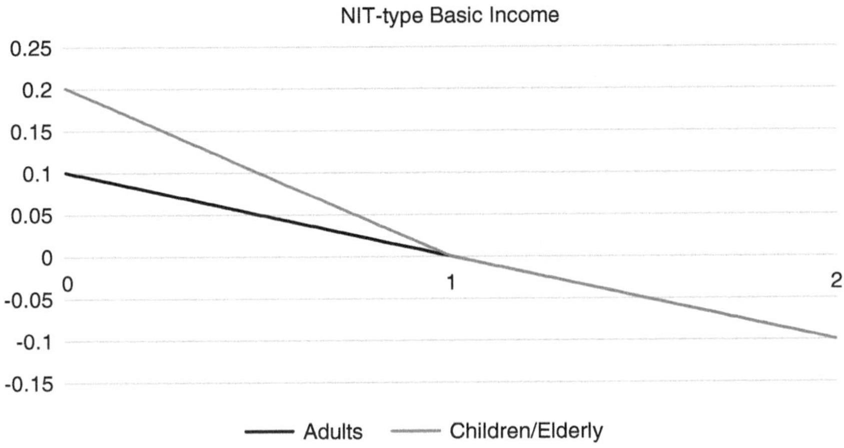


**Fig. 6.1** NIT-Type Basic Income Benefits and Basic Income Tax (Unit: proportion of average income)

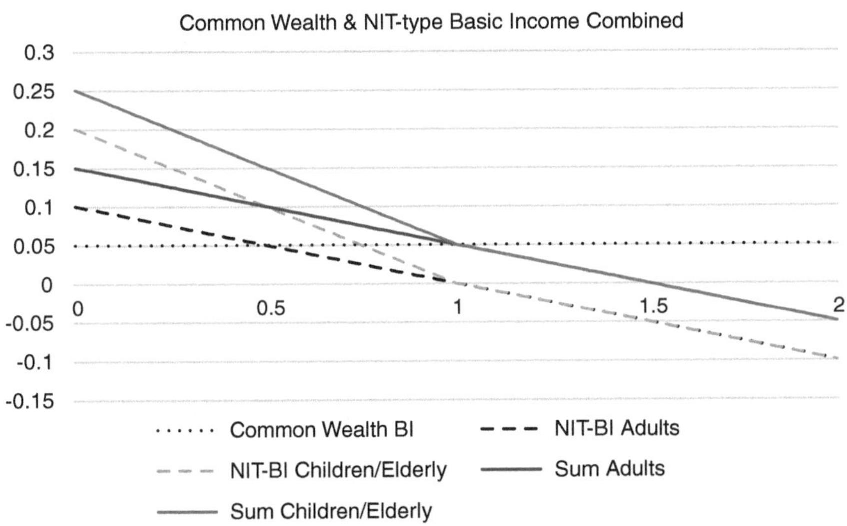


**Fig. 6.2** Combined Common Wealth and NIT-Type Basic Income (Unit: proportion of GNI per capita)

the maximum marginal tax rate for income exceeding 1 billion KRW per year reaches 59.5%.

Whether a 59.5% top marginal rate is excessive is a subject of debate. However, leading economists such as Piketty, Saez, and Stantcheva (2014) estimated the optimal top tax rate to be as high as 83%. Anthony Atkinson (2015) proposed raising the UK's top rate to 65%. Both Atkinson (2015) and Piketty (2020) remind us that countries like the U.S., UK, and France experienced high economic growth even when top rates were in the 80% range. South Korea also achieved rapid growth under a 70% top rate during the Park Chung-hee administration.

Viewed in this historical and academic context, a 59.5% top rate is by no means excessive. Moreover, the real issue for the ultra-wealthy is not necessarily a high tax rate, but rather the fact that a large portion of their wealth—such as financial investment income—is often non-taxable or subject to low-rate separate taxation.

Should there be significant resistance to a 10% Basic Income Tax from the middle and upper classes, we could consider diversifying the funding sources. This might include sharing the fiscal burden with corporate taxes, Value-Added Tax (VAT), or introducing new levies such as Wealth Taxes or Data Taxes. Ideally, maintaining a high proportion of direct taxes is preferable to maximize the redistributive effect. Depending on the extent of such diversification, the specific Basic Income Tax rate could potentially be lowered to a range of 3% to 5%.

## 6.3 Universal Earned Income Tax Credit (Universal EITC)

The Universal EITC provides a fixed percentage of earned income (employment income and business income) up to a certain threshold, and a fixed maximum amount for earned income exceeding that level. Unlike the existing Work Incentive Payment (WIP), it is provided on an individual basis rather than a household basis and features only phase-in and plateau ranges, entirely eliminating the phase-out range. This system consolidates the existing employment income deduction, employment income tax credit, current WIP, and various social insurance premium subsidy programs. Its primary role is to eliminate social insurance blind spots by covering the premiums for low-income workers and entrepreneurs.

To fully cover the social insurance premiums of low-income workers, we propose a 12% credit rate on labor income up to 83.3% of the average income. Under this design, the maximum benefit (plateau) equals 10% of the average income—aligning exactly with the guaranteed income of the NIT-type basic income for adults (Fig. 6.3).

The 12% rate is strategically derived from the social insurance contribution rates for employees. In 2026, the combined rate for employees—including National Pension (scheduled to rise from 4.75% to 6.5%), Health Insurance (3.595%), Long-term Care (0.4724%), and Employment Insurance (0.9%)—is expected to be 9.7174%, rising to over 11.4674% by 2033. A 12% Universal EITC would fully subsidize these contributions for low-income wage earners and cover approximately half for the self-employed. If initial funding is insufficient, the system could start with a 10% rate and a plateau beginning at 80% of the average income, with a maximum benefit of 8%.

Previously, we proposed distributing the tax revenue gained from abolishing employment income deductions equally among all citizens (Kang, 2019b; You, 2018). However, this faced significant resistance from workers who felt that labor income is already treated less favorably than capital income. We acknowledge this concern. Therefore, we propose that while the Basic Personal Allowance should be converted into a nationwide UBI, the Employment Income Deduction and Credit should be consolidated into a Universal EITC that encompasses all workers—including the self-employed—thereby unifying the current fragmented system.

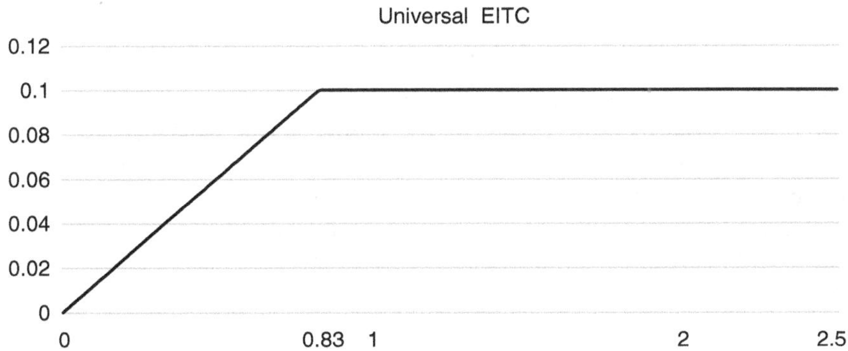


**Fig. 6.3** Universal EITC by Level of Earned Income (Unit: proportion of average income)

The Universal EITC is a form of Participation Income (PI) because, unlike UBI, it is contingent on labor market participation. However, it is more restrictive than the models proposed by Atkinson (1996) or Hiilamo (2022), which recognize unpaid social contributions such as domestic work, caregiving, and volunteering.

To overcome this limitation, the central government should provide financial support to local governments to offer PI for a wider range of social, ecological, and care services. A prime example is the "Opportunity Income" (e.g., for artists, the disabled, and climate action) currently implemented by Gyeonggi Province Governor Kim Dong-yeon. Expanding these models to more regions would allow for the recognition of "work with social value" that meets the unmet needs of local communities (Lee, 2025).

## 6.4 Partial Replacement of Existing Social Assistance

When introducing a Partial Basic Income rather than a Full Basic Income, a crucial principle is ensuring that existing welfare recipients do not suffer any net loss. According to Van Parijs and Vanderborght (2017: 11–12, 135), while basic income can fully replace social assistance benefits that are lower than the basic income amount, for benefits that exceed it, only the portion equivalent to the basic income should be replaced. This approach prevents current recipients from being disadvantaged while reducing overall dependency on social assistance by decreasing the number of recipients and the total payout amounts. Furthermore, as the number of social assistance recipients shrinks, the administrative costs associated with means testing will also decline (You, 2018).

Following the recommendation of the Basic Income Korean Network (2021: 103), cash benefits from social insurance should be maintained even after basic income is introduced. Unlike social assistance, which is funded by general tax revenue, social insurance benefits are grounded in the contributions (premiums) of the insured.

Under these principles, existing social assistance programs—including the Child Allowance, Child Incentive Payment, and Basic Pension—will be fully replaced by the NIT-type Basic Income. The Work Incentive Payment, along with the Employment Income Deduction and Credit, will be consolidated into the Universal EITC. While the National Basic

Livelihood Security System (NBLSS) remains in place, the NIT-type basic income payouts will be included in the "Recognized Income" calculation for NBLSS, thereby achieving a partial replacement effect. Crucially, the Common Wealth Basic Income and the Universal EITC will *not* be included in the NBLSS Recognized Income. Regarding income tax, the Basic Personal Allowance will be converted into a UBI, while Additional Allowances for Seniors and the Child Tax Credit will be replaced by the NIT.

A contentious issue in the introduction of basic income is whether it should be fully included in the NBLSS Recognized Income. If basic income is fully included, NBLSS recipients see their Livelihood Benefits reduced by the exact same amount, effectively nullifying the benefit of the basic income for the most vulnerable. Van Parijs and Vanderborght (2017) argue for full inclusion as a means of replacing existing assistance within the scope of the basic income. However, some Korean scholars have proposed alternatives: Baek and Seo (2021) suggest excluding a 300,000 KRW partial basic income from recognized income entirely, while Kang (2019a) proposed a middle ground where only half (150,000 KRW) of a 300,000 KRW basic income is replaced within the Livelihood Benefit.

We propose a nuanced approach: NIT-type Basic Income payouts should be included in the NBLSS Recognized Income, while Common Wealth Basic Income and the Universal EITC should be excluded. Including the NIT payout is necessary to minimize and prevent the "income reversals" that occur under the current system. This honors the vested rights of existing recipients while significantly enhancing horizontal equity between recipients and the working poor who currently do not receive benefits.

The Common Wealth Basic Income should be excluded from Recognized Income because it represents the distribution of "what belongs to all to everyone." However, we may consider treating common wealth dividends as taxable income. By including them in global taxable income, they would be taxed at low rates for the poor and high rates for the wealthy, effectively creating a graduated net benefit that favors low-income groups. Finally, the Universal EITC should be excluded from Recognized Income to ensure it can effectively perform its role as a subsidy for the social insurance premiums of low-income earners.

## 6.5 Total Combined Benefits

Figure 6.4 provides a comprehensive overview of the integrated benefits of Common Wealth Dividends, NIT-type Basic Income, the Basic Income Tax, and the Universal EITC for working persons.

When earned income (the sum of employment and business income) is zero, the total benefit for an adult is 15% of the average income, while for children and the elderly, it reaches 25%. As earned income increases to the level of the average income, the total benefit amount stabilizes at 15% for all age groups. This occurs because, while the NIT payout reaches zero at the average income threshold, the Common Wealth Dividend (5%) and the Universal EITC (10%) remain in effect. For earned income exceeding the average, the total benefit of 15% is maintained, though individuals begin to contribute a 10% Basic Income Tax on their excess earnings. Notably, the total benefit amount remains higher than the Basic Income Tax until earned income reaches approximately 250% of the average income.

However, it is important to clarify that the total benefit amount exceeding the Basic Income Tax in this figure does not automatically imply that the "net benefit" (total gain minus all costs) is positive for everyone. This specific visualization does not account for the increased tax burden resulting from the abolition of the Basic Personal Allowance, Additional Allowances, Employment Income Deductions and Credits, Work Incentive

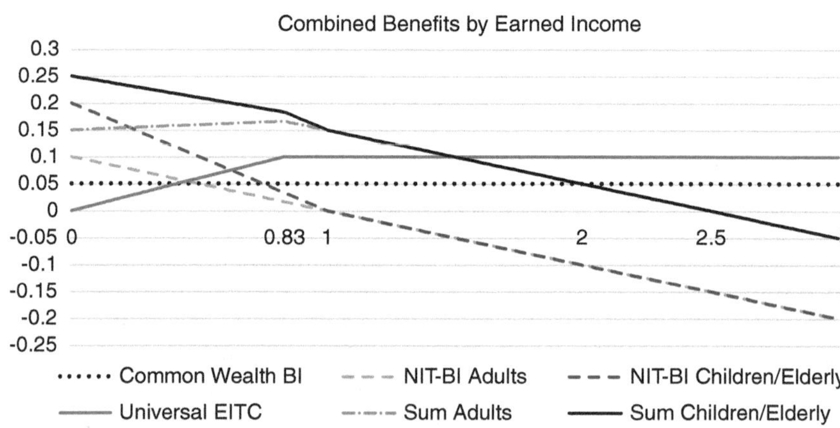


**Fig. 6.4** Integrated Benefits of Common Wealth and NIT Basic Incomes, and Universal EITC by Earned Income (Unit: proportion of average income)

Payment, Child Incentive Payment, and Child Tax Credits, nor the impact of Land Value Taxes and Carbon Taxes.

The real-world impacts of these variables are complex. Land Value and Carbon Taxes, as well as income tax adjustments, are not determined solely by income. For instance, the tax savings from the current Basic Personal Allowance depend on the number of dependents, and eligibility for the WIP is determined by household structure and assets rather than just individual earned income. Furthermore, existing Employment Income Deductions and Credits do not currently apply to business income of the self-employed or daily laborers who do not file tax returns. Finally, determining the exact net benefit requires calculating the specific amount of social assistance that is replaced within the scope of the NIT payments.

Consequently, the full impact of tax increases and the partial replacement of existing benefits must be analyzed through micro-simulations using household data (refer to the simulation results in Chapter 8). Broadly, however, we anticipate that the tax increase for low-income groups will be negligible. For middle-income households, while there will be some tax increases, the total benefit received is expected to outweigh the costs in most cases.

While the partial replacement of existing social assistance will result in a net benefit for current recipients that is lower than the gross payout, it will have no such impact on the many low-income individuals who are currently excluded from the welfare system. Even for current recipients, replacements will often be partial, and even in cases of full replacement, they will still experience a net gain through the Common Wealth Dividend and the Universal EITC.

CHAPTER 7

# Fiscal and Administrative Feasibility

In the previous chapter, we proposed specific implementation plans for NIT-type and Common Wealth Basic Income, as well as the Universal EITC. This chapter examines the fiscal and administrative feasibility of this "Basic Income Policy Package" composed of these three programs.

To assess fiscal feasibility, we estimate several key indicators: Gross Benefits, Actual Refunds, Net Benefits, Gross Tax Increases, Net Tax Increases, and the Net Fiscal Cost.

- Actual Refunds refer to the amount returned to individuals after deducting portions allocated to taxes or social insurance premiums from the gross benefits.
- Net Benefits are the actual refunds minus the reduction in existing social assistance benefits.
- Net Tax Increases represent the gross tax increases minus the portions of benefits that are allocated to taxes and social insurance contributions.
- Net Fiscal Cost is defined as either Gross Benefits minus Gross Tax Increases and existing benefit replacements, or Net Benefits minus Net Tax Increases.



J. S. You et al., *UBI from Idea to Reality*, Exploring the Basic Income Guarantee,
https://doi.org/10.1007/978-3-032-26200-4_7

The closer the Net Fiscal Cost is to zero—indicating Fiscal Neutrality—the higher the fiscal feasibility. However, even if the net cost is near zero, the feasibility may still be challenged if the absolute scale of Net Benefits and Net Tax Increases is large. We project these indicators for each of the three programs individually and for the package as a whole.

When implementing an NIT-type basic income, the threshold income varies depending on the definition of income used, which in turn affects benefit amounts and tax implications, thereby altering the required fiscal resources. As discussed earlier, we have argued for using a "comprehensive income" concept that includes imputed rental income for homeowners and capital gains such as realized gains from stocks and real estate, based solely on income, unlike current social assistance which relies on asset tests applying income conversion rates to assets.

However, actual analysis is constrained by data limitations. We utilize the Survey of Household Finances and Living Conditions (SHFLC) by the Ministry of Data and Statistics (2025a), which is considered relatively accurate for income distribution, complementarily with the National Tax Statistics Yearbook (NTS, 2024) and microdata on income tax from the National Tax Service (NTS, 2026), as well as statistical data from relevant administrative agencies.

We also address administrative feasibility by proposing concrete execution strategies. A common pitfall in policy design is the discrepancy between survey data and actual administrative data. If a policy designed using survey data is executed based on administrative records, the results may deviate significantly. For example, when the Seoul Metropolitan Government distributed disaster relief funds in the spring of 2020, the number of eligible households was double the initial projection. This suggests that administrative data captures high-income brackets more accurately, while survey data is better at identifying low-income groups (You, 2023). We minimize such issues by cross-referencing SHFLC data with NTS records.

We propose implementing the NIT-type basic income as a Refundable Tax Credit. By offsetting a portion of the benefits against taxes owed, we can reduce the actual cash refund volume. Furthermore, by allocating a portion of the tax-funded benefits to social insurance premiums, we can mitigate the increase in the overall tax-to-GDP ratio (or the national burden ratio). In essence, as social insurance burdens are reduced through tax-funded support, the scale of the Net Tax Increase is minimized.

Our simulations using 2023 income data indicate that:

- Gross Benefits for the three programs amount to 10.2% of GNI.
- Actual Refunds through the refundable tax credit system are estimated at 6.0% of GNI.
- Net Benefits (after replacing 1.6% of GNI in existing public transfers) represent a net expenditure increase of 4.3% of GNI.
- Gross Tax Increases stand at 8.2% of GNI, with a Net Tax Increase of 4.0% of GNI.
- The Net Fiscal Cost—the ultimate gap between Net Benefits and Net Tax Increases—is a mere 0.33% of GNI.

We compare our proposal with Seoul's "Stepping Stone Income" (디딤돌소득)—a household-based NIT—assuming its adoption as a national policy. Simulations show that the Gross Payout for Stepping Stone Income is much smaller at 1.35% of GNI. However, because it only replaces a portion of social assistance without a corresponding tax increase, its Net Fiscal Cost is 1.06% of GNI.

In contrast, our proposal's Net Fiscal Cost is less than one-third of that of the Stepping Stone Income, making it virtually fiscally neutral. Nevertheless, a Net Tax Increase of 4.0% of GNI warrants an examination of long-term sustainability amidst rapid aging. Our long-term analysis indicates that while gross benefits relative to GNI may increase over time, the expansion of existing benefit reductions will lead to a slight decrease in both Net Benefits and Net Tax Increases, ensuring fiscal sustainability. The long-term impact on economic growth will be discussed in the following chapter.

## 7.1 Data and Methodology

To ensure the accuracy of our fiscal projections, we utilize both household survey data and administrative records, thereby overcoming the inherent discrepancies between the two. As evidenced by Piketty and Saez (2003), top-income earners are often underrepresented in survey data, and their incomes are frequently underreported. Consequently, many recent studies rely on tax administrative data to measure the income share of the ultra-wealthy. However, administrative data tends to under-capture the income of low-income groups compared to survey data (You, 2023). This discrepancy poses a significant challenge: a policy designed solely on survey data may yield results in actual administrative execution that differ substantially from initial projections.

**Survey of Household Finances and Living Conditions (SHFLC)**: Our primary source for fiscal projections and the redistributive analysis in the following chapter is the 2024 SHFLC (MODS, 2025a). This dataset provides information on household composition and assets as of late March 2024, along with income data for the 2023 fiscal year, including earned, business, and property income, as well as private/public transfers, taxes, and social insurance premiums.

The SHFLC offers several advantages:

- It captures income streams that the National Tax Service (NTS) does not provide to researchers, such as financial income (interest and dividends) under 20 million KRW, non-taxable agricultural income, and social insurance benefits.
- It allows for a higher capture rate of low-income earners and enables the estimation of existing public transfers that could be replaced by an NIT-type basic income.
- It is recognized for providing accurate income distribution data because it adjusts for the underreporting of high-income earners by cross-referencing survey responses with NTS administrative records (MODS, 2020; Kim, 2020).

However, the SHFLC has limitations. It lacks data on non-recurring income, such as retirement income and realized capital gains from real estate or stocks. Despite significant improvements in sample representativeness compared to previous household trend surveys, it still tends to under-capture the highest income brackets. On the positive side, while it does not directly provide imputed rent, it does provide data on household real estate holdings, which allows us to estimate both imputed rent and land value taxes—tasks that are impossible using NTS data alone.

**NTS Micro-Tax Data**: We supplement SHFLC with anonymized micro-level tax data from the National Tax Service (NTS, 2026). This includes global income tax records, year-end settlement data for employment and business income, and payment statements for daily laborers. It also includes data on the Work Incentive Payment (WIP) and Child Incentive Payment (CIP) programs directly administered by the NTS. However, it does not provide information on income subject to separate taxation (interest and dividend income of 20 million KRW or less), other income, and pension income. For these incomes not provided by the NTS, income data from SHFLC is useful.

Like SHFLC, the NTS does not provide capital gains and retirement income. Furthermore, it does not provide information on household composition and lacks information on public and private transfers and taxes other than income tax, making it difficult to use for estimating income redistribution effects in the next chapter.

Despite these limitations, income tax data has advantages in fiscal estimation. The most important point is that actual policy implementation cannot rely on survey data but must calculate benefit amounts and impose taxes based on income data identified by the NTS. In particular, fiscal estimation using income tax data can be more accurate than SHFLC data for calculating benefit amounts for NIT-type basic income and Universal EITC, as well as for estimating the tax increase from abolishing the basic personal deduction and employment income deduction in income tax, and for employment income tax credits and child tax credits. Therefore, we intend to use SHFLC data, which enables the estimation of imputed rental income, Land Value Tax, and public transfer income that can be replaced by NIT-type basic income—which cannot be estimated with income tax data—while using income tax data complementarily.

**Establishing the Break-even Threshold and Imputed Rent**: The national average income—the break-even threshold for the NIT-type Basic Income—varies depending on whether imputed rent is included. We adhere to the principle of including imputed rent in our definition of comprehensive income.

We calculated imputed rent by applying an annual rate of 1.2% to the value of owner-occupied housing. This is slightly lower than Kim's (2022) estimate of 1.38% for net imputed rent relative to housing value, reflecting the relatively lower rent levels in South Korea due to the unique *Jeonse* (전세) system.[1] As of 2023, approximately 59.4% of households owned their primary residence (averaging 430 million KRW in value), resulting in an estimated average imputed rent of 5.15 million KRW. For our analysis, this imputed rent is distributed equally among all household members and treated as individual income.

[1] Jeonse, often referred to as a "lump-sum deposit rental system," is a unique housing lease system in South Korea. Instead of paying monthly rent, the tenant provides a large, one-time deposit to the landlord at the beginning of the lease.

**Table 7.1** Comparison of Primary Income and Break-even Thresholds: SHFLC vs. NTS Micro-data (2023)

| *Income Category* | *Source* | *Population (10k)* | *Average (1k KRW)* | *Total (bn KRW)* |
|---|---|---|---|---|
| Employment Income | SHFLC | 2,695 | 37,314 | 1,005,764 |
| | NTS Micro | 2,581 | 37,856 | 977,080 |
| Business Income | SHFLC | 1,173 | 23,515 | 275,936 |
| | NTS Micro | 1,122 | 13,452 | 150,928 |
| | NTS statistics | | | 10,249 |
| Property Income | SHFLC | 3,632 | 3,338 | 121,226 |
| | NTS Micro | 319 | 20,498 | 65,404 |
| | NTS statistics | | | 129,898 |
| Primary Income | SHFLC | 4,312 | 32,533 | 1,402,926 |
| | NTS Micro | 3,227 | 36,983 | 1,193,441 |
| | NTS consolidated | | | 1,268,154 |
| Primary Income per capita | SHFLC | 5,170 | 27,134 | 1,402,926 |
| | NTS Micro | 5,170 | 23,083 | 1,193,441 |
| | NTS consolidated | 5,170 | 24,529 | 1,268,154 |
| Public Pension | SHFLC | 729 | 8,917 | 65,005 |
| | NTS Statistics | 705 | 8,057 | 56,811 |
| Soc Insure Income | SHFLC | 213 | 8,023 | 17,053 |
| Imputed Rent | SHFLC | 3,401 | 1,737 | 59,066 |
| Break-even Threshold | SHFLC | 5,170 | 29,866 | 1,544,050 |
| | NTS Micro | 5,170 | 27,100 | 1,401,084 |
| Capital gains | NTS Statistics | 44 | 144,561 | 63,223 |
| Retirement Income | NTS Statistics | 332 | 17,479 | 58,073 |
| Break-even Threshold | NTS consolidated | 5,170 | 29,446 | 1,522,380 |
| 60% of GNI per Capita | | 5,170 | 28,350 | 1,465,695 |

Table 7.1 illustrates the comparison between SHFLC and NTS micro-data by income category. The SHFLC captures Primary Income (the sum of earned, business, and property income) for 43.12 million individuals, with an average of 32.53 million KRW and a total of 1,402.9 trillion KRW. In contrast, the NTS micro-data represents 32.27 million

individuals with a higher average of 36.98 million KRW but a lower total of 1,193.4 trillion KRW.[2]

The discrepancy in primary income between the two datasets is particularly pronounced in business and property income. Business income tends to be underreported to the NTS; furthermore, most agricultural income (including crop cultivation and rural sideline income) is non-taxable, and certain business incomes are classified as "other income" by the tax authorities. The difference in property income is primarily due to the omission of financial income (interest and dividends) under 20 million KRW, which is subject to separate withholding taxation, from the NTS micro-data provided to researchers. When total property income is adjusted by calculating the withheld taxes on interest, dividends, and real estate rental income from the NTS *Statistical Yearbook*, the totals become comparable. Regarding employment income, although NTS data shows slightly higher figures for top earners, the total is lower than SHFLC because NTS data fails to capture informal sector income prevalent among low-income groups.

**Estimating the Per Capita Market Income**: Using the 2023 SHFLC data, we calculated the average per capita market income for the entire population, including non-earners such as children and the elderly. We summed primary income, social insurance benefits (public pensions, employment, and industrial accident compensation), and imputed rent. Due to data constraints in the SHFLC, capital gains were excluded.

The resulting national average per capita market income was 29.87 million KRW, equivalent to 63.2% of the 2023 GNI per capita (47.25 million

[2] In the NTS micro-data, employment income refers to "gross pay" (excluding non-taxable income) and the total payment for daily laborers, rather than "employment income amount" after deductions. For business income for the self-employed, we used the "business income amount" (gross revenue minus necessary expenses) for global income filers and year-end settlers. For "personal service providers" without a physical place of business, 60% of the total payment was considered income, assuming a 40% expense ratio. Interest and dividends are only included in total global income if they exceed 20 million KRW annually. Similarly, pension and other incomes are only included if they are subject to global taxation. Thus, a direct comparison of property income between SHFLC and NTS is difficult. Primary income in SHFLC is the sum of employment, business, and property income, while in NTS data, it is the sum of employment and business income plus the remaining global income components. Unlike Park (2022), who considered the total payment as income for personal service providers, this study assumes a 60% income ratio to align with the generous expense recognitions granted to similar workers (e.g., insurance agents and door-to-door salespeople) for year-end settlement.

KRW). Excluding imputed rent, the average market income was 28.72 million KRW, or 60.8% of GNI per capita.

Since NTS micro-data cannot track social insurance benefits or imputed rent, we initially calculated only "primary income" (global income under the Income Tax Act). Dividing the total 2023 primary income of the 32.27 million individuals represented in the NTS 5% sample by the total population (51.71 million) results in an average of 23.08 million KRW.

However, when we supplement the NTS micro-data with other income records held by the NTS, the per capita primary income rises to 24.53 million KRW. Adding social insurance benefits and imputed rent further narrows the gap with the SHFLC baseline to 27.10 million KRW. Finally, by including transfer (capital gains) and retirement income—which are present in NTS general statistics but absent in the SHFLC—the figure reaches 29.45 million KRW, or 62.3% of GNI per capita. Therefore, we conclude that it is entirely feasible for the NTS to capture an average per capita income level equivalent to 60% of GNI per capita when implementing our proposed basic income policy.

## 7.2 Fiscal Projections for the Proposed Basic Income Programs

### *Common Wealth Basic Income*

The Common Wealth Basic Income is composed of three components: (1) converting the Basic Personal Allowance of the income tax into a basic income; (2) Land Dividends based on the previous year's land ownership tax revenue (after compensating for existing land-related property taxes and the Comprehensive Real Estate Tax); and (3) Carbon and Renewable Energy Dividends based on carbon tax revenues and returns on public renewable energy investments. These three programs are designed to be fiscally neutral, meaning they are funded strictly within the limits of their respective revenue sources. Consequently, the net fiscal requirement for these programs is essentially zero.

We proposed that a universal basic income equivalent to 3% of GNI per capita (approximately 5% of average individual market income) is achievable through this package: 0.5% from the converted basic allowance, 1.5% from land dividends, and 1.0% from carbon/renewable energy dividends.

Below, we verify the feasibility of these revenue sources using SHFLC data, NTS records, and other administrative statistics.

**(1) Conversion of the Basic Personal Allowance:** Simulations using the 2023 SHFLC data indicate that abolishing the Basic Personal Allowance (currently 1.5 million KRW per person) would generate approximately 10 trillion KRW in additional tax revenue. NTS statistical data suggests a slightly higher figure of 11 trillion KRW. Providing 0.5% of the 2023 GNI per capita (236,250 KRW) to the entire population requires 12.2 trillion KRW, leaving a shortfall of about 1.2 to 2.2 trillion KRW. However, several amendments to the Income Tax Act are currently proposed in the National Assembly to increase the allowance to 2.0 or 3.0 million KRW. As discussed in Chapter 4, converting a potential 2.0 million KRW allowance into a universal basic income rather than maintaining the regressive deduction system would provide more than enough revenue to meet the fiscal requirement. See Appendix 7.1 about the simulations.

**(2) Land Dividends**: Land dividends can be operated in a fiscally neutral manner based on the previous year's revenue. According to the Bank of Korea's 2023 land asset statistics, private land value totaled 9,253 trillion KRW (Corporate: 2,359 trillion; Households: 6,894 trillion). Ministry of Land, Infrastructure and Transport (MOLIT) statistics show a lower figure of 5,773 trillion KRW for private/unincorporated land, largely because the "Officially Assessed Land Value" (Gongsijiga) reflects only about 65% of market value.

Applying a 1% tax rate on the *Gongsijiga* (roughly 0.65% of market value) would yield over 57.7 trillion KRW. Deducting the 15.2 trillion KRW currently collected from existing land/housing property taxes and the Comprehensive Real Estate Tax leaves approximately 42.5 trillion KRW—sufficient for land dividends. Using SHFLC data, we estimated a tax revenue of 38 trillion KRW (applying 1% to the land portion of real estate holdings), which allows for a land dividend of 735,000 KRW per person (1.56% of GNI per capita) .

**(3) Carbon and Renewable Energy Dividends**: The carbon dividend is inherently fiscally neutral as it distributes the entire previous year's carbon tax revenue equally to all citizens. With Korea's greenhouse gas emissions at 690 million tons in 2024 (approx. 13.3 tons per capita), a tax of 40,000 KRW per ton would enable a dividend of 530,000 KRW (1.1% of GNI per capita). As Korea aims to reduce emissions by over 50% by 2035, gradually raising the tax to 80,000 KRW or more will sustain a dividend of 1% of

GNI per capita. As emissions decline further, we anticipate that renewable energy dividends will supplement the shrinking carbon tax revenue. In the interim, renewable energy dividends will serve as the primary funding for Rural Basic Income.

**(4) Rural Basic Income and Solar Income**: Beyond the national projections, "Rural Basic Income" and "Solar (Wind) Income" are vital regional applications of the common wealth principle. As of 2026, a pilot project provides 150,000 KRW monthly to residents in 10 counties (*Gun*), with plans to expand to all 69 designated population-declining areas.

Simultaneously, "Solar Income Village" projects are gaining traction. Following the Sinan-gun model ( Chapter 3), residents invest in renewable power plants through cooperatives or funds to secure a share of the profits. The Ministry of Agriculture plans to establish over 500 such villages annually starting in 2026. The target model involves 100 residents sharing a 1MW facility to receive an annual "Solar Income" of 1 million KRW per person. These initiatives significantly enhance the fiscal feasibility and public acceptance of the common wealth basic income.

### *NIT-Type Basic Income*

The NIT-type basic income sets the national average per capita market income (including primary income, social insurance benefits, imputed rent, and capital gains) as the break-even threshold. If an individual's income falls below this threshold, they receive a payout equivalent to 10% of the shortfall for adults, and 20% for children (under 18) and the elderly (65 and older). For those exceeding the threshold, a 10% Basic Income Tax is levied on the excess income, separate from existing personal income taxes.

If the payout for all groups were fixed at 10% of the shortfall, the system would be inherently fiscally neutral, as the 10% Basic Income Tax would perfectly cover the expenditures. However, since we provide a higher 20% payout to children and the elderly, fiscal neutrality depends on whether the shortfall—equivalent to half of the total payouts to these groups—can be covered by: (1) the full replacement of Child Allowance, Child Tax Credit, and Basic Pension; (2) the partial replacement of the NBLSS Livelihood Benefit; and (3) the revenue recovered from abolishing Additional Allowances for the elderly (aged 70+) and Child Tax Credits.

**Simulation Results using SHFLC Data**: Using 2023 SHFLC data, we set the break-even threshold at 29.87 million KRW (the average per capita market income, excluding capital gains due to data constraints). The corresponding guaranteed income for those with zero income is 2.99 million KRW for adults and 5.97 million KRW for children/the elderly.

The simulation shows that 61.6% of the total population falls below the threshold, receiving an average NIT payout of 3.39 million KRW.

- Children: 99.9% receive an average of 5.76 million KRW.
- Adults: 47.9% receive an average of 1.83 million KRW.
- Elderly: 78.7% receive an average of 4.28 million KRW.

Conversely, 38.4% of the population exceeds the threshold, paying an average Basic Income Tax of 3.47 million KRW (Adults: 52.1% pay an average of 3.54 million KRW; Elderly: 21.3% pay an average of 2.91 million KRW) .

As shown in Table 7.2, the gross payout totals 108 trillion KRW, while Basic Income Tax revenue reaches 68.9 trillion KRW. Combined with 32.5 trillion KRW in replaced social assistance and 1.5 trillion KRW recovered

**Table 7.2** Fiscal Projections for NIT-Type basic income (2023 Baseline) (Unit: bn KRW, % of GNI)

| *Category* | *SHFLC* | *NTS* | *SHFLC (Adj.)* | *NTS (Adj.)* | *Consolidated* | *% of GNI* |
|---|---|---|---|---|---|---|
| Gross Benefits | 107,991 | 100,864 | 102,509 | 123,877 | 111,056 | 4.55% |
| Basic Income Tax | 68,899 | 66,546 | 65,402 | 81,728 | 75,198 | 3.08% |
| Elderly Allowance Replacement | 546 | 546 | 546 | 546 | 546 | 0.02% |
| Child Tax Credit Replacement | 961 | 771 | 961 | 771 | 771 | 0.03% |
| Child Incentive Replacement | 971 | 971 | 971 | 971 | 971 | 0.04% |
| Social assistance Replacement | 32,454 | 32,454 | 32,454 | 32,454 | 32,454 | 1.33% |
| Net Fiscal Cost | 4,160 | -423 | 2,176 | 7,407 | 1,117 | 0.05% |

*Note:* "Consolidated" figures apply a 60:40 weight for Payouts and a 40:60 weight for Tax Revenues between adjusted SHFLC and NTS data.

from abolished tax credits/allowances, the Net Fiscal Requirement is 4.2 trillion KRW, or a mere 0.17% of GNI. See Appendix 7.2 about the simulations.

**Simulation Results using NTS Micro-Data**: Using NTS micro-data, the break-even threshold was set at 23.08 million KRW (average per capita primary income). Both the threshold and the guaranteed income are significantly lower than the SHFLC-based estimates. Consequently, both the gross payout (100.9 trillion KRW) and tax revenue (66.5 trillion KRW) are lower. While the NTS data lacks information on social assistance and certain allowances, the analysis yielded a negative net fiscal requirement (surplus), primarily due to the lower threshold.

**Comprehensive Fiscal Projection**: The primary reason for the discrepancy between the two simulations lies in the definition of the break-even threshold. To project the fiscal impact if the NTS were to execute the policy using comprehensive income (aiming for a threshold of 60% of GNI per capita), we adjusted both datasets to a unified threshold of 28.35 million KRW (60% of the 2023 GNI per capita).

Recognizing that SHFLC is superior at capturing low-income informal income while NTS micro-data is more accurate for high-income brackets, we applied a weighted averaging method. For the Gross Payout, we assigned a 60% weight to the adjusted SHFLC results and 40% to the NTS results. For Basic Income Tax Revenue, the weights were reversed (40% for SHFLC; 60% for NTS).

In conclusion, we estimate the Gross Benefits of the NIT-type basic income at 4.55% of GNI, with Basic Income Tax Revenue at 3.08% of GNI. After accounting for tax increases and benefit replacements, the Net Fiscal Cost is estimated at approximately 0.05% of GNI, making the proposal virtually fiscally neutral.

As shown in Table 7.2, while there are discrepancies between the SHFLC and NTS datasets, the integrated "Consolidated" estimate provides a robust baseline for the fiscal requirement of the NIT-type Basic Income.

### *Universal Earned Income Tax Credit (Universal EITC)*

The Universal EITC provides 12% of earned income for those earning less than 50% of GNI per capita (23.63 million KRW as of 2023). For those earning above this threshold, a fixed maximum benefit of 6% of GNI per capita (2.84 million KRW)—roughly 10% of the average income—is provided. This program replaces the current employment income deduction,

**Table 7.3** Fiscal Projections for Universal EITC (2023 Baseline) (Unit: bn KRW, % of GNI)

| *Category* | *SHFLC* | *NTS* | *Consolidated* | *% of GNI* |
|---|---|---|---|---|
| Gross Benefits | 73,428 | 63,300 | 63,868 | 2.61% |
| Employment Income Deduction Replacement | 42,961 | 42,404 | 42,404 | 1.74% |
| Employment Income Tax Credit Replacement | 10,450 | 8,047 | 8,047 | 0.33% |
| WIP Replacement | 4,564 | 4,564 | 4,564 | 0.19% |
| Social Insurance Subsidies | 1,800 | 1,800 | 1,800 | 0.07% |
| Net Fiscal Cost | 13,653 | 6,485 | 6,485 | 0.27% |

employment income tax credit, Work Incentive Payment, and various social insurance subsidy programs.

Using 2023 SHFLC data, the beneficiaries of the Universal EITC include 3.1% of children (aged less than 20), 84.3% of adults, and 46.7% of the elderly (aged 65 or more), covering 64.8% of the total population (approx. 33.5 million people).

- Gross Benefits: Estimated at 73.4 trillion KRW (3.01% of GNI) .
- Funding: Abolishing the employment income deduction and credit increases tax revenue by 53.4 trillion KRW (2.19% of GNI).[3] Adding 4.6 trillion KRW from the current Work Incentive Payment and social insurance subsidy budgets brings the total available resources to 59.8 trillion KRW.
- Net Fiscal Cost: Estimated at 13.7 trillion KRW (0.56% of GNI).

Simulations using NTS micro-data yield a significantly lower gross benefit amount and net fiscal cost (Table 7.3). While the revenue from tax reform is slightly lower, the gross benefits drop to 63.3 trillion KRW, resulting

[3] See Appendix 7.3 about the simulation of the abolition of the employment income deduction and credit.

in a Net Fiscal Cost of 6.5 trillion KRW (0.27% of GNI)—about half the SHFLC-based estimate. See Appendix 7.3 for simulations of the accompanied tax reform (repeal of employment income deduction and employment income tax credit).

**Reconciling the SHFLC and NTS projections:** Table 7.4 compares the average earned income by decile between the SHFLC and NTS data. While the total number of earners and average income levels identified in both datasets differ slightly, the discrepancy is not substantial. However, the income distribution shows a significant divergence. For the low-income brackets (1st to 3rd deciles), the earned income reported in SHFLC is more than 1.6 times higher than that in the NTS data. This gap narrows as income deciles rise, and in the 10th decile SHFLC income drops to 93% of the NTS data.

Specifically, among middle-to-low income groups whose income falls below the universal WIP threshold (23.625 million KRW), earned income in SHFLC is considerably higher than in the NTS data. Consequently, the total amount of universal EITC—calculated as 12% of earned income—is inevitably higher when using SHFLC data compared to simulations based on NTS records. The substantial difference in middle-to-low income levels

**Table 7.4** Average Earned Income and Universal EITC Benefits by Decile (Unit: 1,000 KRW)

| *Earned Income Decile* | *Avg. Earned Income (SHFLC)* | *Avg. Earned Income (NTS)* | *Ratio (SHFLC/ NTS)* | *Avg. Benefit (SHFLC)* | *Avg. Benefit (NTS)* |
|---|---|---|---|---|---|
| 1 | 1,498 | 902 | 1.66 | 180 | 108 |
| 2 | 6,169 | 3,614 | 1.71 | 740 | 434 |
| 3 | 12,866 | 7,933 | 1.62 | 1,544 | 952 |
| 4 | 20,641 | 14,368 | 1.44 | 2,470 | 1,724 |
| 5 | 27,352 | 22,132 | 1.24 | 2,835 | 2,621 |
| 6 | 33,394 | 28,592 | 1.17 | 2,835 | 2,835 |
| 7 | 40,494 | 36,034 | 1.12 | 2,835 | 2,835 |
| 8 | 50,921 | 46,527 | 1.09 | 2,835 | 2,835 |
| 9 | 67,574 | 64,073 | 1.05 | 2,835 | 2,835 |
| 10 | 123,118 | 132,510 | 0.93 | 2,835 | 2,835 |
| Average | 38,249 | 35,662 | 1.07 | 2,191 | 2,001 |

between the two datasets likely stems from the underreporting of business income to tax authorities, informal sector earnings among low-income groups, and the tax-exempt status of most agricultural income.

Since the implementation of a universal EITC would necessarily rely on income reported to the NTS, estimates using tax data are considered more accurate than those based on SHFLC. NTS micro-data provides comprehensive information on earned income, including daily labor income (subject to separate taxation) and business income from personal services that may have been omitted from global income tax returns.

However, a portion of business income is classified as "other income" by the NTS and is thus missing from the NTS micro-data. After adjusting the NTS micro-data by adding 10.2 trillion KRW—the portion of "other income" in the Statistical Yearbook of the NTS that appears to be business income—the total benefit amount rose to 63.9 trillion KRW (2.61% of GNI). Accordingly, the net fiscal cost increased slightly to 7.1 trillion KRW, representing 0.29% of GNI, as the "Consolidated" column in Table 7.3 indicates.

### *Integrated Fiscal Projection and Implementation Strategy*

The consolidated gross benefits for the three programs amount to 10.16% of GNI (Common Wealth: 3%; NIT-type: 4.55%; Universal EITC: 2.61%). Funding is derived from tax reforms (8.20% of GNI) and the replacement of existing social assistance (1.63% of GNI). The resulting Net Fiscal Cost is only 0.33% of GNI, successfully achieving the goal of keeping the gap within 1% of GNI.

While the net cost is minimal, the gross benefits and tax scale appear substantial. To enhance administrative feasibility and social acceptance, we propose two primary strategies to reduce the scale of actual cash transfers and net tax increases.

**Offsetting Social Insurance Premiums**: Rather than issuing a full cash payout, a significant portion of the Universal EITC (UEITC) is automatically diverted to cover social insurance premiums. For low-income wage earners (those earning below 50% of GNI per capita), the 12% UEITC credit would fully cover their premiums (approx. 9.72% in 2026), with the remainder issued as a cash refund. Even if National Pension rates rise to 13% (6.5% for employees, and 6.5% for employers) as planned by 2033, the UEITC remains sufficient to cover entire social insurance premiums for low-wage earners and substantial portion for the higher wage earners.

UEITC can cover more than half of the social insurance premiums for low-income self-employed. This mechanism converts 2.48% of GNI from the gross benefits (2.61% of GNI) into social insurance contributions, reducing the net cash payout of the UEITC to just 0.13% of GNI.

**The Refundable Tax Credit Offset**: Portions of the Common Wealth and NIT benefits can be used to automatically offset Basic Income Tax and Land Value Tax liabilities. By offsetting benefits against basic income tax obligations for those above the break-even threshold, 1.36% of GNI is accounted for through internal tax settlement rather than cash refunds. Additionally, 0.35% of GNI from these benefits is estimated to offset Land Value Tax liabilities.

Through these strategies, the actual cash refund volume is reduced from a gross 10.16% to 5.97% of GNI. Furthermore, after replacing 1.63% of GNI in existing welfare spending, the Net Benefit (actual increase in social spending) is 4.34% of GNI.

On the revenue side, although the gross tax increase is 8.20% of GNI, the net increase in the National Burden Ratio (the combined burden of taxes and social insurance) is reduced to 4.01% of GNI after accounting for the offsets. These consolidated findings are summarized in Table 7.5.

**Fiscal Feasibility in the OECD Context**: As demonstrated in the projections, while the net fiscal cost for our proposed triple-program package is minimal, the Net Benefit (Net increase in fiscal expenditure) and Net Tax Increase represent significant shifts, amounting to 4.3% and 4.0% of GNI, respectively. However, these figures are well within a manageable range when considering that South Korea's public social spending and tax-to-GDP ratio remain substantially lower than the OECD average.

As of 2024, South Korea's public social expenditure stands at 15.3% of GDP, significantly trailing the OECD average of 21.2%. An expenditure increase of approximately 4.4% of GDP (equivalent to 4.3% of GNI) would simply move Korea closer to the international standard rather than imposing an undue burden.

Similarly, the tax-to-GDP ratio in Korea remains low. In 2023, it stood at 19.0%, which was 6.3 percentage points below the OECD average of 25.3%, and it further declined to 17.7% in 2024. While the tax burden had been on a steady upward trend—rising from 16.6% in 2015 to 22.1% in 2022—it plummeted by 4.4 percentage points within just two years due to the tax cuts for the wealthy implemented by the Yoon Suk-yeol administration. This implies that the required net tax increase for our basic income proposal could be largely met simply by restoring tax rates to their pre-cut levels.

**Table 7.5** Consolidated Fiscal Projection for the Integrated Basic Income Package (2023 Baseline)(Unit: % of GNI)

| *Program & Benefits* | *% of GNI* | *Funding Sources* | *% of GNI* |
|---|---|---|---|
| Common Wealth basic income | 3.00 | Common Wealth Revenue | 3.00 |
| Basic Allowance | 0.50 | Basic Personal Allowance Conversion | 0.50 |
| Land Dividend | 1.50 | Land Value Tax | 1.50 |
| Carbon Dividend | 1.00 | Carbon Tax | 1.00 |
| *(Less: Basic Income Tax Offset)* | 1.36 | | |
| *(Less: Land Value Tax Offset)* | 0.35 | | |
| Actual Refund | 1.29 | | |
| NIT-Type basic income | 4.55 | NIT Funding | 4.50 |
| | | Basic Income Tax | 3.08 |
| | | Elderly/Child Credit Repl. | 0.05 |
| | | Social Assistance Replacement | 1.37 |
| Universal EITC | 2.61 | Universal EITC Funding | 2.33 |
| *(Less: Social Insurance Premiums Offset)* | *−2.48* | Employment Income Deduction/Credit Replacement | 2.07 |
| | | WIP Replacement | 0.19 |
| Actual Refund | 0.13 | Social Insurance Subsidies | 0.07 |
| Gross Benefits (Total) | 10.16 | Total Funding | 9.83 |
| *(Less: Basic Income Tax Offset)* | 1.36 | Gross Tax Increase | 8.20 |
| *(Less: Land Value Tax Offset)* | 0.35 | *(Less: BIT & LVT Offset)* | 1.71 |
| *(Less: Social Insurance Premiums Offset)* | 2.48 | *(Less: Social Insurance Premiums Offset)* | 2.48 |
| Actual Refund (Total) | 5.97 | Net Tax Increase | 4.01 |
| Net Benefits (Total) | 4.34 | Social Assistance Replacement | 1.63 |
| | | Net Fiscal Cost | 0.33 |

**The "Tax Wedge" on Employment Income**: Korea notably maintains a very low tax and social insurance burden on employment income. A comparison of the tax wedge—the difference between labor costs to the employer and the net take-home pay of the employee (including personal income tax and social insurance contributions)—shows that Korea's rate is only 24.5%. This is composed of personal income tax (6.2%), employee-paid social insurance (8.5%), and employer-paid social insurance (10.0%).

This is significantly lower than the OECD average of 34.9% (Tax: 13.4%; Employee SI: 8.1%; Employer SI: 13.4%) and pales in comparison to countries like Belgium (52.6%), Germany (47.9%), and France (47.2%). This low tax wedge on labor provides significant fiscal room to increase revenue while implementing a more robust social safety net. However, given the rapid aging of the population, it is essential to examine whether this basic income model remains sustainable in the long term, a topic we will address in the following section.

### *Comparison of Net Fiscal Costs: Basic Income Package vs. "Stepping Stone" Income*

We further compare the fiscal requirements of our three-program basic income package with those of the Seoul Metropolitan Government's "Stepping Stone" Income—a household-based NIT—assuming its adoption as a national policy. This comparison is essential because UBI is frequently criticized as being fiscally infeasible due to its large gross expenditure compared to targeted NIT models.

**Key Differences in Design**: The Stepping Stone Income differs from our proposal in several fundamental ways:

- Unit of Distribution: It operates on a household basis rather than an individual basis.
- Thresholds and Rates: The break-even threshold is set at 85% of the Standard Median Income (as announced annually by the government), with the guaranteed income set at 50% of that threshold (i.e., 42.5% of the standard median income). It applies a clawback rate of 50%.
- Taxation: Unlike our model, it does not include additional taxation for those above the threshold.
- Eligibility: While benefits are calculated based on income alone, households exceeding a specific asset threshold (326 million KRW) are disqualified.

Both policies share the objective of replacing the cash components of major existing social assistance programs, such as the NBLSS and Basic Pension. The primary policy goal of the Stepping Stone Income is poverty alleviation by closing gaps in the safety net and maintaining work incentives through a 50% marginal tax rate—significantly lower than the high marginal tax rates found in the current NBLSS (70% on earned income; 100% on other income).

**Simulation Results and Fiscal Comparison**: Our simulation using SHFLC data for the 2023 baseline reveals that under a national Stepping Stone Income policy, 22.6% of all households would receive an average of 6.6 million KRW per year. After replacing existing social assistance (avg. 1.41 million KRW), the average net benefit per household would be 5.18 million KRW.

As shown in Table 7.6, while the Gross Benefits for the Stepping Stone Income (1.35% of GNI) is much smaller than our package (10.16% of GNI), its Net Fiscal Cost (1.06% of GNI) is more than three times larger than ours (0.33% of GNI). This paradox is explained by our comprehensive funding strategy involving tax reform, whereas the Stepping Stone Income model relies solely on existing budget reallocations without new revenue streams.

**Household vs. Individual Units**: The Stepping Stone Income's relatively small gross expenditure, despite a high guarantee level, is largely due to its operation as a household unit and its high 50% clawback rate. Household-based programs leverage the internal income-redistribution function of the family, which significantly reduces the fiscal outlay.

For instance, an individual-based NIT program proposed by five former senior economic officials (Kim et al., 2021) estimated a gross payout

**Table 7.6** Fiscal Comparison: Basic Income Package vs. Stepping Stone Income (2023 Baseline)

| *Indicator* | *Proposed Basic Income Package* | *Stepping Stone Income (National)* |
|---|---|---|
| Gross Benefits (% of GNI) | 10.16% | 1.35% |
| Net Fiscal Cost (% of GNI) | 0.33% | 1.06% |
| Funding Strategy | Tax Reform + Benefit Replacement | Benefit Replacement Only |
| Unit of Distribution | Individual | Household |

of 172.7 trillion KRW—vastly higher than the Stepping Stone Income model—even though their guaranteed income (approx. 500,000 KRW/month) was lower. This underscores that the choice of the distribution unit is a primary driver of fiscal scale. However, as discussed in Chapter 2, Section 4, household-based income security programs carry the inherent risk of creating perverse incentives for household dissolution to maximize benefits.

## 7.3 Long-term Sustainability Amidst Rapid Population Aging

As noted in Chapter 5, the *5th Social Security Fiscal Projections* (Ministry of Health and Welfare, 2024) warn that even under the current system, rapid aging will drive public social spending to 27.1% of GDP by 2065. While our proposed basic income package initially increases social spending by 4.3% of GDP (as of 2023), concerns may arise regarding whether this fiscal burden will spiral out of control as the population ages.

To test the long-term sustainability, we focus on the population aged 65 and older. Under our proposal, seniors are guaranteed a floor of 15% of GNI per capita (25% of the average market income) through a combination of Common Wealth and NIT-type basic income, plus a Universal EITC for those who work. Crucially, the NIT-type benefit for seniors is reduced by 20% of their market income (including public pensions), and those above the average income pay a 10% Basic Income Tax. The primary stabilizer in this model is the full replacement of the Basic Pension with the NIT-type Basic Income.

According to the Ministry of Data and Statistics' median population projections, the elderly population (65+) will surge from 18.3% in 2023 to over 40% by 2050, reaching 49% by 2080. By approximately 2065, South Korea will become a precedent-setting nation where the elderly outnumber the working-age population, with an old-age dependency ratio exceeding 100%.

Table 7.7 compares the fiscal outlook under the status quo versus our basic income model through 2100, assuming current income distributions and benefit levels remain constant relative to GNI to isolate the impact of aging.[4]

[4] Projections assume the Basic Pension remains at approximately 8% of GNI per capita (approx. 334,000 KRW/month) while incorporating the government's plan to reduce the couple's benefit reduction from 20% to 10% by 2030.

**Table 7.7** Fiscal Outlook for the Population Aged 65+ (2023–2100) *(Unit: % of GNI)*

| *Category* | *2023* | *2030* | *2040* | *2050* | *2065* | *2080* | *2100* |
|---|---|---|---|---|---|---|---|
| Elderly Population (%) | 18.25 | 25.30 | 34.26 | 40.14 | 46.57 | 49.08 | 44.44 |
| [Status Quo] | | | | | | | |
| Public transfers | 3.13 | 4.44 | 6.01 | 7.04 | 8.17 | 8.61 | 7.79 |
| Basic Pension | 0.89 | 1.34 | 1.81 | 2.12 | 2.46 | 2.59 | 2.35 |
| Public Pension | 1.76 | 2.44 | 3.30 | 3.87 | 4.49 | 4.73 | 4.28 |
| Other benefits | 0.48 | 0.66 | 0.89 | 1.05 | 1.22 | 1.28 | 1.16 |
| Taxes & SSCs | 0.62 | 0.86 | 1.16 | 1.36 | 1.58 | 1.67 | 1.51 |
| Net transfers | 2.51 | 3.48 | 4.71 | 5.52 | 6.40 | 6.74 | 6.11 |
| [Basic Income Package] | | | | | | | |
| Gross benefits | 2.09 | 2.90 | 3.93 | 4.60 | 5.34 | 5.63 | 5.09 |
| Replacing current benefits | 1.05 | 1.56 | 2.12 | 2.48 | 2.88 | 3.03 | 2.75 |
| Net benefits | 1.04 | 1.34 | 1.81 | 2.12 | 2.46 | 2.59 | 2.35 |
| Increased taxes | 0.94 | 1.31 | 1.77 | 2.08 | 2.41 | 2.54 | 2.30 |
| Net fiscal cost | 0.09 | 0.03 | 0.04 | 0.04 | 0.05 | 0.05 | 0.05 |
| [Combined Result] | | | | | | | |
| Gross public transfers | 4.16 | 5.77 | 7.82 | 9.16 | 10.63 | 11.20 | 10.14 |
| Taxes & SSCs | 1.56 | 2.17 | 2.93 | 3.44 | 3.99 | 4.20 | 3.81 |
| Net transfers | 2.60 | 3.61 | 4.88 | 5.72 | 6.64 | 6.99 | 6.33 |

Under the current system, net transfers to the elderly will soar from 2.51% of GNI in 2023 to 6.74% by 2080, as tax revenues from the elderly cannot keep pace with the explosion in pension and healthcare spending. In contrast, while the gross benefits of our basic income model for the elderly rise from 2.09% to 5.63% of GNI, the net fiscal cost does not increase. It is projected to slightly decreases from 0.09% in 2023 to 0.05% by 2080. This counter-intuitive result is driven by two factors:

1. Dynamic Replacement: The fiscal savings from replacing the Basic Pension—which grows exponentially with the number of seniors—offset the costs of the NIT.
2. Enhanced Revenue: The Basic Income Tax and the abolition of deductions increase contributions from high-income seniors.

In reality, the fiscal outlook is likely to be even more favorable than these projections suggest. As the National Pension system matures and senior employment rates rise, the average NIT benefit will likely decrease, while tax revenues increase. Furthermore, the Universal EITC's social insurance subsidies will help eliminate blind spots in public pensions, significantly alleviating old-age poverty in the long run.

By maintaining a low 20% clawback rate, the NIT-type basic income does not discourage healthy seniors from working. Combined with the Universal EITC, this model incentivizes labor participation and promotes "Active Aging," allowing seniors to contribute to economic growth while simultaneously reducing the net fiscal cost of the basic income system (You, 2025).

While aging is often cited as the primary driver of fiscal pressure, our basic income policy also provides robust support for children, a group with limited tax-bearing capacity. Simultaneously, a shrinking working-age population may reduce the overall tax base. Therefore, a comprehensive long-term fiscal projection for the entire population is essential.

Table 7.8 summarizes these projections through 2080, assuming current income distributions remain constant to isolate the impact of demographic shifts. As of 2023, under the status quo, the household sector is a "net contributor (2.50% of GNI)," with taxes and social insurance contributions (7.85% of GNI) exceeding public cash transfers (5.35% of GNI). Our basic income package slightly reduces the net contribution to 2.17% of GNI by increasing gross benefits by 4.34% of GNI and tax revenues by 4.01% of GNI.

By 2080, when the elderly population reaches its peak, the total benefits under the current system increase to 9.99% of GNI, while taxes and social insurance contributions decrease to 6.16% of GNI. Hence, the household sector becomes a net beneficiary of 3.83% of GNI. This indicates substantial increases in taxes and social insurance contributions will be required to achieve fiscal sustainability of the current social security system.

Our basic income package is projected to increase the household sector's net benefits by a mere 0.2% of GNI. The net fiscal cost of the basic income system—the actual fiscal pressure—remains remarkably small. While gross benefits of the system will slightly increase to 10.7% of GNI, increases in taxes (7.1% of GNI) and replacement of existing benefits (3.4% of GNI) will bring down the net fiscal cost.

This stability is achieved because the expansion of existing benefit replacements—particularly the Basic Pension—grows in tandem with the

**Table 7.8** Comparative Long-term Fiscal Projections: Status Quo vs. Basic Income Policy(Unit: % of GNI)

| | *2023/2024* | | *2050* | | *2065* | | *2080* | |
|---|---|---|---|---|---|---|---|---|
| | *Status quo* | *BI system* | *Status quo* | *BI system* | *Status quo* | *BI system* | *Status quo* | *BI system* |
| Elderly (65+) | 18.25 | | 40.14 | | 46.57 | | 49.08 | |
| Net Benefit | 2.51 | 2.60 | 5.68 | 5.72 | 6.59 | 6.64 | 6.94 | 6.99 |
| Adults (19–64) | 67.16 | | 49.59 | | 44.62 | | 41.74 | |
| Net Benefit | -5.28 | -6.68 | -3.90 | -4.93 | -3.51 | -4.43 | -3.28 | -4.15 |
| Children (≤18) | 14.59 | | 49.59 | | 44.62 | | 41.74 | |
| Net Benefit | 0.28 | 1.93 | 0.20 | 1.36 | 0.17 | 1.17 | 0.17 | 1.21 |
| Total Population | 100 | | 100 | | 100 | | 100 | |
| Net Benefit | -2.50 | -2.14 | 1.97 | 2.15 | 3.24 | 3.37 | 3.83 | 4.06 |
| Net fiscal cost | 0.34 | | 0.18 | | 0.12 | | 0.23 | |

elderly population. Furthermore, the fiscal cost is mitigated by the drastic reduction in the child population due to low birth rates. While an increase in the birth rate triggered by our policy might raise fiscal requirements for child benefits in the short term, this would be a welcome development. In the long run, a larger youth population will expand the working-age tax base, brightening both economic growth prospects and the national fiscal outlook.

### *Fiscal Sustainability in the Context of Long-term Social Security Projections*

Our previous projections assumed that the 2023 income distribution and benefit levels would remain constant. However, given the expected rise in public pension coverage and benefit levels, along with increases in employment insurance and the National Basic Livelihood Security System

**Table 7.9** Long-term Fiscal Outlook of Basic Income Policy (Based on the 5th Social Security Projections)(Unit: % of GDP/GNI)

| *Category* | *2023/24* | *2040* | *2050* | *2060* | *2065* |
|---|---|---|---|---|---|
| Government Proj. (Cash) | 6.3 | 9.1 | 11.1 | 12.5 | 13.2 |
| Government Proj. (In-kind) | 9.3 | 11.4 | 12.9 | 13.7 | 13.9 |
| Projected Total (Status Quo) | 15.7 | 20.5 | 24 | 26.2 | 27.1 |
| Net Benefit (BI Increase) | 4.3 | 3.5 | 3.2 | 3 | 2.9 |
| Total Expenditure with BI | 20.0 | 24.0 | 27.2 | 29.2 | 30.0 |
| Net Tax Increase | 4.0 | 3.8 | 3.6 | 3.6 | 3.5 |

(NBLSS) benefits, the status quo projections in Table 7.7 likely underestimate future expenditures. This is confirmed by the *5th Mid-to-Long-term Social Security Fiscal Projections* (Ministry of Health and Welfare, 2024), which estimates that cash benefits relative to GDP will double from 6.3% in 2024 to 13.2% by 2065. While this increase is larger than our 1.87-fold projection, it reaffirms that nearly 90% of the expenditure growth is driven by demographic shifts.

Table 7.9 provides a long-term outlook by integrating our basic income policy with the government's *5th Fiscal Projections.* We assume that common wealth dividends remain stable and that NIT-type benefits may slightly decrease as existing social insurance benefits rise.

Under this model, if our basic income policy had been implemented in 2023, total social spending (including in-kind benefits) would have reached 20.0% of GDP, nearing the OECD average. By 2065, total spending would reach 30.0% of GDP—a level comparable to contemporary France (31.6% in 2022). Given that Korea's old-age dependency ratio in 2065 (104.6%) is projected to be double that of France (51.3%), a 30% expenditure level is not excessive; rather, it is a necessary adjustment to demographic reality.

**Which path is more fiscally stable?** Social spending reaching 27% of GDP without a basic income system, or 30% with our proposed basic income system? Current government projections predict massive spending increases primarily in social insurance (rising from 8.5% to 19.8% of GDP) without proposing a corresponding funding plan. Most social insurance funds, including the National Pension, are projected to face widening deficits unless radical reforms are undertaken.

Our basic income policy offers a superior alternative for three reasons:

1. Integrated Funding: Unlike current projections, our model includes a specific, pre-funded tax reform plan. After 2040, the scale of Net Tax Increases is projected to exceed the growth of Net Benefits, enhancing fiscal robustness.
2. Social Insurance Stabilization: The Universal EITC subsidizes premiums for low-income and precarious workers, thereby increasing social insurance revenue and stabilizing its fiscal base.
3. Reform Catalyst: By eliminating "blind spots" in the social safety net, our policy makes it politically and socially easier to implement the necessary structural reforms to the social insurance system.

In conclusion, our proposed basic income policy does not impose a long-term fiscal burden. Instead, it serves as a proactive fiscal stabilizer that addresses the inherent weaknesses of the current social security framework amidst a demographic crisis.

## 7.4 Administrative Implementation Strategies

Along with fiscal feasibility, administrative feasibility is a prerequisite for introducing innovative policies like basic income. When planning the Finnish basic income experiment, designers excluded the Negative Income Tax (NIT) model, assuming that real-time monthly income tracking was an essential but unattainable requirement (Kangas et al., 2016).

However, as argued in Chapter 4, we do not view real-time monthly tracking as a strict necessity. For the majority of citizens, calculating benefits and taxes based on the previous year's annual income is sufficient. The payment cycle—whether monthly or quarterly—can be chosen by individuals based on their needs. For those facing sudden income loss, a system for quarterly or semi-annual self-reporting and year-end reconciliation can be implemented. This approach was proven feasible during the COVID-19 pandemic in the United States, where the refundable Child Tax Credit was successfully distributed through advanced monthly payments (Lee, forthcoming). Conversely, the UK's experience with Universal Credit suggests that fluctuating monthly payments can often cause unnecessary confusion (Bennett, 2025).[5]

**Leveraging Korea's Tax Infrastructure**: South Korea's National Tax Service (NTS) already operates "Hometax," a sophisticated online platform that simplifies tax filing and provides high-level income tracking. Therefore, the NTS is well-equipped to manage a basic income system based on annual calculations with options for monthly or quarterly distributions through a Refundable Tax Credit mechanism.

The primary administrative challenge is not tracking income in real-time, but ensuring that all adults, including those currently below the tax threshold, file comprehensive income tax returns. This requires a government-wide effort, supported by civil society and the media, to shift public perception: filing taxes should be seen as a gateway to exercising one's right to basic income. Initially, close cooperation between the NTS, local government welfare officers, and social security agencies will be essential. Furthermore, the expansion of Rural Basic Income can serve as a catalyst for integrating farmers and rural residents—who have historically been exempt from income reporting—into the formal tax system.

**Implementing a Comprehensive Income Definition**: Another challenge for the NTS is managing a system based on our proposed comprehensive income definition, which includes capital gains and imputed rent. By moving away from the complex "asset-to-income conversion" used in current social assistance, we eliminate the punitive effective tax rates often imposed on the near-poor. This ensures fairness by capturing "invisible" income from owner-occupied housing (imputed rent) while simplifying the treatment of other assets that already generate cash flow.

To avoid immediate administrative chaos, we propose a dual-track implementation in the short term. Rather than overhauling the entire existing income tax code overnight, we suggest adding a specific "Basic Income Supplementary Form" to the current tax return. In this form, taxpayers would report non-taxable income, capital gains, and the publicly notified prices of their land and primary residence. This allows for the

[5] Bennett (2025) discusses the administrative hurdles and recipient confusion associated with high-frequency adjustments in the UK system.

calculation of Common Wealth Dividends, NIT payouts, and Universal EITC benefits without disrupting the existing tax structure.

The NTS should proactively gather as much of this data as possible from other administrative agencies to pre-populate these forms, allowing taxpayers to simply verify or correct the information.[6] As the public becomes familiar with these new concepts and recognizes their benefits, the tax system can eventually be unified under a single comprehensive income definition. If concepts like imputed rent remain socially difficult to accept initially, a grace period for their inclusion could be considered.

**Integration of Social Insurance and Step-by-Step Tax Filing**: A critical next step for administrative success is empowering the National Tax Service (NTS) to consolidate social insurance collection and utilize the Universal EITC for the automatic payment of premiums. This is a vital prerequisite for shifting toward an income-based social insurance system and eliminating blind spots in the safety net (You, 2025).

While the gross payout and tax scale of our proposal are substantial, the Refundable Tax Credit system significantly reduces the volume of actual cash transfers. Benefits for children are distributed through parents or household heads, and the Universal EITC is primarily used for automatic insurance contributions. This process not only streamlines administration but also serves as an educational tool for citizens. To this end, the tax filing form should be designed to help taxpayers intuitively understand the principles of basic income.

We propose a step-by-step filing process on the NTS Hometax platform to enhance public understanding:

1. Step 1: Basic Income vs. Basic Income Tax: Calculate the sum of Common Wealth and NIT-type benefits for the individual and their dependents, then offset this against the total Basic Income Tax and Land Value Tax. The system should clearly display both the individual shares and the combined result to show whether the person is a net recipient or payer in this category.

[6] For example, for crop cultivation income, the NTS could provide an estimate based on "Agricultural Management Body" registration data, allowing taxpayers to file an amended return with supporting evidence if they disagree with the estimate.

2. Step 2: Universal EITC vs. Social Insurance: Compare the Universal EITC amount with the required social insurance premiums. If the premiums are higher, the individual pays the difference; if the EITC is higher, the surplus is issued as a refund after the premiums are fully covered.[7]
3. Step 3: Final Consolidation: Aggregate the results from the previous steps with existing personal income tax liabilities (refunds or additional payments) .

This phased approach ensures that taxpayers recognize the Universal EITC as a subsidy for their social insurance. Citizens can choose to receive refunds monthly, quarterly, or as a lump sum, and those with tax liabilities can opt for installment plans. For the Land Value Tax, we recommend allowing payments in the form of land equity rather than cash to ease liquidity concerns. By integrating this into a modified Hometax interface and moving the filing deadline to late March, quarterly refunds for the first quarter can be distributed promptly based on the previous year's income. **A Gradual and Natural Tax Strategy**: While our model assumes a 10% Basic Income Tax on excess earnings, the tax rate could be lowered by diversifying funding sources through corporate or value-added taxes. Furthermore, we can utilize a natural and incremental tax increase strategy. During the Park Geun-hye and Moon Jae-in administrations, the share of income tax relative to GDP rose from 3.3% in 2014 to 5.76% in 2022 without drastic rate hikes. This was achieved by:

- Converting certain deductions into tax credits.
- Expanding tax brackets (e.g., lowering the 38% threshold).
- Introducing new high-income brackets (42% and 45% rates).

Even without changing rates or brackets, economic growth naturally pushes taxpayers into higher brackets—a phenomenon known as bracket creep. By combining these moderate methods with the proposed tax reforms, the fiscal targets of the basic income policy can be achieved in a politically sustainable manner.

[7] To facilitate this, social insurance should not be withheld at the source for part-time wage earners below the Universal EITC threshold. For daily laborers and personal service providers, social insurance should be reconciled during the tax filing process rather than withheld at the source.

CHAPTER 8

# Expected Effects: Redistribution and Sustainable Efficiency

In the previous chapter, we examined the fiscal feasibility of three programs: a negative income tax-type basic income, a Common Wealth basic income, and a Universal Earned Income Tax Credit as a form of participation income. In this chapter, for each of these programs individually and for the case in which all three are implemented simultaneously, we examine the expected effects not only on the promotion of equality but also on freedom and sustainable efficiency.

To assess the impact on income inequality and poverty, we analyze the increase and decrease in disposable income by income bracket—that is, the distribution of net benefits—and estimate the degree of change in various inequality and poverty indicators.. We also examine income redistribution effects at the individual level by demographic characteristics and at the household level by household type. For this purpose, we use data from The Survey of Household Finances and Living Conditions (SHFLC), which is widely regarded as the most accurate source of information on income distribution.

Although it is difficult to empirically analyze the expected effects on freedom and sustainable efficiency, we consider at least how the level of guaranteed minimum income and the effects on participation tax rates and effective marginal tax rates may influence real freedom and labor supply. We also examine, through effects by household type, whether these programs can actually mitigate the incentives for household dissolution that



J. S. You et al., *UBI from Idea to Reality*, Exploring the Basic Income Guarantee,
https://doi.org/10.1007/978-3-032-26200-4_8

are created by existing household and needs-based welfare programs. For this analysis, we use the OECD tax-benefit simulation model by household type (the OECD Tax-Benefit Calculator).

In the previous chapter, we estimated the required fiscal resources under the assumption that a negative income tax-type basic income would be implemented based on a comprehensive income definition that includes imputed rent (owner-occupied housing expenses). In analyzing income redistribution effects in this chapter, we adopt the same definition of income. If these programs were implemented based on an income definition that excludes imputed rent, the redistribution effects would differ slightly. It can easily be anticipated that owner-occupiers would benefit somewhat more than in the former case. For comparison purposes, we therefore also briefly present the income redistribution effects under an income definition that excludes imputed rental income.

However, due to limitations of the SHFLC data—such as the lack of information on capital gains from real estate and stock transactions—our analysis of income redistribution effects is also subject to limitations. If capital gains were included in the income definition for implementing the basic income programs and in measuring income redistribution, the redistribution effects would be larger than those estimated in this chapter. Moreover, although the SHFLC provides information on household-owned real estate, it does not separately provide land price information within real estate holdings. As a result, the income redistribution effects of a land dividend-type basic income are likely to be somewhat underestimated.

Next, we estimate the expected effects of Seoul's household-based negative income tax program, the Stepping Stone Income, on inequality and poverty, and compare them with our three policy packages. The results show that improvements in inequality indicators such as the Gini coefficient are weaker than under our policies, while the poverty-reduction effect is stronger. However, although the Stepping Stone Income provides a high guaranteed income level and lowers participation tax rates and effective marginal tax rates relative to the current system, these rates remain relatively high. Consequently, the program is expected to somewhat reduce labor supply, and concerns remain regarding incentives for household dissolution.[1]

[1] The household-based Safety Income proposed by Park and Byun (2017), which served as a model for Seoul's Stepping Stone Income Program, did not link benefit levels to the government-announced median income by household size but instead scaled in proportion to household size, which could reduce incentives for household dissolution.

The income redistribution analysis presented in this chapter is based on income accrued in 2023 as reported in the SHFLC. Average per capita market income (including employment income, business income, property income, social insurance income such as benefits from the public pension and employment insurance, as well as imputed rent for owner-occupiers) amounts to 29.866 million KRW, which corresponds to 63.2% of per capita GNI (47.249 million KRW) in the same year. When policies are actually implemented, they will be administered based on administrative data rather than survey data. Accordingly, depending on the scope and accuracy of income information available to tax authorities, average per capita market income and the estimated income redistribution effects may differ somewhat. However, microdata from national tax statistics lack information on household composition and do not provide data on capital gains, retirement income, financial income under 20 million KRW, and other income under 3 million KRW that are separately taxed, as well as tax-exempt income. As such, they are difficult to use for income redistribution analysis. Because the SHFLC adjusts survey data using administrative records from the National Tax Service and other sources and thus presents a relatively accurate picture of income distribution, its analytical results can generally be regarded as not substantially different from reality.

A comparison of SHFLC data and NTS tax data in Chapter 7 shows that informal-sector labor income among low-income groups and business income (including tax-exempt agricultural income) among the lower-middle-income groups are higher in the SHFLC than in the NTS tax data, while employment and financial income among the top income group tend to be lower in the SHFLC than in the NTS tax data. Accordingly, benefit levels from the negative income tax-type basic income for lower-middle-income groups may be slightly higher than those estimated by the SHFLC simulation, while Universal Earned Income Tax Credit benefits may be slightly lower. In addition, the tax burden on the highest-income group may be somewhat higher than suggested by the SHFLC results.

## 8.1 Impact on Inequality and Poverty

### *Common Wealth Basic Income*

The common wealth basic income is designed to replace the basic personal deduction and to combine land dividends and carbon dividends. Under this scheme, every individual receives a basic income equivalent to 3% of gross national income per capita (1,418 thousand KRW in 2023, approximately 1.8 million KRW projected by 2030). Accordingly, each household receives basic income in proportion to the number of its members, while bearing different levels of burden depending on income level, land ownership status and value, and the level of carbon consumption.

Table 8.1 presents the results of an analysis of the income redistribution effects of introducing the Common Wealth basic income by income decile, based on household disposable income that includes imputed rental income. The analysis simultaneously takes into account the amount of the Common Wealth basic income received, the increased tax burden resulting from the abolition of the basic personal deduction, the burden of the land value tax, and the increase in household carbon expenditures due to the introduction of a carbon tax. Because the SHFLC does not provide household-level information on land assets separately, a uniform tax rate was applied to the total value of household real estate holdings. Likewise, due to lack of information on carbon-related expenditures, a fixed proportion was applied to total household consumption expenditure to estimate the increase in carbon spending.

Before the introduction of the Common Wealth basic income, the average disposable income of all households in 2023 was estimated at 63,963 thousand KRW. The average disposable income of households in the lowest income decile was only 13,834 thousand KRW, whereas that of households in the highest decile reached 197,958 thousand KRW, implying an income gap of 14.3 times between the two groups.

Household characteristics exhibit clear differences across income deciles in terms of household composition and age structure. In the lowest decile, the average household size is only 1.3 persons, while the mean age of the household head is relatively high at 65.2 years, indicating a high prevalence of elderly single-person households. By contrast, as income deciles increase, household size rises gradually and the age of the household head becomes relatively younger. In the highest decile, the average household size is 3.5 persons and the mean age of the household head is 53.4 years.

Because the basic income is paid on an individual basis, households with more members receive larger total benefits at the household level. As a result, low-income elderly households with fewer members receive relatively smaller amounts of basic income, but they also have less burdens due to low levels of land ownership and carbon consumption, leading to net benefits. In contrast, high-income households with more members receive larger basic income payments, but their burdens—such as land holding

**Table 8.1** Income Redistribution Effects of the Common Wealth Basic Income Based on Household Disposable Income (Unit: 10,000 KRW, persons, %)

| *Income Decile* | *Household Disposable Income* | *Household Size* | *Household Head Mean Age* | *Common Wealth Dividend Basic Income* | *Tax Increase from Abolition of Basic Deduction* | *Land Value Tax* | *Increase in Carbon Expenditure* | *New Household Disposable Income* | *Net Household Benefit(Burden)* | *Share of Net Beneficiaries* |
|---|---|---|---|---|---|---|---|---|---|---|
| 1 | 1,383.4 | 1.3 | 65.2 | 184.4 | 7.8 | 46.9 | 46.5 | 1,466.5 | 83.1 | 87.6% |
| 2 | 2,871.5 | 1.7 | 55.7 | 239.0 | 20.8 | 85.7 | 72.5 | 2,931.5 | 60.0 | 77.9% |
| 3 | 4,053.5 | 2.0 | 52.4 | 284.8 | 32.0 | 97.8 | 88.8 | 4,119.7 | 66.2 | 76.2% |
| 4 | 5,150.6 | 2.4 | 52.2 | 341.8 | 41.8 | 126.1 | 107.1 | 5,217.4 | 66.8 | 74.2% |
| 5 | 6,229.1 | 2.7 | 51.5 | 376.7 | 49.0 | 155.3 | 120.4 | 6,281.0 | 52.0 | 69.2% |
| 6 | 7,323.7 | 3.0 | 51.2 | 419.3 | 59.0 | 189.4 | 137.6 | 7,356.9 | 33.2 | 65.4% |
| 7 | 8,581.6 | 3.1 | 51.1 | 433.5 | 66.5 | 213.9 | 146.1 | 8,588.7 | 7.0 | 60.4% |
| 8 | 10,135.4 | 3.3 | 51.3 | 462.8 | 75.3 | 264.3 | 163.9 | 1,0094.7 | -40.7 | 56.9% |
| 9 | 12,366.0 | 3.4 | 52.6 | 488.1 | 91.1 | 336.0 | 188.9 | 1,2238.1 | -127.9 | 41.2% |
| 10 | 19,795.8 | 3.5 | 53.4 | 501.2 | 119.0 | 623.5 | 233.9 | 1,9320.6 | -475.2 | 20.5% |
| Total | 6,396.3 | 2.4 | 54.9 | 337.8 | 46.5 | 175.2 | 114.0 | 6,398.6 | 2.2 | 68.0% |

Note: Household disposable income includes imputed rental income from owner-occupied housing (1.2% of housing value). The figures are based on results from static microsimulation using 2023 income data and 2024 real estate asset data from the SHFLC.

taxes and increased carbon expenditures—also rise, causing net benefits to decline gradually or to shift into net contributions.

After the introduction of the Common Wealth basic income, the average disposable income of all households becomes 63,986 thousand KRW, virtually unchanged from the pre-introduction level. This outcome is expected, as the Common Wealth basic income is designed to be fiscally neutral. However, when examining changes by income decile, net benefits are clearly more pronounced among lower-income households.

Specifically, households in the lowest income decile receive an average of 1,844 thousand KRW per household in basic income. In contrast, their average burden amounts to only 78 thousand KRW from replacing the basic deduction, 469 thousand KRW in land holding taxes, and 465 thousand KRW from increased carbon expenditures. As a result, these households record an average net benefit of 831 thousand KRW per household, equivalent to 6.0% of household disposable income. This net-benefit structure persists consistently up to the sixth income decile, although the size of the net benefit gradually declines as income increases.

From the eighth decile onward, the combined burdens from land value tax and increased carbon expenditures exceed basic income receipts, resulting in a shift to a net contributor structure. In particular, households in the highest decile receive an average of 5,012 thousand KRW in basic income but incur an average net burden of 4,752 thousand KRW per household, equivalent to 2.4% of household disposable income. This indicates that the burden is concentrated on the highest-income households, which also tend to have highly concentrated land asset ownership.

Looking at the share of net beneficiary households, 68% of all households fall into the net beneficiary category. In the lowest income decile, approximately 88% of households are net beneficiaries, and a high proportion—around 70%—is maintained across the second to sixth deciles. By contrast, in the ninth and tenth deciles, the share of net beneficiary households falls to about 40% and 20%, respectively, reflecting a substantial increase in the proportion of net contributor households.

In sum, the Common Wealth basic income increases disposable income for low-income and middle-income households, while imposing net burdens on high-income households with concentrated land asset ownership. It thus exhibits a progressive income redistribution effect and represents a policy design under which a majority of households become net beneficiaries.

Nevertheless, several limitations remain due to constraints in the SHFLC data. Specifically, the share of land value within total household real estate assets cannot be identified, leading to uniform estimation assumptions, and the incidence of land ownership held by corporations cannot be fully reflected. Although, on average, approximately 65% of housing prices are attributable to the value of the underlying land, this share varies depending on housing type, location, and year of construction.[2] Land ownership is more highly concentrated at the very top of the distribution than housing ownership, and land value taxes imposed on corporate-owned land are ultimately borne largely by corporate shareholders, who predominantly belong to the highest income groups. As a result, the present analysis may underestimate the contribution of the top income group to land value taxes and somewhat overestimate the burden on upper-middle-income households. In addition, the assumption that carbon tax burdens are proportional to total household consumption expenditure likely overestimates the burden on low-income households and underestimates the burden on high-income households, given that lower-income households rely more on public transportation while higher-income households more frequently use private vehicles and air travel.[3] Taking these data limitations into account, the actual redistributive effects of the common wealth dividend basic income are likely to be somewhat larger than those estimated in this analysis.

As noted earlier, lower income deciles tend to have smaller household sizes. To account for this, we further analyzed the redistributive effects of the Common Wealth basic income using equivalized household disposable income—calculated by dividing household disposable income by the square root of household size. Figure 8.1 shows, by income decile, the ratios (%) of equivalized Common Wealth basic income receipts, increased

[2] According to the Bank of Korea's National Balance Sheets, as of the end of 2023, the total value of land attached to residential buildings amounted to 4,385 trillion won, while the total value of residential buildings within construction assets was 2,357 trillion won. Of the combined total housing asset value of 6,741 trillion won, land accounts for 65% and buildings for 35%.

[3] The facts that the decile ratio of carbon expenditures in Table 8.1 is 5.0, which is significantly lower than the decile ratio of disposable income (14.3), and that Fig. 8.1 shows higher tax increase rates for households in the first and second income deciles compared to other income groups appear to result from an overestimation of the carbon tax burden on low-income households.

tax burdens (including higher taxes due to the abolition of the basic deduction, land value taxes, and carbon taxes), and the resulting net benefits (or net burdens) relative to equivalized household disposable income.

The redistributive effects based on equivalized household disposable income are similar to those based on non-equivalized household disposable income but are slightly stronger. In the lowest decile, the equivalized net benefit amounts to 9.2% of equivalized household disposable income, while in the highest decile, the equivalized net contribution amounts to 2.5%. These effects are larger than those obtained using non-equivalized household disposable income (a 6.0% net benefit in the lowest decile and a 2.4% net contribution in the highest decile). The share of net beneficiary individuals also increases slightly to 69.4% (see Appendix Table 8.A1 for detailed figures by income decile and component) .

Overall, Fig. 8.1 demonstrates that, although the Common Wealth basic income provides the same basic income to all individuals, it generates different net redistribution effects across income levels, producing net benefits for low-income households and net burdens for high-income households, thereby yielding a clearly progressive distributional structure.

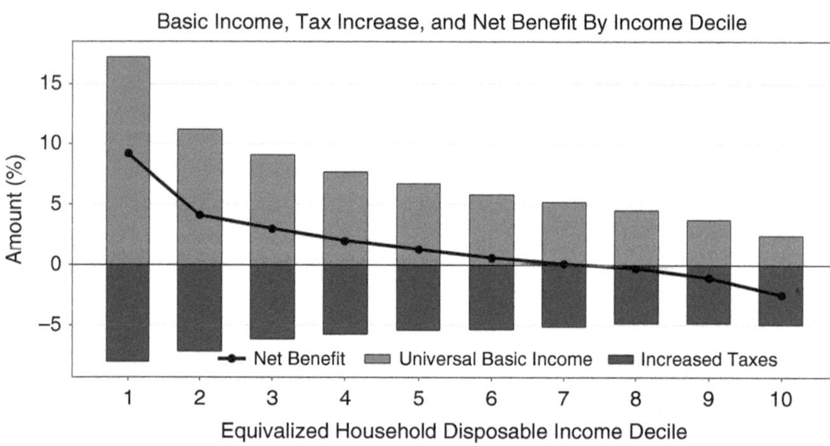


**Fig. 8.1** Ratios (%) of Equivalized Common Wealth Basic Income, Increases in Tax Burdens (Tax Increases from the Abolition of the Basic Deduction, Land Holding Taxes, and Carbon Tax Burdens), and Net Benefits (Net Burdens) Relative to Equivalized Household Disposable Income: Distribution by Income Decile

### *Negative Income Tax-Type Basic Income*

Under the Negative Income Tax-type basic income that we propose, a guaranteed income is provided at a level equivalent to 20% of average individual market income (approximately 12% of gross national income per capita) for children and older adults, and 10% of average individual market income (approximately 6% of gross national income per capita) for adults. The reference income is set at average individual market income, which corresponds to about 60% of gross national income per capita. In addition, the benefit reduction rate as income increases is set at 20% for children and older adults and 10% for adults.

This institutional design is intended to generate relatively large net transfer effects for groups with limited earned income, such as children, adolescents, and older adults, while making it more likely that net burdens arise—through benefit reductions and tax liabilities—among the core working-age population, where earned income is concentrated.

Based on 2023 income, Table 8.2 presents, by age group, the net benefits (or net contributions) after the introduction of the Negative Income Tax-type basic income, combining benefit receipts, increases in taxes, and reductions in public transfers, as well as the shares of net beneficiaries and net contributors. The results show that the income redistribution effects of the Negative Income Tax-type basic income differ markedly across age groups.

**Table 8.2** Income Redistribution Effects of the NIT-Type Basic Income by Age Group (Unit: 10,000 KRW, %)

| *Age Group* | *NIT-Type Benefits* | *Increase in Taxes* | *Reduction in Public Transfers* | *Net Benefit (Burden)* | *Share of Net Beneficiaries* | *Share of Net Contributors* |
|---|---|---|---|---|---|---|
| Aged 18 or younger | 574.8 | 0.1 | 78.8 | 495.9 | 95.5% | 0.1% |
| 19–29 | 166.1 | 33.0 | 0.4 | 132.7 | 76.4% | 23.4% |
| 30–49 | 63.8 | 226.9 | 2.0 | -165.1 | 36.7% | 63.0% |
| 50–59 | 72.3 | 236.7 | 7.6 | -172.0 | 39.7% | 59.0% |
| 60–64 | 88.8 | 176.9 | 10.7 | -98.8 | 47.6% | 50.5% |
| Aged 65 or older | 336.5 | 65.5 | 252.8 | 18.2 | 61.0% | 38.2% |
| Total | 208.9 | 136.2 | 62.8 | 9.9 | 56.4% | 42.3% |

For the age group aged 18 or younger, the average benefit received from the Negative Income Tax-type basic income is very high at 5,748 thousand KRW, while increases in taxes are virtually nonexistent. Despite reductions in some public transfers (such as child allowances and the child tax credit), an average net benefit of 4,959 thousand KRW is generated. The share of net beneficiaries reaches 95.5%, whereas net contributors account for only 0.1%.

In the 19–29 age group, an average Negative Income Tax-type basic income of 1,661 thousand KRW is provided, and the increase in taxes is relatively limited at 329 thousand KRW. Reductions in public transfers are also negligible, resulting in an average net benefit of 1,327 thousand KRW. In this age group, 76.4% are net beneficiaries, indicating that a large majority of young adults benefit on net after the introduction of the scheme.

By contrast, among the most economically active age groups—those aged 30–49 and 50–59—the net effect of the Negative Income Tax-type basic income is reversed. For individuals aged 30–49, the average benefit received amounts to only 638 thousand KRW, while the increase in taxes is substantial at 2,269 thousand KRW, resulting in an average net burden of 1,651 thousand KRW. Accordingly, the share of net contributors reaches 63.0%, far exceeding the share of net beneficiaries (36.7%). A similar pattern is observed for the 50–59 age group, resulting in an average net burden of 1,720 thousand KRW.

In the 60–64 age group, the magnitude of the net burden becomes somewhat smaller, with an average amount of 988 thousand KRW. In this age group, the shares of net beneficiaries (47.6%) and net contributors (50.5%) are relatively balanced.

For the older population aged 65 or older, the income redistribution effect of the Negative Income Tax-type basic income shifts back toward a net-benefit outcome. The average benefit received is relatively high at 3,365 thousand KRW, while the increase in taxes is limited to 655 thousand KRW. However, reductions in existing public transfers—such as the basic pension—are substantial at 2,528 thousand KRW, constraining the average net benefit to 182 thousand KRW. Nevertheless, the share of net beneficiaries reaches 61.0%, suggesting that a majority of older individuals are expected to benefit on net.

Overall, after the introduction of the Negative Income Tax-type basic income, the average net benefit amounts to 99 thousand KRW, which is relatively modest, while the share of net beneficiaries reaches 56.4%, exceeding a simple majority. In particular, strong net transfer effects emerge among children and young adults, whereas net burdens are clearly concentrated on the core working-age population in middle and older adulthood. This pattern suggests that the Negative Income Tax-type basic income produces a form of horizontal income redistribution across age groups and, at the same time, provides each individual with a minimum income floor. In doing so, it not only reduces the risk of falling into severe poverty but also functions as an insurance mechanism that smooths income and consumption over the life course.

We next examine the income redistribution effects of the Negative Income Tax-type basic income using equivalized household disposable income. Table 8.3 presents, by income decile based on equivalized household disposable income, the net benefits (or net burdens) after the introduction of the Negative Income Tax-type basic income—combining benefit receipts, increases in taxes, and reductions in existing public transfers—along with the shares of net beneficiaries and net contributors.

**Table 8.3** Income Redistribution Effects of the Negative Income Tax-Type Basic Income Based on Equivalized Household Disposable Income (Unit: 10,000 KRW, %)

| *Income Decile* | *Household Disposable Income* | *Household NIT Benefits* | *Increase in Household Taxes* | *Reduction in Household Public Transfers* | *New Household Disposable Income* | *Net Benefit (Burden)* | *Share of Net Beneficiaries* |
|---|---|---|---|---|---|---|---|
| 1 | 1,130.6 | 546.3 | 4.5 | 281.4 | 1,391 | 260.4 | 84.3% |
| 2 | 1,993.1 | 467.6 | 18.2 | 155.9 | 2,286.5 | 293.5 | 93.1% |
| 3 | 2,611.1 | 433.0 | 45.5 | 114.3 | 2,884.3 | 273.2 | 89.6% |
| 4 | 3,146.2 | 390.6 | 87.4 | 84.2 | 3,365.2 | 219 | 82.5% |
| 5 | 3,662.6 | 368.3 | 125.3 | 67.0 | 3,838.6 | 176 | 79.8% |
| 6 | 4,227.8 | 332.1 | 167.6 | 58.9 | 4,333.4 | 105.6 | 67.5% |
| 7 | 4,832.4 | 327.5 | 225.7 | 59.6 | 4,874.6 | 42.2 | 57.6% |
| 8 | 5,605.7 | 293.3 | 301.3 | 43.4 | 5,554.2 | -51.4 | 35.8% |
| 9 | 6,782.2 | 264.7 | 437.5 | 33.6 | 6,575.8 | -206.4 | 12.4% |
| 10 | 10,701.6 | 236.7 | 937.5 | 25.9 | 9,974.9 | -726.7 | 1.2% |
| Total | 4,468.6 | 366.0 | 235.0 | 92.5 | 4,507.2 | 38.6 | 60.4% |

Note: Household disposable income refers to household income that includes imputed rental income from owner-occupied housing—calculated as 1.2% of housing value—and is equivalized by dividing by the square root of household size.

Clearly, net benefits from the Negative Income Tax-type basic income are observed among households in the lower income deciles. In particular, for households in the first through fourth income deciles, the benefit effect of the basic income substantially exceeds the combined increases in taxes and reductions in public transfers, resulting in equivalized net benefits of more than 2 million KRW per household. For the fifth and sixth deciles, equivalized net benefits exceed 1 million KRW. Consistent with this pattern, the share of net beneficiaries exceeds 80% up to the fifth decile, and even in the sixth decile it remains above two-thirds, implying that 60.4% of the total population are net beneficiaries. This confirms that the scheme effectively supplements disposable income not only for low-income households but also for a segment of the middle-income group.

By contrast, as income deciles rise, basic income receipts decline rapidly while tax increases expand gradually, leading to an offsetting of net benefits and net burdens among the upper-middle-income groups in the seventh and eighth deciles. In the ninth decile, the average equivalized net contribution exceeds 2 million KRW, and in the tenth decile, it exceeds 7 million KRW.

Overall, the average equivalized net benefit amounts to 386 thousand KRW, and the share of net beneficiaries is 60.4%. The NIT-type basic income exhibits a progressive income redistribution effect, providing substantial net benefits to low-income households while imposing net burdens on high-income households with minimal fiscal input.

Figure 8.2 presents, by income decile based on equivalized household disposable income, the ratios of equivalized Negative Income Tax-type basic income benefits, increases in taxes, reductions in existing public transfer income, and the resulting net equivalized benefits (or net burdens). In the lower income deciles, the ratio of equivalized net benefits to equivalized household disposable income is very large. Specifically, it reaches 23.0% in the first decile, 14.7% in the second decile, and 10.5% in the third decile, indicating a substantial poverty-alleviation effect. This ratio then declines progressively to 7.0% in the fourth decile, 4.8% in the fifth decile, and 2.5% in the sixth decile.

In the seventh and eighth income deciles, the ratios of equivalized net benefits and net contributions relative to equivalized household disposable income are both negligible, at approximately 0.9%. In contrast, the ratios of equivalized net contributions rise to 3.0% in the ninth decile and 6.8% in the tenth decile. Although higher-income groups thus make a substantial contribution in absolute terms, the resulting burden does not appear to be excessive.

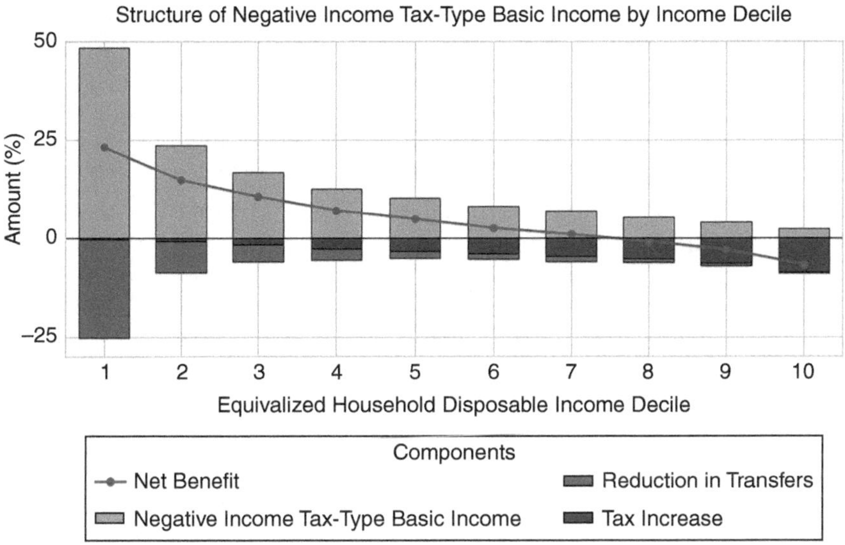


**Fig. 8.2** Ratios of Equivalized Negative Income Tax-Type Basic Income Benefits, Taxes, Reductions in Public Transfer Income, and Net Benefits (Net Burdens) by Income Decile Based on Equivalized Household Disposable Income

### *Universal Earned Income Tax Credit*

The Universal Earned Income Tax Credit (EITC) proposed in this study is designed to address the regressive nature of the existing employment income deduction and to offset the social insurance contribution burden faced by low-income and precarious workers. It applies to all working persons, including both wage earners and the self-employed. Under this scheme, individuals whose earned income (employment income plus business income) is less than or equal to 50% of gross national income per capita (equivalent to five-sixths of average individual market income) receive a credit equal to 12% of their earned income. For individuals whose earned income exceeds this threshold, a lump-sum earned income tax credit equivalent to 6% of gross national income per capita (approximately 10% of average individual market income) is provided. To implement this system, the existing employment income deduction, employment income tax credit, and Work Incentive Payment are integrated and unified into a single refundable tax credit structure.

**Table 8.4** Income Redistribution Effects of the Universal Earned Income Tax Credit by Decile Based on Individual Earned Income (Unit: 10,000 KRW, %)

| *Earned Income Decile* | *Earned Income* | *Employment Income Deduction / Tax Credit* | *Work Incentive Payment* | *Universal Earned Income Tax Credit* | *Net Benefit (Net Contribution)* | *Share of Net Beneficiaries* |
|---|---|---|---|---|---|---|
| 1 | 149.8 | 3.9 | 14.0 | 18.0 | 0.1 | 89.1% |
| 2 | 616.9 | 21.4 | 21.5 | 74.0 | 31.1 | 86.3% |
| 3 | 1,286.6 | 44.8 | 23.9 | 154.4 | 85.7 | 88.3% |
| 4 | 2,064.1 | 80.1 | 22.7 | 247.0 | 144.1 | 93.9% |
| 5 | 2,735.2 | 139.9 | 15.8 | 283.5 | 127.8 | 94.6% |
| 6 | 3,339.4 | 191.0 | 12.8 | 283.5 | 79.8 | 92.9% |
| 7 | 4,049.4 | 204.8 | 12.5 | 283.5 | 66.2 | 92.5% |
| 8 | 5,092.1 | 220.8 | 7.3 | 283.5 | 55.4 | 93.6% |
| 9 | 6,757.4 | 263.1 | 7.2 | 283.5 | 13.3 | 41.6% |
| 10 | 12,311.8 | 435.8 | 3.7 | 283.5 | -156.0 | 15.6% |
| Total | 3,824.9 | 159.4 | 14.2 | 219.1 | 45.5 | 78.8% |

Note: Earned income is defined as the sum of employment income and business income.

Table 8.4 presents the results of an analysis of the income redistribution effects of the UEITC by decile based on individual earned income.

The results show that the net benefit effect of the universal earned income tax credit is particularly pronounced among the lower-middle income groups rather than the lowest-income group. In the lowest (first) decile, average earned income is relatively low at 1,498 thousand KRW. While the average net benefit from the UEITC—replacing the existing Work Incentive Payment and employment income deduction and credit—is very small at one thousand KRW, the share of net beneficiaries is 89.1%. In the second and third deciles, net benefits increase to 311 thousand KRW and 857 thousand KRW, respectively, while the shares of net beneficiaries remain high at 86.3% and 88.3%.

The fourth and fifth income deciles exhibit the highest average net benefits, at 1,441 thousand KRW and 1,278 thousand KRW, respectively. Although average net benefits gradually decline to 554 thousand KRW by the eighth decile, the share of net beneficiaries remains very high, exceeding 90% across all of these deciles.

By contrast, for the top income deciles, the net benefit effect reverses into a net burden due to the removal of tax reductions associated with the existing employment income deduction. In the ninth decile, the average net benefit shrinks to 133 thousand KRW, and the share of net beneficiaries drops sharply to 41.6%. In the highest (tenth) decile, average earned income reaches 123,120 thousand KRW, while the net effect turns into a substantial net burden of −1,560 thousand KRW, with only 15.6% remaining net beneficiaries.

Looking at the overall averages, mean individual earned income amounts to 38,249 thousand KRW. The average net benefit associated with the introduction of the UEITC is 455 thousand KRW, and the share of net beneficiaries reaches 78.8%. This suggests that the Universal Earned Income Tax Credit functions as a scheme that delivers net benefits to the vast majority of working persons, excluding the top income decile, with only minimal net fiscal input.

Taken together, these results demonstrate that the refundable Universal Earned Income Tax Credit proposed in this study can correct the regressive features of the employment income deduction and provide social insurance contribution support as well as income support to a broad range of workers, including low-income and precarious workers.

Figure 8.3 illustrates, by income decile based on individual earned income, the effects of introducing the Universal Earned Income Tax Credit in terms of benefits, increases in taxes, replacement of existing Work Incentive Payment, and the resulting net benefits (or net burdens) .

### *Combined Redistribution Effects of the Three Programs*

In the preceding sections, we examined and compared the individual income redistribution effects of the three basic income programs. We now estimate their combined effects when all three programs are implemented simultaneously.

Table 8.5 presents the redistribution effects by income decile based on equivalized disposable income (including imputed rent) under a comprehensive model that combines the three basic income programs. Looking first at the total equivalized benefit amounts, relatively similar levels of benefits are provided across all income deciles. These range from 7,950 thousand KRW in the lowest (first) decile to 8,620 thousand KRW in the seventh decile, with an overall average of 8,410 thousand KRW. This is because the benefit level of the NIT-type basic income is higher for lower-income households, whereas the common wealth dividend basic

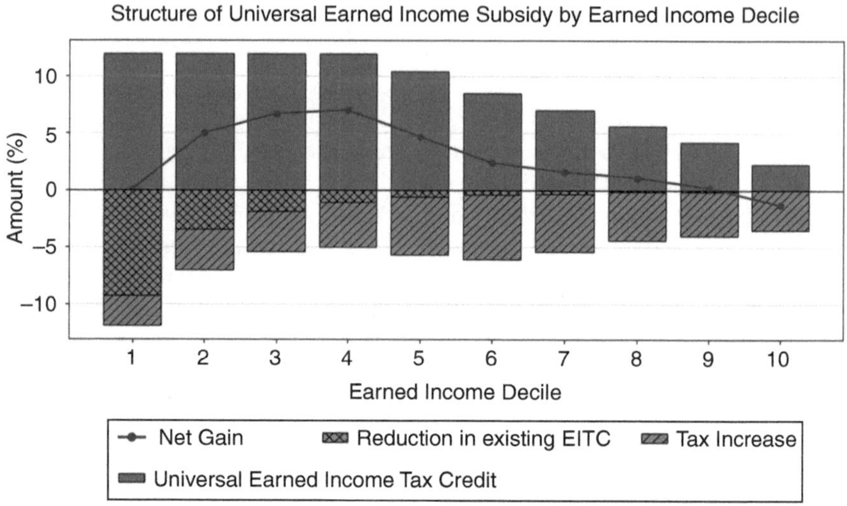


**Fig. 8.3** Structure of Net Benefits (Net Burdens) Under the Universal Earned Income Tax Credit by Individual Earned Income Decile

**Table 8.5** Combined Effects of the Three Basic Income Programs by Equivalized Household Disposable Income Decile (Unit: 10,000 KRW, %)

| *Income Decile* | *Household Disposable Income* | *Total Benefits* | *Increase in Taxes* | *Reduction in Existing Benefits* | *Net Benefit (Burden)* | *Net Benefit as a Share of Disposable Income* | *New Household Disposable Income* | *Share of Net Beneficiary Households* |
|---|---|---|---|---|---|---|---|---|
| 1 | 1,132.4 | 795.2 | 109.7 | 314.0 | 371.6 | 32.8% | 1,504.1 | 90.9% |
| 2 | 1,993.1 | 834.0 | 211.2 | 192.5 | 430.2 | 21.6% | 2,423.3 | 94.4% |
| 3 | 2,611.1 | 861.5 | 296.7 | 140.0 | 424.8 | 16.3% | 3,035.9 | 95.6% |
| 4 | 3,146.2 | 853.8 | 388.0 | 99.8 | 366.0 | 11.6% | 3,512.2 | 91.2% |
| 5 | 3,662.6 | 860.4 | 468.9 | 80.4 | 311.1 | 8.5% | 3,973.7 | 86.9% |
| 6 | 4,227.8 | 847.9 | 567.0 | 69.4 | 211.5 | 5.0% | 4,439.3 | 81.4% |
| 7 | 4,832.4 | 862.8 | 675.9 | 66.9 | 120.0 | 2.5% | 4,952.4 | 69.4% |
| 8 | 5,605.7 | 852.3 | 820.8 | 49.6 | -18.1 | -0.3% | 5,587.6 | 50.8% |
| 9 | 6,782.2 | 829.9 | 1,060.6 | 37.2 | -267.9 | -3.9% | 6,514.4 | 17.7% |
| 10 | 10,701.6 | 816.7 | 1,845.7 | 28.3 | -1,057.0 | -9.9% | 9,644.6 | 2.2% |
| Total | 4,468.8 | 841.4 | 644.3 | 107.9 | 89.3 | 2.0% | 4,558.1 | 68.1% |

Note: Household disposable income refers to household income including imputed rental income, equivalized by household size. All other measures are also expressed in equivalized terms.

income is higher among high-income deciles with larger household sizes, and the UEITC is higher for middle- and upper-income groups than for low-income groups with lower earned income.

By contrast, equivalized tax increases expand markedly as income deciles rise. In the first decile, the increase in taxes amounts to only 1,097 thousand KRW, but it rises rapidly to 4,689 thousand KRW in the fifth decile and 10,606 thousand KRW in the ninth decile, reaching 18,457 thousand KRW in the tenth decile.

Equivalized reductions in existing social assistance benefits are larger in the lower income deciles. In the first decile, the replacement of existing public transfers amounts to 3,140 thousand KRW, the largest reduction observed. As income deciles increase, however, benefit reductions gradually diminish, falling below 1 million KRW from the fourth decile onward.

Combining equivalized total benefits, tax increases, and reductions in existing benefits, the resulting net benefits (or net burdens) display a clear redistributive pattern across income deciles. From the first through the fifth income deciles, the equivalized net benefit exceeds 3 million KRW, with particularly large gains of more than 4 million KRW observed in the second and third deciles. Substantial net benefits are also maintained in the sixth and seventh deciles, exceeding 2 million KRW and 1 million KRW, respectively. In the eighth decile, the net effect becomes nearly neutral at –180 thousand KRW, while in the ninth and tenth deciles it shifts to net burdens of –2,680 thousand KRW and –10,570 thousand KRW, respectively.

Examining the ratio of equivalized net benefits to equivalized disposable income further clarifies the intensity of income-decile–specific redistribution effects. In the first decile, the equivalized net benefit amounts to 32.8% of pre-BI equivalized disposable income, representing a very large share. Substantial gains are also observed in the second and third deciles, at 21.6% and 16.3%, respectively. As income rises, this ratio declines steadily—to 8.5% in the fifth decile and 2.5% in the seventh decile—and turns negative at –0.3% in the eighth decile. In the ninth and tenth deciles, the ratios reach –3.9% and –9.9%, respectively. These results show that the comprehensive model substantially increases real disposable income for low-income households while imposing meaningful net burdens on higher-income households. At the same time, even for the highest-income group, the net burden remains below 10%, indicating that the model does not impose excessively large burdens.

The share of net beneficiary households follows a pattern consistent with these findings The share of net beneficiary households exceeds 90%

from the first through the fourth income deciles and remains above 80% in the fifth and sixth deciles. By contrast, the share drops sharply to 50.8% in the eighth decile, and further to 17.7% in the ninth decile and 2.2% in the tenth decile, indicating that most households in the upper income groups become net contributors.

In sum, our model is designed to provide relatively even benefits across income deciles on the benefit side, while progressively strengthening tax increases toward the upper end of the income distribution. As a result, substantial net benefits are concentrated among low-income and lower-middle-income households; the net effect tapers off across the middle of the distribution; and clear burdens accrue to the highest-income households, yielding a progressive redistributive structure.

Next, Table 8.6 presents the income redistribution effects of introducing the comprehensive model of the three programs by households' sociodemographic characteristics, including household size, the household head's gender and age, disability status, and homeownership.

First, when examined by household size, one- and two-person households exhibit a small net burden on average after the introduction of the comprehensive model. For one-person households, total benefits amount to 4,831 thousand KRW, but increases in taxes (3,516 thousand KRW) and reductions in existing social assistance benefits (1,676 thousand KRW) more than offset these gains, resulting in an average net burden of 361 thousand KRW. Likewise, two-person households experience a modest net burden of 99 thousand KRW on average, indicating little change relative to the current system. Nevertheless, the median net benefit for both one- and two-person households remains positive, and the shares of net beneficiary households reach 55.5% and 65.7%, respectively, exceeding a majority.

Among households with three or more members, net benefits increase clearly as household size grows. Three-person households shift to a net benefit of 401 thousand KRW, which rises to 1,435 thousand KRW for four-person households and expands substantially to 4,648 thousand KRW for households with five or more members. In particular, for households with five or more members, the average equivalized net benefit amounts to approximately 10.5% of equivalized disposable income, and the share of net beneficiary households is exceptionally high at 87.5%. This pattern contrasts with the current social assistance system, which tends to favor smaller households and disadvantage larger ones.

Differences also emerge by the gender of the household head. Male-headed households record an average equivalized net benefit of

**Table 8.6** Income Redistribution Effects by Household Type and Sociodemographic Characteristics (Unit: 10,000 KRW, %)

| *Household Type* | *Household Disposable Income* | *Total Benefits under the Comprehensive Model* | *Increase in Household Taxes* | *Reduction in Existing Benefits* | *New Household Disposable Income* | *Net Household Benefit* | *Share of Net Beneficiaries* |
|---|---|---|---|---|---|---|---|
| One-person household | 2903.8 | 483.1 | 351.6 | 167.6 | 2867.7 | –36.1 | 55.5% |
| Two-person household | 3986.6 | 665.5 | 528.2 | 147.2 | 3976.7 | –9.9 | 65.7% |
| Three-person household | 4880.5 | 827.0 | 699.4 | 87.6 | 4920.6 | 40.1 | 66.5% |
| Four-person household | 5179.1 | 1022.9 | 814.2 | 65.3 | 5322.6 | 143.5 | 70.4% |
| Five-or-more-person household | 4526.0 | 1247.7 | 671.6 | 111.3 | 4990.9 | 464.8 | 87.5% |
| Male-headed household | 4704.6 | 869.9 | 693.7 | 95.6 | 4785.3 | 80.7 | 67.2% |
| Female-headed household | 3380.3 | 710.0 | 416.9 | 164.4 | 3509.1 | 128.8 | 72.1% |
| Adult-headed household | 4764.5 | 867.1 | 706.6 | 64.1 | 4860.9 | 96.4 | 67.7% |
| Elderly-headed household | 3361.2 | 745.3 | 411.4 | 271.5 | 3423.7 | 62.5 | 69.5% |
| Household with a disabled head | 3825.6 | 867.8 | 478.0 | 195.2 | 4020.3 | 194.6 | 77.7% |
| Household with a non-disabled head | 4555.4 | 837.9 | 666.8 | 96.1 | 4630.4 | 75.0 | 66.8% |
| Non-homeowner household | 3757.8 | 808.2 | 484.0 | 130.9 | 3951.2 | 193.3 | 75.4% |
| Homeowner household | 4838.4 | 858.7 | 727.7 | 95.9 | 4873.5 | 35.1 | 64.3% |

Note: Household disposable income refers to household income including imputed rental income, equivalized by household size. All other measures are also expressed in equivalized terms.

807 thousand KRW, with 67.2% classified as net beneficiaries. Female-headed households experience larger gains, with an average equivalized net benefit of 1,288 thousand KRW and a higher share of net beneficiaries at 72.1%.

With respect to the age of the household head, adult-headed households exhibit slightly larger net benefits than elderly-headed households. The average equivalized net benefit for adult-headed households is 964 thousand KRW (about 2.0% of equivalized disposable income), compared with 625 thousand KRW (about 1.9%) for elderly-headed households. Among elderly-headed households, smaller household size leads to somewhat lower benefit amounts, while reductions in existing social assistance, including the Basic Pension, are relatively larger; as a result, net benefits are smaller despite relatively modest tax increases. In terms of beneficiary shares, however, elderly-headed households show a slightly higher proportion of net beneficiaries (69.5%) than adult-headed households (67.7%).

Next, considering disability status, households headed by a person with a disability experience relatively large net benefits under our model. Their average equivalized net benefit amounts to 1,946 thousand KRW, substantially exceeding the 750 thousand KRW observed for households headed by a non-disabled individual. The share of net beneficiary households is also higher among disabled-headed households (77.7%) than among non-disabled-headed households (66.8%).

Finally, with respect to homeownership, non-homeowner households benefit more than homeowner households. Non-homeowner households record an average equivalized net benefit of 1,933 thousand KRW, with 75.4% classified as net beneficiaries. In contrast, homeowner households experience a much smaller average equivalized net benefit of 351 thousand KRW, and the share of net beneficiaries is lower at 64.3%.

Taken together, the results in Table 8.6 indicate that our model generates differentiated redistribution effects by sociodemographic characteristics. It delivers stronger redistributive effects for households with larger sizes and for groups with relatively vulnerable sociodemographic characteristics—particularly female-headed households, households headed by persons with disabilities, and non-homeowner households.

Figure 8.4 compares the redistributive effects of the comprehensive model that combines the three basic income programs with the overall redistributive effects of the existing social security system. Using equivalized market income quintiles that include imputed rent, the figure contrasts market income, current disposable income under the existing

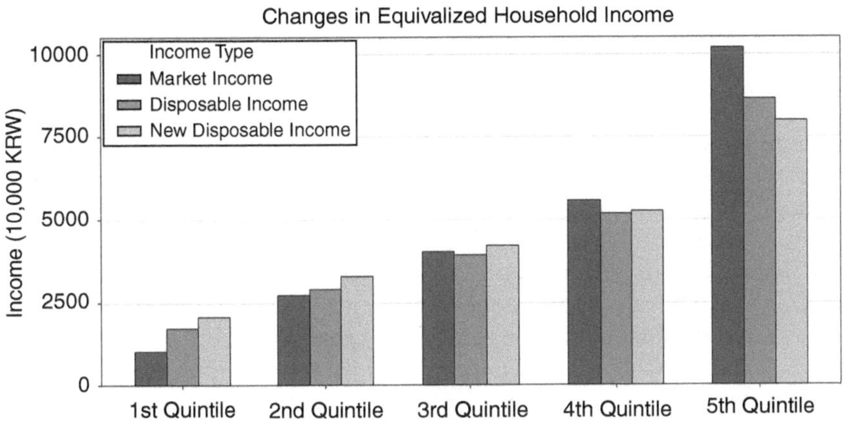


**Fig. 8.4** Combined Effects of the Three Basic Income Programs: Comparison with the Existing Social Security System by Equivalized Market Income Quintile (Including Imputed Rent)

system, and disposable income after the introduction of the comprehensive model.[4] This figure shows that while the current social security system makes only low-income groups net beneficiaries, the proposed model extends net beneficiary status to the middle-income groups as well. In addition, our model increases the contribution of high-income groups relative to the current system, thereby achieving a greater reduction in income inequality.

In the first quintile, equivalized household market income amounts to only 10,249 thousand KRW, but current disposable income rises to 17,246 thousand KRW, and further increases to 20,726 thousand KRW after the introduction of our model. In the second quintile, equivalized disposable income increases from 29,019 thousand KRW under the current system to 32,953 thousand KRW after our model is implemented, compared with an equivalized market income of 27,195 thousand KRW. In the third quintile, current equivalized disposable income (39,218 thousand KRW) is

[4] Appendix Table 8.A2 presents the same comparison of redistributive effects between the current system and our proposed model by income decile, based on equivalized household market income including imputed rent, extending the analysis shown in this figure. Appendix Table 8.A3 presents the corresponding results by income decile based on equivalized household market income excluding imputed rent.

lower than equivalized market income (40,292 thousand KRW), whereas our proposed model raises equivalized disposable income to 42,094 thousand KRW, exceeding equivalized market income. In the fourth quintile, our model increases equivalized disposable income relative to the current system, although it remains below equivalized market income. Compared with the existing social security system, our proposed model not only substantially improves disposable income for low-income households but also delivers meaningful gains to middle-income households. By contrast, in the highest quintile, equivalized market income is 101,882 thousand KRW and current equivalized disposable income is 86,327 thousand KRW, while equivalized disposable income under our proposed model declines further to 79,720 thousand KRW. This clearly illustrates that our model places a greater contribution burden on high-income households than the current system, thereby enhancing its overall redistributive effect.

Figure 8.5 compares the effects of the Seoul "Stepping Stone (*Didimdol*) Income" Program when implemented nationwide with the proposed model based on equivalized disposable income (excluding imputed rent). The Stepping Stone Income Program operates as a

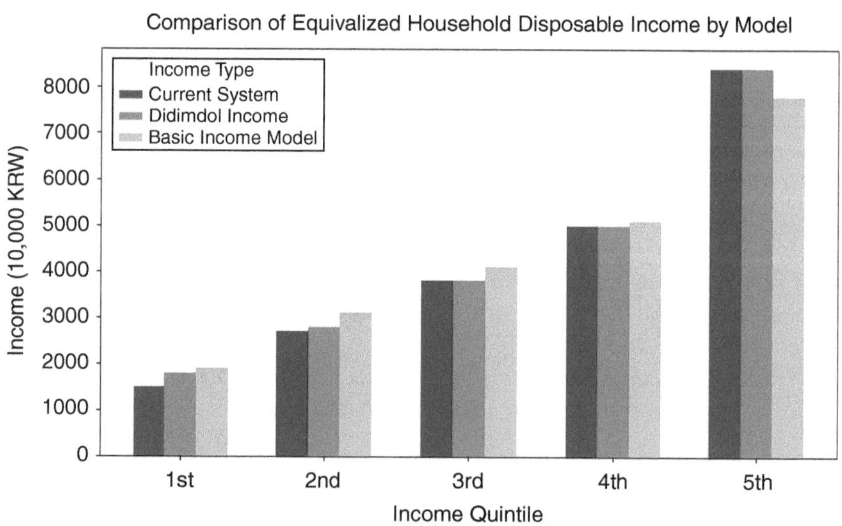


**Fig. 8.5** Comparison of Income Redistribution Effects with the Stepping Stone Income (*Didimdol* Income) Program

household-based negative income tax scheme, with a threshold income set at 85% of the standard median income, a guaranteed income at 42.5% of the standard median income, and a clawback rate of 50%; no additional taxation is imposed on households with income above the threshold income. Similarly to our NIT-type basic income model, it replaces cash benefits from major social assistance programs such as the National Basic Livelihood Security and the Basic Pension. Because imputed rent is not included in the income definition used for Stepping Stone Income, we adopt the same income definition—excluding imputed rent—when comparing our policy with the Stepping Stone Income program.

In the first quintile, current equivalized disposable income amounts to 14,630 thousand KRW, rising to 17,810 thousand KRW with the introduction of Stepping Stone Income and further to 18,440 thousand KRW under our proposed model. In the second quintile, equivalized disposable income under Stepping Stone Income increases only modestly to 27,750 thousand KRW relative to the current system, whereas it rises substantially to 31,300 thousand KRW under our model. Similarly, in the third quintile, Stepping Stone Income leaves equivalized disposable income largely unchanged from the current level (37,760 thousand KRW), while our model produces a meaningful increase to 40,350 thousand KRW. The difference persists in the fourth quintile, a middle-income group: Stepping Stone Income maintains equivalized disposable income at roughly the current level (about 50,160 thousand KRW), whereas our model provides an additional, albeit modest, improvement to 50,710 thousand KRW. These patterns suggest that, whereas Stepping Stone Income is a selective income-support scheme with effects concentrated on the lowest-income group, our model generates continuous income improvements extending to the lower-middle and middle-income groups.

By contrast, in the highest (fifth) quintile based on equivalized disposable income, the two systems diverge sharply. Stepping Stone Income maintains equivalized disposable income at the current level (83,910 thousand KRW), imposing no additional burden on high-income households. Under our model, however, it declines to 77,560 thousand KRW.

In sum, our comprehensive model that combines the three basic income programs produces a clearly progressive redistributive effect across the entire income distribution. Importantly, redistribution is not confined to the lowest-income group but extends continuously to the lower-middle and middle-income groups, distinguishing our model from approaches centered on narrowly targeted income support. On the benefit side, relatively similar benefit amounts are provided across income deciles, while tax burdens increase progressively with income. As a result, low- and middle-income groups become net beneficiaries, whereas high-income groups become net contributors—achieving universality in benefits alongside progressivity in burdens (See Appendix Table 8.A4 for further details).

Moreover, the sociodemographic analysis indicates that our model delivers differentiated redistributive effects not only by income level but also by household structure and social vulnerability. The tendency for net benefits to increase with household size and to be larger among relatively vulnerable groups—such as female-headed households, households headed by persons with disabilities, and non-homeowner households—suggests that our model operates in a manner that preserves universality while providing stronger cushioning effects for groups facing greater social risks. Accordingly, our proposed model should be understood not merely as a poverty-alleviation policy, but as a comprehensive basic income package that simultaneously promotes income stability for lower and middle strata and reduces overall inequality across society.

### *Effects of Each Basic Income Program on Inequality and Poverty Indices*

In the preceding section, we examined the income redistribution effects of the three basic income programs—the common wealth dividend basic income, the Negative Income Tax-type basic income, and the Universal Earned Income Tax Credit—as well as the comprehensive model that implements all three programs simultaneously. The analysis focused on the magnitude of net benefits or net burdens by income group and by sociodemographic characteristics. In this section, we compare the impacts of each individual program and the comprehensive model on the income distribution using more official inequality and poverty indices. To ensure comparability with the current system and the Stepping Stone Income Program, all indices when the basic income programs are implemented are measured using an income definition that excludes imputed rent. Table 8.7 presents a comprehensive comparison of inequality- and poverty-reducing effects using a range of indicators for the Common wealth dividends basic income, the Negative Income Tax-type basic income, the Universal Earned Income Tax Credit, the comprehensive model combining the three programs, and the Stepping Stone Income program. As shown in the table, all three basic income programs, as well as Stepping Stone Income, operate in a direction that mitigates inequality and poverty relative to the current

**Table 8.7** Comparison of Income Redistribution and Poverty Alleviation Effects by Program

| *Inequality and Poverty Indicators* | *Under the Current System (as of 2023)* | *Common wealth Dividends Basic Income* | *NIT-type Basic Income* | *UEITC* | *Comprehensive Model* | *Stepping Stone Income* |
|---|---|---|---|---|---|---|
| Gini Coefficient | 0.3233 | 0.3149 | 0.2884 | 0.3177 | 0.2732 | 0.3056 |
| Quintile Ratio | 5.74 | 5.45 | 4.65 | 5.62 | 4.31 | 4.76 |
| Decile Ratio | 11.09 | 9.20 | 7.59 | 9.74 | 7.33 | 7.21 |
| Top 1% Income Share | 4.01% | 3.90% | 3.55% | 3.93% | 3.35% | 3.94% |
| Top 10% Income Share | 25.24% | 24.71% | 20.94% | 24.83% | 22.35% | 24.84% |
| Middle 40% Income Share | 51.19% | 51.14% | 50.71% | 51.24% | 50.66% | 50.37% |
| Bottom 50% Income Share | 23.58% | 24.16% | 25.95% | 23.94% | 27.00% | 24.81% |
| Headcount Ratio | 14.91 | 14.15 | 12.20 | 14.71 | 11.54 | 10.84 |
| Poverty Gap | 32.80 | 32.25 | 29.93 | 34.01 | 29.99 | 22.33 |
| Headcount Ratio among Those Aged 66 and Over | 39.90 | 39.52 | 37.37 | 39.98 | 37.51 | 33.63 |
| Poverty Gap among Those Aged 66 and Over | 35.36 | 34.52 | 32.42 | 36.81 | 31.59 | 22.98 |

Note: In this table, the indices for the basic income programs are calculated using a definition of income that excludes imputed rent income. When an income definition that includes imputed rent income is applied to the comprehensive model, the results show further improvements in inequality and poverty indices, with a Gini coefficient of 0.2703, a headcount ratio of 10.90, a poverty gap of 28.97, an elderly headcount ratio (aged 66 and over) of 35.21, and an elderly poverty gap of 30.12.

system. However, there are clear differences in the magnitude and nature of their effects. Among the three basic income programs, the Negative Income Tax-type basic income produces the largest improvements across most inequality and poverty indices, and the comprehensive model further amplifies these effects.

First, the Gini coefficient, which summarizes overall inequality, based on current disposable income stands at 0.3233. The NIT-type basic income lowers the Gini coefficient substantially to 0.2884, while the comprehensive model further reduces it to 0.2732, indicating a very strong inequality-reducing effect. This is comparable to that of Norway (0.285 in 2021 and 0.262 in 2022) and Finland (0.274 in 2022 and 0.269 in 2023), and is lower than both the OECD average (0.319 in 2022) and Sweden (0.289 in 2023). Stepping Stone Income also lowers the Gini coefficient to 0.3056, but the magnitude of improvement is smaller than that achieved by the NIT-type basic income or the comprehensive model.

A similar pattern emerges for the quintile and decile share ratios, which capture income gaps across the distribution. Under the current system, the quintile share ratio is 5.74 and the decile share ratio is 11.09, reflecting very large disparities between upper and lower income groups. The NIT-type basic income substantially lowers the ratios to 4.65 and 7.59, and the comprehensive model achieves the largest reductions, to 4.31 and 7.33. Likewise, Stepping Stone Income reduces the ratios to 4.76 and 7.21.

Differences in the profile of each program become even clearer when examining income share indicators. Under the current system, the income shares of the top 1% and top 10% are 4.01% and 25.24%, respectively. The NIT-type basic income reduces these to 3.93% and 24.38%, while the comprehensive model lowers them substantially further to 3.35% and 22.35%. By contrast, under the Stepping Stone Income Program, the magnitude of the reduction is negligible.

The income share of the bottom 50% rises from 23.58% under the current system to 25.95% under the NIT-type basic income, while it increases most strongly to 27.00% under the comprehensive model. Under Stepping Stone Income, the bottom -50% share shows a modest improvement to 24.81%

Poverty outcomes are examined using improvements in the headcount ratio and the poverty gap. The headcount ratio measures the proportion of individuals living in households below the poverty line—defined as 50% of the median equivalized disposable income—within the total population, and is useful for identifying the overall structure and extent of poverty. In contrast, the poverty gap indicates how far the average income of poor households falls below the poverty line, making it an appropriate indicator for assessing the depth or severity of poverty.

The headcount ratio declines substantially from 14.91 under the current system to 12.20 under the NIT-type basic income, with a further improvement to 11.54 under the comprehensive model, which is comparable to the OECD average (11.5 in 2022). Stepping Stone Income records the lowest headcount ratio at 10.84, indicating the largest poverty-reducing effect among the programs.

A similar pattern is observed for the poverty gap. From 32.80 under the current system, it declines to 29.93 under the NIT-type basic income and to 29.99 under the comprehensive model, while the Stepping Stone Income Program achieves the largest improvement, reducing the poverty gap to 22.33. These differences are repeated for elderly poverty indices. Under the current system, the poverty rate among those aged 66 and over stands at a very high level of 39.90, with a poverty gap of 35.36. The NIT-type basic income and the comprehensive model moderately reduce the elderly poverty rate and poverty gap to 37.51 and 31.59, respectively, while the Stepping Stone Income Program shows a relatively larger effect, lowering the elderly poverty rate to 33.63 and the poverty gap to 22.98.The aforementioned inequality and poverty indices for each basic income program and for the comprehensive model are measured following the conventional practice of excluding imputed rent from the definition of income. When an income definition that includes imputed rent is applied, the overall effects on reducing inequality and poverty become more pronounced. For example, under the comprehensive model, the Gini coefficient improves to 0.2703, the headcount ratio to 10.90 (35.21 for the elderly), and the poverty gap to 28.97 (30.12 for the elderly).

Even though our model provides a higher guaranteed income for the elderly than for adults, its impact on reducing elderly poverty is limited, and the elderly headcount ratio under the Stepping Stone Income Program remains above 30%, indicating that meaningful reductions in elderly poverty require stronger old-age income security, including improved public pension coverage. The UEITC—by supporting social insurance contributions including National Pension premiums—may indirectly contribute to reducing elderly poverty over time by reducing blind spots and enhancing the real income replacement rates, with effects expected to grow gradually.

Taken together, the evidence from a wide range of inequality and poverty indices shows that the common wealth dividends basic income and the UEITC produce gradual, moderate improvements across the income distribution, whereas the NIT-type basic income and the comprehensive model generate strong redistributive effects that meaningfully reshape the inequality structure itself. By contrast, the Stepping Stone Income Program clearly exhibits relatively stronger improvements in poverty alleviation than in inequality indicators..

## 8.2 Effects on Freedom and Sustainable Efficiency

In Chapter 5, we pointed out several fundamental problems of the current social assistance system: the unfairness arising from income reversals between beneficiaries and non-beneficiaries; the suppression of work incentives due to excessively high participation tax rates and marginal effective tax rates; the resulting de facto restriction on freedom of labor choice that makes it difficult to escape poverty through work and fosters welfare dependency; and the incentives the system creates for household dissolution. In this section, we examine the extent to which our basic income model alleviates these problems.

Figure 8.6 presents simulation results, using the OECD Tax-Benefit Calculator (Korea, based on 2022 income), showing how disposable income (net income) changes as gross earned income increases for a four-person household consisting of a single-earner couple with two children. The figure compares outcomes under the current system (left panel) and under the implementation of the three proposed basic income programs (right panel, thick line), for both households that receive all major social assistance benefits and those that do not receive social assistance other than child allowances and the work incentive payment. The x-axis plots household earned income as a percentage of the average monthly wage (4,338 thousand KRW), while the y-axis shows household disposable income (in thousand KRW).

The left panel illustrates that under the current system there is a substantial income reversal between social assistance recipient households (net w/ SA) and non-recipient households (net w/o SA). By contrast, the right panel shows that when our basic income model is implemented, disposable income increases markedly for previously non-recipient low-income households. For households with zero earned income, disposable income rises from 492 thousand KRW to 2,196 thousand KRW. Although

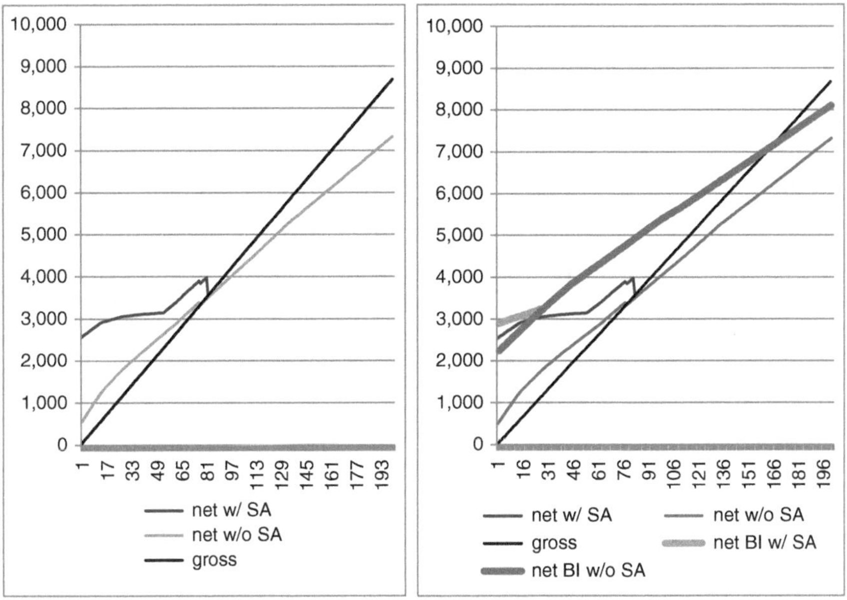


**Fig. 8.6** Disposable Income by Labor Income for a Single-Earner Couple with Two Children (Four-Person Household): Comparison of Current Beneficiaries, Non-Beneficiaries, and Our Basic Income Model (for Both Former Beneficiaries and Non-Beneficiaries). *Notes*: This household is assumed to have no income other than labor income and no assets. The x-axis shows total labor income ranging from 1% to 200% of the average wage in 2022 (4,337,964 KRW). The y-axis indicates disposable income. "Gross" refers to total labor income (gross wages). "Net w/ SA" denotes disposable income under the current system when all major social assistance benefits are received. "Net w/o SA" denotes disposable income when no social assistance is received except child allowances and the work incentive payment. "Net BI w/ SA" and "net BI w/o SA" denote disposable income when all three proposed basic income programs are implemented, for former social assistance beneficiaries (w/ SA) and non-beneficiaries (w/o SA), respectively. Source: Data from the OECD Tax-Benefit Calculator (gross, net w/ SA) and the authors' simulations based on these data (net w/o SA, net BI w/ SA, net BI w/o SA)

the rate of increase in disposable income gradually diminishes as earned income rises, disposable income continues to increase up to 200% of the average wage. For existing recipient households, the increase in disposable income is relatively modest in the very low-income range but becomes substantial in the lower-middle-income range. In particular, at 82% of the average wage (3,557 thousand KRW per month)—the point at which housing benefits under the National Basic Livelihood Security System are phased out—disposable income increases by 1,417 thousand KRW (from 3,506 thousand KRW to 4,923 thousand KRW), after which the rate of increase gradually tapers off.

Under the current system, net benefits accrue only to the very lowest-income group. In contrast, our basic income model generates net benefits even for lower-middle-income households, resulting in negative effective tax rates, whereby disposable income increases by more than earned income. Specifically, under the current system, the effective tax rate for a single-earner four-person household remains negative only up to 81% of the average wage, turning positive at 82%. Under our basic income model, however, the effective tax rate remains negative up to 164% of the average wage (7,114 thousand KRW per month), turning positive only at 165% or above. Although the figure does not display income levels beyond 200% of the average wage, the slopes of the disposable income curves indicate that at higher income levels, disposable income under our basic income model would fall below that under the current system.

As discussed in Chapter 5, the current system's very high asset-to-income conversion rates result in many low-income individuals being deemed ineligible for social assistance, while others who are eligible refrain from applying due to stigma or administrative barriers. This leads to unfair income reversals between beneficiaries and low-income non-beneficiaries, a phenomenon clearly illustrated in the left panel by the stark gap in disposable income between recipient households and non-recipient households (net w/o SA). The NIT-type basic income partially replaces existing social assistance benefits when its payment level is lower than those benefits, ensuring that current beneficiaries are not made worse off. Consequently, under our basic income model shown in the right panel, final disposable income differs between recipient and non-recipient households only up to 27% of the average wage. From 28% upward, the difference disappears entirely, and even below 27% the gap is substantially reduced. At zero earned income, disposable income under the current system is 2,545 thousand KRW for recipient households and 492 thousand KRW for non-recipient households—a large gap of 2,052 thousand KRW. With our basic income model in place, disposable income becomes 2,883 thousand KRW for former recipient households and 2,196 thousand KRW for former non-recipient households, reducing the gap to 687 thousand KRW. Thus, while our proposed model does not completely eliminate disparities between recipients and non-recipients, it substantially mitigates the problem and significantly reduces both the share of the population dependent on social assistance and the degree of such dependence.

Under the current system, income reversals occur not only between recipients and non-recipients but also between recipients and the near-poor. These reversals disappear entirely under our basic income model. For example, under the current system, at 81% of the average wage (3,514 thousand KRW) recipients have disposable income of 3,978 thousand KRW, but at 82%, when all cash benefits including housing assistance are withdrawn, disposable income falls to 3,506 thousand KRW, and remains at only 3,976 thousand KRW even at 96% of the average wage (4,164 thousand KRW). Under our proposed model, however, disposable income at 81%, 82%, and 96% of the average wage is 4,894 thousand KRW, 4,923 thousand KRW, and 5,324 thousand KRW, respectively, rising steadily with earned income.

The reason why income reversals, in which disposable income declines even as earned income rises, occur under the current system is that there are income ranges in which the effective marginal tax rate (EMTR) exceeds 100%. The left panel of Fig. 8.7 shows the EMTR as a function of earned income for the single-earner head in the four-person household discussed above. Under the current system, a single-earner social assistance recipient faces an EMTR of 216% at 76% of the average wage, and an extraordinarily high 1,189% at 81% of the average wage, implying that increases in earned income actually reduce disposable income. In the income range between 27% and 52% of the average wage, the EMTR exceeds 90%, so disposable income barely increases even when earned income rises. Such extremely high EMTRs restrict freedom of labor choice and weaken work incentives, thereby reducing labor supply and generating economic inefficiency, including deadweight losses.

By contrast, under our basic income model, existing social assistance recipients are allowed to retain their social assistance benefits. As a result, in the very low-income range up to 25% of the average wage, EMTRs remain relatively high—above 60%—but beyond this range they are generally much lower. For previously non-recipient households,

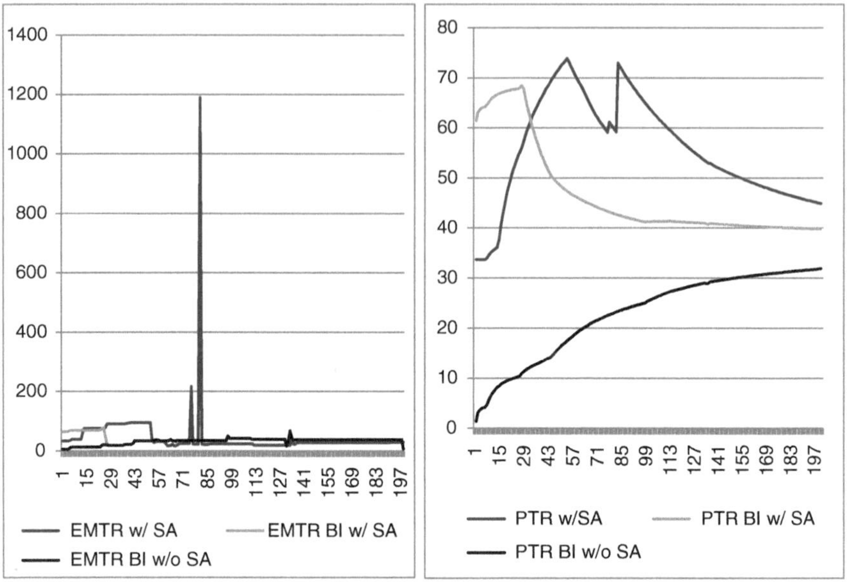


**Fig. 8.7** Effective Marginal Tax Rates and Participation Tax Rates by Earned Income for a One-Earner Couple with Two Children: Effective Marginal Tax Rates (EMTR, left panel) and Participation Tax Rates (PTR, right panel) for Current Social Assistance Recipients (w/ SA) and, Under the Basic Income Policies, Former Recipients (BI w/ SA) and Non-Recipients (BI w/o SA)

EMTRs remain low across all income levels. In our model, the NIT-type basic income imposes a tax (withdrawal) rate of 10%, while a UEITC of 12%—equivalent to a −12% tax rate—is provided up to five-sixths of the average income. As a result, low-income employed individuals, including both wage earners and the self-employed, face an effective tax rate of −2%, thereby reducing EMTRs relative to the current system. Even for middle- and higher-income groups, a relatively low tax rate of 10% applies. Accordingly, concerns and criticisms that basic income or negative income tax schemes may reduce labor supply and thus hinder economic growth due to high effective marginal tax rates do not apply to our model. Moreover, because the guaranteed income level in our model is not high, any labor supply disincentives arising from income effects are likely to be negligible or minimal.[5]

Equally important for freedom of labor choice and work incentives is the participation tax rate (PTR). While the effective marginal tax rate influences the decision of whether to increase labor hours in order to earn additional income, a high participation tax rate affects the decision of whether to engage in paid work at all. If disposable income increases little compared to non-employment, the incentive to participate in paid labor is severely weakened.

As shown in the right panel of Fig. 8.7, under the current system the single-earner head in a four-person household faces a PTR exceeding 60% over the income range from 31% to 110% of the average wage. In particular, between 82% and 87% of the average wage, the PTR exceeds 70%. Under our basic income model, PTRs for previously non-recipient low-income households start at very low levels and increase gradually: they remain below 20% up to 62% of the average wage, below 30% up to 149%, and even beyond that remain below 32% up to 200% of the average wage.

[5] Recent work by Chang et al. (2024) suggests that, in light of labor supply and economic growth considerations, the optimal basic income corresponds to 7.2% of average income with a tax rate of 8%, while the optimal negative income tax entails a guaranteed income equal to 19.5% of average income combined with an 8% tax rate on income above the 40th percentile. The authors caution that excessively high guaranteed income levels or excessively high tax rates may adversely affect labor supply and economic growth. By contrast, our model provides a universal basic income equivalent to 5% of average income for adults and a guaranteed income equal to 10% of average income. It applies an effective tax rate of −2% to low-income workers—reflecting a 10% withdrawal rate offset by a 12% Universal Earned Income Tax Credit—and a relatively low tax rate of 10% to individuals with above-average incomes. In this way, our model pursues economic efficiency through more moderate guaranteed income levels and lower tax rates than those implied by the optimal models proposed by Chang et al(2024). Moreover, the analysis by Chang et al.(2024) does not incorporate demand-expansion effects arising from fiscal multipliers. Once such demand-side effects are taken into account, our model is expected to exert a substantially more positive impact on economic growth. Meanwhile, a study by Lee (2025) examining the labor supply effects of the basic income proposal pledged by presidential candidate Lee Jae-myung during South Korea's 2022 election finds that the policy has negligible negative effects on currently employed individuals, while it increases labor market participation among those who were previously not employed.

For existing social assistance recipients, however, PTRs remain above 60% up to 33% of the average wage, and below 32% of the average wage they are even higher than under the current system. Beyond this point, PTRs gradually decline. Under the current system, PTRs above 50% persist up to 153% of the average wage, whereas under our basic income model PTRs fall below 50% from 45% of the average wage onward, and below 40% beyond 184% of the average wage.

Next, we consider the incentive effects on household formation and dissolution. As discussed in Chapter 5, under the current system households can enjoy substantially higher disposable income with the same earned income if they dissolve, while household formation—such as marriage—can reduce disposable income, thereby creating disincentives for household formation. By contrast, all of our basic income programs operate on an individual basis, so disposable income does not change as a result of household formation or dissolution.

Consider a scenario in which a one-earner four-person household receiving social assistance engages in a sham divorce: the single earner formally becomes a one-person household, while the non-working spouse forms a separate three-person household with the two young children. Figure 8.8 assumes that after the sham divorce the non-working spouse remains out of employment and relies entirely on social assistance, while the former household head works as a one-person household from 1% to 100% of full-time employment at the average wage, so that earned income gradually increases. The figure shows how the sum of disposable incomes of the two separated households compares with the disposable income of the original four-person household under the current system and under our basic income model. Under our basic income model, there is no difference between pre- and post-separation outcomes: the sum of disposable incomes conditional on earned income is identical before and after household separation (net BI w/ SA). By contrast, under the current system, the combined disposable income of the two separated households (Separated 1+3) becomes larger than the disposable income of the original four-person household (net w/ SA), and even exceeds the disposable income under our basic income model (net BI w/ SA). If the former household head earns 100% of the average wage (4,338 thousand KRW per month) after separation, the combined disposable income of the non-working three-person household and the one-person working household reaches 5,979 thousand KRW, which is 1,870 thousand KRW (or 45.5%) higher than the 4,109 thousand KRW received before separation. This constitutes a strong economic incentive

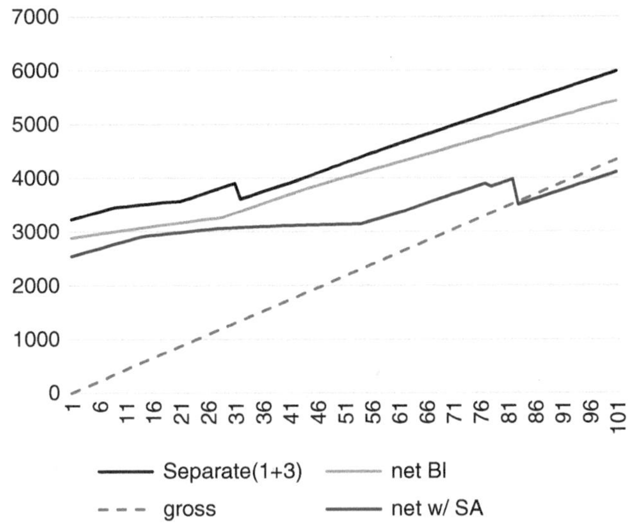


**Fig. 8.8** Changes in Disposable Income by Earned Income When a Single-Earner Four-Person Social Assistance Household Separates into a One-Person Household and a Three-Person Non-Earning Household, Under the Current System and Under Our Basic Income System. Note: Separated (1+3) refers to the case under the current system in which the household separates into a one-person household and a three-person non-earning household. Net w/ SA denotes the case in which the household remains a four-person household under the current system. Net BI denotes the case under our basic income model, which yields the same disposable income whether the household remains a four-person household or separates into a one-person household and a three-person non-earning household

for household dissolution. The current social assistance system, by creating marriage penalties and incentives for household breakup, may therefore contribute to reinforcing low fertility.[6]

[6] We also conducted a preliminary analysis of the participation tax rate, effective marginal tax rate, and incentives for household formation and dissolution under the Seoul Stepping Stone Income Program. As expected, participation tax rates and effective marginal tax rates are not as extremely high as those observed under the current system, but they remain substantially elevated. As a result, the income effect generated by the high guaranteed income, combined with the substitution effect, is likely to create significant disincentives to labor supply. Empirical evidence from an evaluation of the Stepping Stone Income pilot by Lee

As discussed above, our basic income model is capable of addressing several fundamental problems inherent in the current social assistance system: the unfairness arising from income reversals between beneficiaries and non-beneficiaries; the suppression of work incentives due to excessively high participation tax rates and effective marginal tax rates, which in practice restrict freedom of labor choice and trap individuals in poverty; and the incentives for household dissolution created by household-based benefit designs.

In conclusion, although the guaranteed income level under our basic income model is not particularly high, it generates substantial redistributive effects that reduce income inequality to levels comparable to those observed in Nordic countries. By maintaining low participation tax rates and effective marginal tax rates, our model preserves work incentives and, as discussed in Chapter 7, enhances the long-term sustainability of social security finances in the context of population aging, thereby contributing positively to long-run economic growth. At the very least, it is unlikely to produce adverse economic effects. In particular, the UEITC is expected to encourage labor supply among low-income workers through a de facto wage increase, to reduce incentives for underreporting business income, and to narrow blind spots in social insurance coverage through the automatic linkage of social insurance contributions to reported income, thereby generating synergistic effects between employment promotion and the strengthening of social protection. Although the guaranteed income floor may not be sufficient on its own, it nonetheless provides a minimum income base, while social insurance further enables income maintenance and consumption smoothing over the life course. Moreover, our model eliminates the unfair income reversals that arise at eligibility thresholds between social assistance recipients and non-recipients, removes welfare dependency incentives and poverty traps, and promotes unconditional minimum income security without social stigma. By guaranteeing a basic income floor while dismantling poverty traps, our proposed model enhances real freedom for all individuals.

et al. (2025) supports this prediction, showing that household heads in the treatment group experienced a 13.8 percentage point reduction in labor supply relative to those in the control group. Although that study does not analyze incentives for household dissolution, the generous household-based benefit structure, which becomes more advantageous as household size decreases, can be expected to generate substantial marriage penalties and incentives for household breakup.

In addition, a carbon and renewable energy dividends basic income can facilitate a desirable energy transition and enhance ecological sustainability in response to the climate crisis. By eliminating marriage penalties and household dissolution incentives inherent in household and needs-based social assistance, the policy also encourages marriage and household formation, reduces the financial burden of childrearing, and may contribute to higher fertility rates. Beyond population decline, it is expected to strengthen demographic sustainability in Korea, particularly in rural and fishing communities facing the risk of depopulation. Ultimately, our model is expected to simultaneously advance freedom, equality, and sustainable efficiency.

CHAPTER 9

# Political Feasibility

Chapter 7 confirmed that our basic income policy is both fiscally and administratively feasible. In this chapter, we examine the political feasibility of our proposed model and suggest measures to enhance it. If fiscal and administrative viability are considered necessary conditions for realizing basic income, political feasibility can be viewed as the sufficient condition.

As demonstrated in Chapter 8, our policy ensures that the majority—approximately 70% of the population, including both low- and middle-income groups—becomes net beneficiaries, while only the top 30% act as net contributors. According to the Median Voter Theorem, a policy should be politically viable if it benefits the majority, including the median voter. Furthermore, one might anticipate that once introduced, political support would expand over time, allowing the system to evolve from a modest beginning into a more robust framework.

However, an optimistic outlook based solely on the Median Voter Theorem is not guaranteed. First, potential net beneficiaries may not accurately perceive their gains. Fear of tax increases or the reduction of existing social security benefits can overshadow the expected advantages. Some may also oppose basic income due to deep-seated beliefs in traditional needs-based welfare. As basic income becomes a prominent political issue, opponents will likely exploit these fears through strategic issue framing.



J. S. You et al., *UBI from Idea to Reality*, Exploring the Basic Income Guarantee,
https://doi.org/10.1007/978-3-032-26200-4_9

Second, even if a majority of voters support basic income, it does not ensure legislative success. Empirical research suggests that on issues of conflicting economic interests, the preferences of elites and vested interest groups often exert a greater influence on policy than those of the median voter. These groups not only shape public opinion but also intensify lobbying efforts toward political parties and leaders. Conversely, basic income supporters face significant organizational challenges, making it difficult to overcome the status quo bias.

Due to these factors, securing a firm majority of public support and overcoming the political influence of opponents remains a daunting task. Political parties or leaders who champion basic income may adopt ambiguous stances or retract their promises once it becomes a contentious electoral issue or after they ascend to power.

This chapter first explores the potential for broad political support based on the Median Voter Theorem. Subsequently, we examine the theoretical counter-arguments and existing literature regarding political obstacles. We will then analyze the shifts in South Korean public opinion on basic income over recent years, focusing on the dynamics of issue framing and the responses of political actors. Building on this analysis, the chapter concludes by proposing strategic measures for the basic income movement to secure majority support and compel political parties and politicians to actually implement the policy.

## 9.1 Optimistic Outlook Based on the Median Voter Theorem

According to the Median Voter Theorem, policies that provide net benefits to a majority of the population possess high political feasibility and tend to maintain long-term support. This explains why universal welfare programs often survive and remain resilient even during periods of welfare retrenchment, whereas selective programs are more vulnerable to cuts (Pierson, 1994).

### *70% of the Population as Net Beneficiaries*

Our model is designed so that approximately 70% of the total population becomes net beneficiaries. Under a democratic system where voters act rationally to maximize their economic interest, such a policy has a strong path to implementation. Unlike traditional social assistance, which only increases the real income of the lowest-income brackets, our proposal enhances the real income of the vast majority of the middle class, creating a powerful democratic mandate through the median voter mechanism.

Based on our simulations using 2023 data, 68.1% of the total population and 66.3% of the voting-age population are net beneficiaries. If we assume that voters make rational choices based on household-level gains—where an individual whose market income exceeds the average may still support the policy because their household (including a spouse and children) benefits overall—we can predict that two out of three voters (66.3%) would support this policy package.

Furthermore, once a basic income policy is introduced and distributions begin, it becomes historically difficult to repeal. A large majority of net beneficiaries transition into powerful "policy advocates" (Pierson, 1994). Examples include the Alaska Permanent Fund Dividend, which has maintained bipartisan support since 1982 despite changes in state leadership, and the enduring support for Social Security and Medicare in the United States. In South Korea, the Basic Pension, which covers two thirds of seniors, continues to expand in benefit levels rather than contract, as no political party dares to risk the backlash of a majority-supported program.

### *The Rise of the "Precariat" Amidst AI Advancements*

Unlike the era of industrial capitalism centered on manufacturing, the post-industrial era is witnessing a global rise in the precariat—workers facing low income and chronic job instability (Standing, 2011). The rapid advancement of Artificial Intelligence (AI) threatens to accelerate this polarization, hollowing out traditional full-time roles and leaving a labor market split between a small group of high-skilled elites and a vast majority of precarious workers.

In South Korea, precarious workers—including temporary and daily laborers, micro-entrepreneurs without employees, unpaid family workers, and platform-based "personal service providers"— account for 40% of the total workforce. As AI substitutes for white-collar jobs—not just blue-collar automation—labor market volatility will intensify. Recent experimental research suggests that white-collar workers who perceive a threat from AI are increasingly supportive of Universal Basic Income (Choi and Kweon, 2025). This growing instability heightens the "insurance motive" among voters. Even those currently acting as net contributors may support basic income as a form of lifelong social insurance that helps smooth consumption and income across their entire life cycle.

Moreover, even the economic elite may support basic income to mitigate social conflict and systemic instability. This is evidenced by the growing support for UBI among Silicon Valley leaders, such as OpenAI's Sam Altman. Just as Bismarck introduced the first social insurance to curb the rise of socialist movements, basic income may eventually be realized as a concession from economic elites to maintain social cohesion in the face of widespread precarious employment.

## 9.2 Factors Hindering Political Feasibility

According to the Median Voter Theorem and rational choice theory, policies that benefit the majority should have a high probability of adoption (Downs, 1957). From this perspective, our proposal—where 70% of voters are net beneficiaries—should naturally gain overwhelming public support and be adopted by political parties.

However, political reality is rarely so straightforward. It is difficult for the general public to process complex policy information and align it with their personal interests and values. History shows that the public sometimes supports policies that contradict their own interests or opposes those that would benefit them. Furthermore, empirical evidence often suggests that economic elites and organized interest groups exert far greater influence over policy outcomes than the median voter. If a significant portion of the 70% net beneficiaries fails to grasp the policy's mechanics, while the 30% net contributors leverage their superior political influence to oppose it, the implementation of basic income becomes a daunting challenge.

**Information Asymmetry and Policy Misperception**: The Bush administration's "tax cuts for the wealthy" serve as a classic example of the public supporting a policy contrary to their own interests. Larry Bartels (2005) found that most Americans supported these cuts not because they were indifferent to inequality, but because they failed to connect public policy with economic disparity or their own material well-being. Despite recognizing that the wealth gap was a problem, they supported regressive tax cuts due to a lack of accurate information and an inability to link the policy to their personal values.

**Elite Influence and Status Quo Bias**: Even when the public understands and supports a policy, it is not always enacted. Gilens and Page (2014) tested four theoretical traditions of American politics and found that while economic elites and business-oriented interest groups have substantial independent impact on government policy, average citizens and mass-based interest groups have little to none. Their study of 1,779 policy issues revealed a powerful status quo bias: even when an overwhelming 80% of the public favored a change, it was implemented only 43% of the time. It is much easier for a motivated minority to block change than for a disorganized majority to realize it.

**Loss Aversion and Framing**: The public's struggle to connect interests with policy is compounded by Loss Aversion and Framing Effects. Behavioral economics suggests that people feel the pain of a potential loss twice as strongly as the joy of an equivalent gain (Kahneman and Tversky, 1979; 1984).

Basic income opponents often exploit this by exaggerating the "burden" of tax increases while downplaying the "benefit" of the payout. This can lead potential net beneficiaries to oppose the policy out of a disproportionate fear of loss. The recent failure of the Canadian Liberal government's Carbon Tax and Dividend policy provides a cautionary tale: despite 80% of households being net beneficiaries, a conservative campaign focusing on rising energy costs and inflation successfully turned public opinion against the policy by misattributing general inflation to the carbon tax.

**Partisanship and "Cheap Political Support"**: Public opinion and political leadership interact in a feedback loop. Voters often align their policy preferences with the stance of the political parties they support (Nam and Kang, 2025).

More concerning is what Jurgen De Wispelaere (2016) calls "cheap political support." Small or fringe parties often endorse radical ideas like basic income when they bear no responsibility for implementation. However, as they gain power or approach an election, they frequently dilute their support or adopt ambiguous stances. Examples include Spain's *Podemos* retreating to a "long-term goal" stance, the Irish government canceling its promised Green Paper on basic income, and the Brazilian parliament passing a basic income law while leaving its funding to a non-existent federal budget provision.

**The Challenge of Ideological Inertia**: Finally, the entrenched concept of needs-based welfare poses a significant ideological hurdle. Many struggle to accept the idea of providing income to the wealthy or those who choose not to work. Surveys in Europe and Korea suggest that public support for basic income often stems from a desire to provide a minimum floor for the poor, rather than an endorsement of its core principles of universality and unconditionality (Roosma and Van Oorschot, 2019; Kim et al., forthcoming; Lee, 2021).

In conclusion, while a basic income policy becomes highly resilient once implemented—as the majority will then defend their tangible benefits (Pierson, 1994)—the initial hurdle of adoption remains immense. The higher the proportion of net beneficiaries, the more intense the resistance from net contributors may become at the implementation stage.

## 9.3 Trends in Public Opinion and the Positions of Political Parties and Actors[1]

Over the past few years, South Korea has witnessed significant shifts in public support for basic income and the stances of major political parties and leaders. During the COVID-19 pandemic, favorable public sentiment surged, prompting a responsive movement among political actors. Leading up to the March 2022 presidential election, Lee Jae-myung—the candidate of the then-ruling party—pledged to implement a Universal Basic Income (UBI) . However, as the election neared, support for basic income plummeted, and Lee shifted from active promotion to a passive defense against criticism from opponents.

The decline in public support and the subsequent election of Yoon Suk-yeol, who opposed the policy, led to skeptical outlooks regarding the political feasibility of basic income. Following the 2025 impeachment of former President Yoon, Lee Jae-myung was elected in a subsequent election. President Lee has not yet clarified his stance on a national UBI, focusing primarily on pilot programs for Rural Basic Income. To forecast future feasibility, we analyze the dynamic interaction between public opinion and political leadership, including the sharp decline in support prior to the 2022 election.

### *Public Interest and Support Trends (2018–2025)*

Figure 9.1 illustrates the changes in public support based on various polls and the search volume trends for "Basic Income" on Google and Naver (representing a standardized average of both).

Search trends reveal that Korean public interest in basic income peaked during the onset of the pandemic in early 2020 and saw a secondary rise

[1] This section is substantially based on Lee and You (2025).

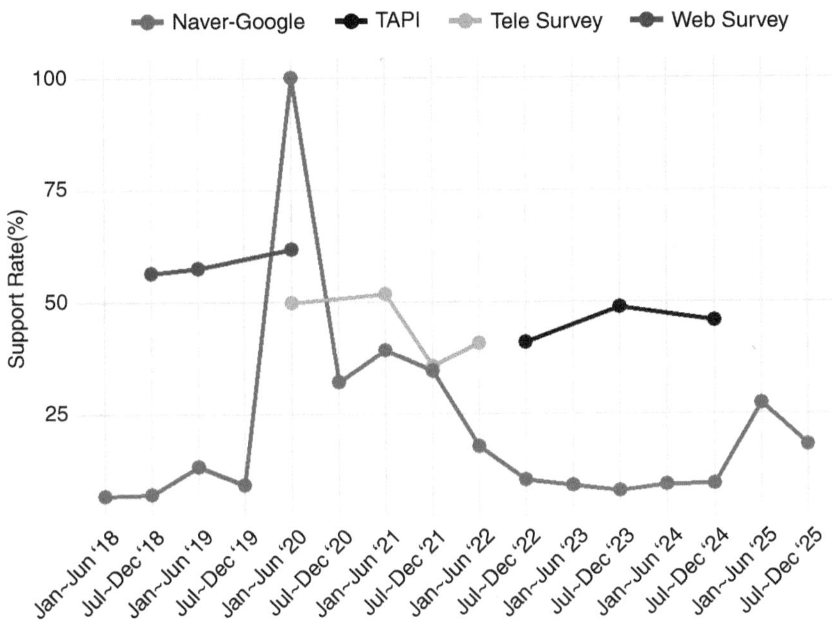


**Fig. 9.1** Trends in Public Support and Interest in Basic Income, 2018–2025. Sources: KIHASA (2024), Naver Data Lab (2026), Google Trends (2026)

in early 2021. Interest surged again in the first half of 2025 as Lee Jae-myung's election prospects increased, though it has leveled off following his inauguration.

**The Pandemic and the "Disaster Basic Income" Catalyst**: The surge in interest during the pandemic was largely driven by discussions regarding the Emergency Disaster Relief Fund. Media coverage of "Disaster Basic Income" and UBI increased exponentially following initial proposals in late February 2020 (Lee and You, 2021). During March 2020, public opinion shifted rapidly from favoring selective distribution to supporting universal distribution. A Realmeter poll on March 3 showed universal distribution trailing (42.6% vs. 47.3%), but just ten days later, it led significantly (48.6% vs. 34.3%).

Political parties reacted to this shift ahead of the April 2020 general election. Remarkably, the leader of the conservative opposition party advocated for universal relief just ten days before the election, followed immediately by the leader of the ruling Democratic Party. The government, which had insisted on selective aid, was forced to concede. By June 2020, 99% of households had applied for and received the relief fund, an experience that significantly bolstered support for the concept of a universal basic income.

Web surveys conducted between 2018 and 2020 show that support for UBI rose from approximately 56–57% to 61.8% following the 2020 relief fund distribution (Lab 2050, 2020).

**Falling Support Ahead of the 2022 Presidential Election**: However, telephone polls conducted between June 2020 and February 2022 tell a different story. While support remained high through early 2021 (averaging 51.8%), it plummeted to an average of 35.75% in late 2021. Although it partially recovered to 40.7% in early 2022, it remained more than 10 percentage points lower than the previous year. Furthermore, the National Perception Survey on Social Policy—conducted via Tablet-Aided Personal Interviews (TAPI)—showed support rising to 48.7% in 2023 but falling slightly to 45.7% in 2024, consistently failing to secure a majority.

The discrepancy between web surveys (61.8% support in May 2020) and telephone polls (51.8% in June 2020) suggests that web-based samples may overrepresent younger, highly educated populations with higher internet usage. Nevertheless, the convergence of telephone and face-to-face (TAPI) results by 2022 provides a more grounded baseline of current public sentiment.

### *Fluctuating Public Opinion and the Politics of Basic Income*

In September 2020, amidst rising favorable public sentiment, the conservative opposition party, People Power Party (PPP), took the surprising step of adopting basic income as the first priority in its official party platform. This move was orchestrated by Kim Chong-in, the interim leader appointed after the party's crushing defeat in the April general elections. A centrist politician and well-known advocate for "economic democratization," Kim held a favorable view of basic income as a means to broaden the party's electoral base.

However, a political paradox emerged. While the PPP officially adopted the policy, the general public continued to perceive basic income as a hallmark of the Democratic Party (DP), the ruling party at the time. This misperception was driven by two factors: Lee Jae-myung, a prominent DP figure, was already the nation's most visible champion of the policy, and the DP had a historical reputation for universal welfare, whereas conservative parties traditionally favored selective assistance.

Polls from June 2020 confirmed this ideological divide. A Realmeter survey showed that 63.4% of progressives supported basic income, compared to only 31.2% of conservatives. Similarly, a Hankil Research poll found that 63.9% of DP supporters favored the policy, while only 35.9% of PPP supporters did.

Following the PPP's official adoption of the policy, several of its leading figures proposed their own versions of a Negative Income Tax (NIT). Oh Se-hoon, the former (and now incumbent) Mayor of Seoul, introduced "Safety Income"—a household-based NIT model. After winning the 2021 by-election and the 2022 regular election, Mayor Oh launched a Randomized Controlled Trial (RCT) for the program, later renaming it "Stepping Stone Income" (Didimdol Income). Meanwhile, another PPP heavyweight, Yoo Seong-min, proposed an individual-based NIT called "Fair Income," but he lost the 2021 presidential nomination to Yoon Suk-yeol.

Notably, Yoon Suk-yeol maintained a consistently critical stance toward basic income both as a candidate and as President, despite it being his party's official platform. The Yoon administration has instead pursued "welfare for the vulnerable," focusing on strengthening selective social assistance, such as incrementally raising the NBLSS Livelihood Benefit from 30% to 35% of the median income.

**Lee Jae-myung and the 2022 Presidential Campaign**: In the ruling Democratic Party, basic income was a source of internal friction. President Moon Jae-in and the party's mainstream remained hesitant, and Lee Jae-myung's rivals criticized the policy to differentiate themselves. Lee's track record was already established; as Mayor of Seongnam in 2016, he introduced the "Youth Basic Income," providing 1 million KRW annually to 24-year-olds. He championed UBI during the 2017 presidential primary, and after being elected Governor of Gyeonggi Province in 2018, he expanded the program to the entire province—home to a quarter of the nation's population—while initiating further experiments in rural areas.

In July 2021, as the DP's presidential nomination candidate, Lee pledged a Universal Basic Income of 1 million KRW per year, funded by land and carbon dividends, with an additional 1 million KRW for youth aged 18–29. However, he faced intense scrutiny during the primary and general election. Critics argued that 83,000 KRW per month was too meager to be meaningful and that it was wasteful to support the wealthy rather than concentrating resources on the poor.

The proposal for a Land Ownership Tax to fund dividends proved particularly controversial. Amidst a backlash from homeowners in the Seoul metropolitan area against the Moon administration's real estate tax hikes, the PPP intensified its attacks on Lee's model. Faced with waning public support and opposition from within his own party's legislators as well as attacks from the PPP, Lee adopted a defensive stance. He eventually stated that he would not implement the land and carbon dividend policies without explicit public consent via a national referendum—a move widely interpreted as a de facto retraction of his core pledge.

The decline in Lee Jae-myung's proactive promotion of basic income and the waning public support appeared to reinforce each other. Support for basic income hit its nadir in November and December 2021, coinciding with the period when Lee trailed Yoon Suk-yeol by the largest margin. Conversely, the slight recovery in favorable sentiment in early 2022 mirrored the period when the race between the two candidates tightened. The fear of increased tax burdens and the perception of universal "small-sum" payouts as wasteful became the dominant frames that eroded the policy's political momentum.

### *Empirical Analysis of the Shift in Public Sentiment: Evidence from KGSS*

The decline in favorable sentiment toward basic income during 2021 appears to be closely linked to the falling approval ratings of the Moon Jae-in administration and the shifting popularity of the Democratic Party and its candidate, Lee Jae-myung. Notably, a significant segment of voters in their 20s and 30s—traditionally a core support base for the Democratic Party—began gravitating toward the People Power Party (PPP) and candidate Yoon Suk-yeol.

Many of these younger voters appeared to embrace the PPP's framing of basic income as a "populist handout" that would eventually impose a heavy fiscal burden on future generations. Consequently, despite the inclusion of "Youth Basic Income" in the campaign pledges, support for basic income among the youth was lower than in other age groups.

Objective data from the Korean General Social Survey (KGSS) conducted in the autumns of 2018 and 2021 provides robust evidence for this shift. By using a consistent question about basic income across both

**Table 9.1** Public Sentiment on Basic Income: 2018 vs. 2021 KGSS (Unit: %)

| *View on Basic Income* | *2018 KGSS* | *2021 KGSS* | *2021 KGSS (If Tax-funded)* |
|---|---|---|---|
| Support | 37.4 | 31.7 | 27.0 |
| Neutral | 31.5 | 34.3 | 32.3 |
| Oppose | 31.1 | 34.0 | 40.6 |

years, the KGSS allows us to identify who changed their minds and why. Furthermore, the 2021 survey introduced a specific question regarding "tax-funded" basic income, highlighting the power of issue framing.

As shown in Table 9.1, support dropped from a lead over opposition in 2018 (37.4% vs. 31.1%) to a trailing position in 2021 (31.7% vs. 34.0%). When "tax funding" was explicitly mentioned, support plummeted to 27.0%, while opposition surged to 40.6%. This underscores that fear of tax increases is a primary hurdle for political feasibility.

**Ideology and Age as Key Drivers:** We conducted a regression analysis using an Ordinal Logit Model to measure the impact of demographic, socioeconomic, and political variables on basic income support.

The findings generally align with existing literature, with one striking exception: Age. While age was not a significant factor in 2018, it became a sharply negative predictor in 2021. This statistically supports the observation that negative sentiment was specifically reinforced among the 20s and 30s age cohorts as they shifted toward the conservative opposition.

The most powerful predictors, however, were welfare attitudes and political orientation:

- Individuals who believe the government should expand benefits for the poor, the elderly, and the unemployed—and those who support minimum wage hikes—were significantly more likely to support basic income.
- Political progressives and those satisfied with the current political climate showed strong support.

Between 2018 and 2021, the South Korean political landscape underwent a significant rightward shift. The proportion of self-identified progressives shrank by 10.8 percentage points, while moderates and conservatives grew.

**Table 9.2** Shifts in Political Ideology and the Decline in Basic Income Support

| *Political Ideology* | *Population Share (2018)* | *Population Share (2021)* | *Change (%p)* | *Support Rate (2018)* | *Support Rate (2021)* | *Change (%p)* |
|---|---|---|---|---|---|---|
| Progressive | 43.7% | 32.9% | −10.8 | 41.2% | 41.9% | 0.7 |
| Moderate | 32.4% | 38.7% | 6.3 | 36.5% | 27.7% | -8.8 |
| Conservative | 23.8% | 28.5% | 4.7 | 32.3% | 24.2% | -8.1 |
| Total | 100% | 100% | 0 | 37.5% | 31.4% | -6.1 |

As Table 9.2 illustrates, while progressives maintained their support level (approx. 41–42%), support among moderates and conservatives dropped sharply. Regression analysis controlling for other variables shows that the "dislike" of basic income associated with moving one point toward the conservative end of a 5-point scale increased from 5% in 2018 to 9% in 2021.

These results suggest that the low support observed in late 2021 was a transitory phenomenon driven by the specific political environment of the time. It should not be interpreted as a fundamental or permanent withdrawal of support for the concept of basic income among South Koreans (Lee and You, 2025).

### *Evolution Below the Surface: Local Pilot Programs and the Post-2025 Resurgence*

Following Lee Jae-myung's narrow defeat by a 0.7 percentage point margin in the March 2022 presidential election, general interest in basic income appeared to wane. However, data from the *National Perception Survey on Social Policy* indicates that public support did not fundamentally collapse. As shown in Fig. 9.1, while support has not returned to the majority levels seen during the pandemic, it recovered significantly to 48.7% in 2023 and 45.7% in 2024 from its late-2021 nadir (35.75%).

Under the Yoon Suk-yeol administration, basic income moved away from the central political spotlight but saw significant bottom-up developments:

- The "Basic Society" Platform: The main opposition Democratic Party (DP), under Lee Jae-myung's leadership, officially adopted the

"Basic Society" framework—including basic income—as its primary policy platform.

- Opportunity Income (Gyeonggi Province): Governor Kim Dong-yeon launched "Opportunity Income," a form of Participation Income. This included targeted pilots for artists, athletes, farmers, the disabled, and those engaged in climate action.
- Stepping Stone Income (Seoul): Mayor Oh Se-hoon conducted a three-year Randomized Controlled Trial (RCT) of "Stepping Stone Income" (a household-based NIT) from 2022 to 2025.

**The Rise of "Renewable Energy Dividends"**: A pivotal shift occurred with the birth of renewable energy-based common wealth dividends in rural areas. In Sinan-gun, "Sunlight Pensions" (1–2 million KRW annually) are distributed to residents of five islands. This model involves organizing residents into cooperatives that hold equity in solar power plants, with profits distributed as dividends. Sinan-gun has further announced plans for a "Wind Pension" (500,000 KRW monthly) once offshore wind farms become operational by 2030. In late 2024, Yeongwang-gun also elected a governor committed to similar renewable energy dividends.

**The 2025 Political Transformation and Current Outlook**: The dramatic political shift in 2025—the impeachment of Yoon Suk-yeol and the election of Lee Jae-myung—has brought basic income back to the forefront. While President Lee prioritized economic growth during his campaign, he has since instructed the cabinet to examine the feasibility of Carbon Dividends and launched Rural Basic Income pilots. Beginning in January 2026, residents in 10 selected counties will receive a regular basic income of 150,000 KRW per month for two years.

Following his inauguration, President Lee distributed "Livelihood Recovery Consumption Coupons." In a compromise between universal and selective approaches, the government provided 150,000 KRW to every citizen, with an additional 100,000 KRW for the bottom 90%. While critics decried this as "irresponsible populism," public opinion revealed a fascinating nuance: overall support for the coupons was 58%, but support for the differentiated (combined) payment method was significantly higher at 67% (Nam and Kang, 2025). This suggests that a hybrid model—much like our proposal combining a Universal Common Wealth Dividend with an NIT-type Basic Income—may possess higher public acceptability.

While the one-time coupons sparked expectations for further transfers, budget constraints have limited subsequent efforts to a few local governments. Our proposal to convert the Basic Personal Allowance into a permanent Refundable Tax Credit offers a fiscally sustainable path to a modest but enduring basic income. As the "Presidential Commission on the Basic Society" is set to launch, our model provides a robust framework for persuading both the political establishment and civil society that a fiscally viable and politically acceptable basic income is within reach.

## 9.4 Strategic Considerations for the Basic Income Movement in Korea

Having examined the theoretical factors and the evolving landscape of public opinion in South Korea, we now turn to the strategic considerations necessary to enhance the political feasibility of basic income.

### *Building a Broad-Based Coalition*

While the introduction of even a modest basic income is expected to create a self-sustaining cycle of support from net beneficiaries, the initial hurdle of adoption remains immense. Basic income activists must prioritize building a wide-ranging alliance that encompasses diverse ideological perspectives.

This requires a pragmatic approach: rather than insisting on a "prototype" Universal Basic Income (UBI) , we must foster dialogue and cooperation with advocates of the Negative Income Tax (NIT)—such as the "Stepping Stone Income"—and proponents of Participation Income, like "Opportunity Income." While politicians often emphasize differences to distinguish themselves from rivals, a successful basic income movement must prioritize a "united front" over differentiation. Our proposal is strategically designed to be flexible, incorporating NIT and participation income elements to facilitate negotiation and minimize the risk of what De Wispelaere (2016) calls "cheap political support"—where abstract coalitions crumble once concrete implementation begins.

### *Strategies to Mitigate Opposition*

One of the primary paradoxes of basic income is that even when two-thirds of the population are net beneficiaries, they are often difficult to organize due to the collective action dilemma (Olson, 1965). In contrast, the top one-third of net contributors—comprising professors, journalists, high-ranking officials, and business leaders—possess disproportionate political influence and media access. Turning this influential group into an antagonistic bloc can be fatal to the policy's success.

To address this, we propose the following strategies to weaken opposition:

- From "Robin Hood" to "Common Wealth": We must move away from the "Robin Hood" narrative—taking from the rich to give to the poor—which can be perceived as punitive. Instead, the discourse should emphasize the shared distribution of common wealth or social production. The logic should be rooted in horizontal alliances and "taxation according to ability" rather than class struggle.
- Addressing Loss Aversion: Behavioral economics teaches us that the fear of loss is more potent than the hope for gain (Kahneman & Tversky, 1984). Opponents often exploit this by exaggerating the tax burden. This is why we propose "in principle" a 10% tax on income exceeding the average, but in our practical implementation, we suggest a lower rate (3–5%) and the use of natural tax increases driven by economic growth and inflation.
- Basic Income as Social Learning: We believe that introducing even a low basic income tax is essential. First, it establishes the principle that the right to basic income is linked to the duty of taxation, fostering a life-cycle perspective where individuals may be net beneficiaries at one stage and net contributors at another. Second, without a broad-based tax foundation, the long-term expansion of basic income levels remains fiscally limited.

Politicians are often tempted to frame policies as Pareto superior—where some gain and no one loses—by claiming they can fund basic income solely through fiscal restructuring without tax hikes. However, meaningful redistribution to alleviate inequality inevitably requires some net contribution from the wealthy. Rather than pursuing populist short-term gains, we should emphasize a spirit of "sharing"—akin to the biblical tithe—to minimize resistance from high-income earners and actively invite supportive members of the elite into the deliberation process.

### *Incremental and Phased Implementation and Expansion Strategies*

A crucial consideration for political feasibility is to work within the existing institutional framework—leveraging path dependency—rather than pursuing a revolutionary overhaul that triggers strong status quo bias. By strategically choosing which elements of the current tax and benefit system to retain, abolish, or transform, we can enhance both political acceptability and administrative viability (Lee, forthcoming).

Our proposal to transform employment income deductions and tax credits into a refundable Universal EITC is a prime example of this incremental approach. In a country like South Korea, which already has generous employment income deductions, this transition is relatively feasible. Furthermore, the conversion of the Basic Personal Allowance into a universal refundable credit provides a stable funding source for a universal dividend. President Lee Jae-myung's recent directive to conduct a comprehensive survey of current tax expenditures suggests a growing political opening for this "Universal Refundable Tax Credit" model.

Additionally, unpaid labor not covered by the Universal EITC can be supported through local Participation Income programs, such as those already active in Gyeonggi Province. Strategically, we recommend an expansion path starting from rural pilot programs (currently in 10 counties) to all 69 designated population-declining counties, and eventually to a national UBI. To mitigate urban-rural friction, we must enforce the principle that the right to basic income is tied to the duty of taxation; this involves reducing tax exemptions for agricultural income and ensuring rural residents participate in annual income tax filing.

### *Policy Experiments and Deliberative Public Debates*

To overcome the public's fear of tax increases and the collective action dilemma, a process of social learning is essential. Policy experiments and deliberative debates can serve as vital tools for this purpose

**Behavioral Policy Experiments**: While static micro-simulations (as presented in Chapter 8) are useful, measuring behavioral changes such as labor supply and macroeconomic effects is challenging. We believe our policy minimizes negative effects on labor supply and economic growth by minimizing income and substitution effects through modest guaranteed income levels and low tax rates. Nevertheless, if the political sphere finds it difficult to accept our proposal immediately, conducting a randomized controlled trial (RCT) for about three years is a viable option.

In policy experiments, conducting experiments on taxes in addition to benefits is politically difficult and may have constitutional issues. To address the “half-experiment” problem (where benefits are tested but taxes are not), we suggest a “Virtual Tax Notification” system for the treatment group. Net contributors in the experiment would receive a notice stating: *“Under this policy, based on last year’s income, you would have contributed X amount; however, you remain eligible for benefits should your income fall below the threshold.”* This fosters an understanding of basic income as a form of horizontal and vertical redistribution over the life cycle.

While the payment of additional taxes cannot be mandated for experimental net contributors, voluntary contribution could be permitted. The government could enclose a survey asking these individuals how they feel about becoming net contributors if the policy were real and whether they think it is a good policy.

Similarly, the government can send a message and survey to net beneficiaries in the experiment. It should explain that if this policy is actually implemented, anyone will be a net beneficiary in years when their income is below the threshold, but will become a net contributor and pay additional taxes in years when it exceeds the threshold. The survey would ask how they feel about being net beneficiaries this year, whether they think it is a good policy, and whether they would be willing to pay taxes if they become net contributors in the future.

Policy experiments can be utilized as a process of social learning through public deliberation. Based on the experiences and reactions of net beneficiaries and net contributors in the experiment, social discussions can be organized and publicized. Through this process of reflection and debate during the experiment, many people will be able to understand the principles of Common Wealth Basic Income, NIT-type Basic Income, and Universal EITC.

**Public Deliberation**: Public understanding can be significantly enhanced through deliberative processes even without full-scale experiments. Gyeonggi Province’s deliberative polls in 2019 and 2020 demonstrated this effect. About 200 participants were selected by lottery, and their support for basic income was surveyed three times: first without any learning, second after studying materials alone, and third after hearing arguments from experts and discussing in randomly assigned groups. As shown in Figs. 9.2 and 9.3, support for basic income based on land and carbon taxes surged by 28 and 24 percentage points, respectively, following deliberation.

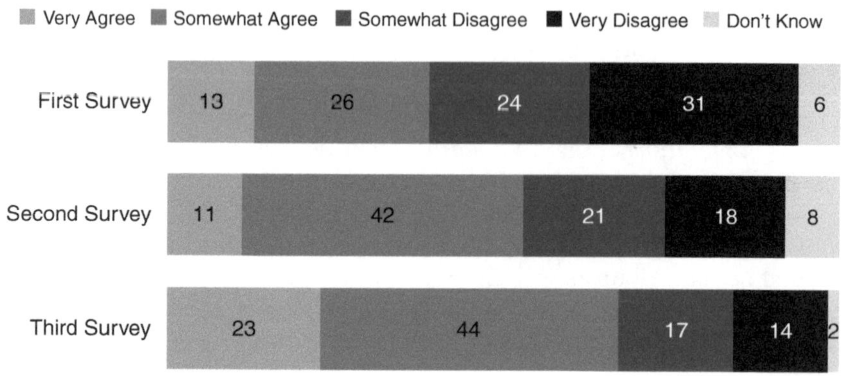


**Fig. 9.2** Change in Support for Land Dividend Basic Income Through Deliberation. Source: 2020 Gyeonggi Province Deliberation Briefing

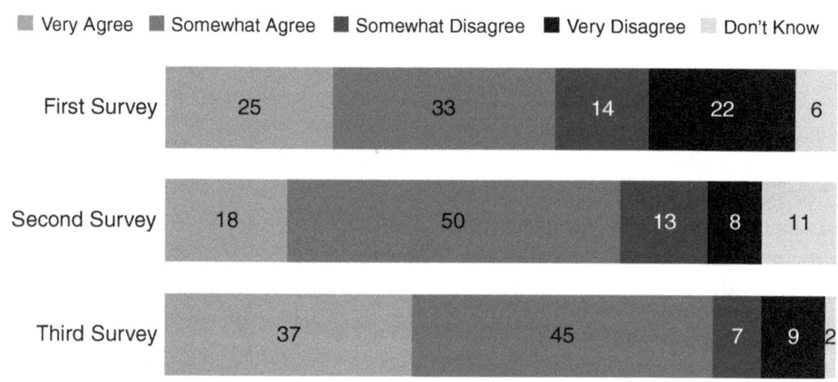


**Fig. 9.3** Change in Support for Carbon Dividend Basic Income Through Deliberation. Source: 2020 Gyeonggi Province Deliberation Briefing

These results demonstrate that when the public purpose of a tax (e.g., curbing real estate speculation or carbon reduction) is clear, and when individuals can accurately calculate their net gains/losses using tools like our Basic Income Simulator App, tax-based basic income can garner majority support. By fostering online debates and expert-led forums, we can move beyond "cheap political support" toward a robust social mandate.

CHAPTER 10

# Conclusion

The idea of basic income is garnering global attention as a definitive alternative to an era of inequality and instability. Nonetheless, it is still frequently perceived as a utopian concept, impractical for real-world implementation. As "idealistic realists" or perhaps "realistic idealists," we have presented a concrete and actionable design for basic income.

While the welfare states developed in the twentieth century played a significant role in reducing inequality, their limitations are becoming increasingly apparent. In the face of deindustrialization and automation, the capacity of the traditional welfare state to respond to the spread of precarious labor and rising inequality has reached its breaking point. Furthermore, the onset of the climate crisis and the unpredictable AI revolution are accelerating systemic instability. Today, the job security of high-skilled white-collar workers is being threatened alongside that of low-skilled blue-collar workers. In this climate, we see ideals of equality and freedom, concepts of equality and efficiency, and goals of efficiency and sustainability clashing across the globe. Welfare capitalism is facing a fundamental crisis.

The allure of basic income lies in its ability to alleviate inequality not by restricting freedom, but by enhancing it. Moreover, basic income promotes equality efficiently without sacrificing productivity, and it pursues



J. S. You et al., *UBI from Idea to Reality*, Exploring the Basic Income Guarantee,
https://doi.org/10.1007/978-3-032-26200-4_10

"sustainable efficiency" without sacrificing the environment for the sake of growth. By simultaneously pursuing freedom, equality, and sustainable efficiency, the introduction of basic income could become the seminal reform of the twenty-first century—following the path of Bismarck's introduction of social insurance and the Beveridge Report's blueprint for the universal welfare state—to overcome the crisis of contemporary capitalism. We have proposed this specific policy alternative within South Korea's historical, socio-political, and institutional context.

South Korea stands at the forefront of substituting simple, repetitive, unskilled labor with automation, leading the world in the use of industrial robots. Now, aiming to be a top-three global power in AI, Korea is focusing all its national strength on AI-driven industrial development. The displacement of jobs by AI is no longer a vague anxiety; it is a reality hitting the younger generation today, evidenced by the contraction of new recruitment for college graduates. Even if Korea's global corporations lead the AI revolution to success, it will only reinforce the nature of "jobless growth," deepening economic polarization. As employment becomes more precarious, income inequality and volatility will surge. In this context, basic income is shifting from an "option" to a "necessity."

Korea's success in rapid industrialization and economic growth in the late twentieth century was underpinned by the dissolution of the landlord class through land reform, the mitigation of landownership inequality, and the rapid expansion of education. Notably, South Korea's land reform was significant because it was achieved through a democratic political process under a liberal democratic system—unlike the top-down reforms in Japan, Taiwan, or the communist bloc (You, 2015). Once praised for "growth with equity" on the foundation of that land reform, Korea is now seeing growth stall amidst deepening inequality. A bold reform is required to drastically lower this inequality. We believe that the introduction of basic income policies—including Land Dividends based on a Land Value Tax—will constitute a "Second Equalization Reform," comparable to the land reform at the dawn of the Korean Republic.

We envision basic income becoming a central pillar of the welfare state, functioning as a low-level foundational social insurance while simultaneously eliminating the blind spots of contribution-based social insurance and minimizing dependence on social assistance. To this end, we have established a theoretical framework for our three basic income policies based on normative and empirical theories and have strictly verified their feasibility and effectiveness.

## 10.1 Summary of Core Arguments and Key Findings

We have established the principle that the "universal right to basic income is grounded in the duty of taxation," addressing the common "free-rider" critique. To implement this, we proposed an integrated tax-and-benefit model where every adult is mandated to file an income tax return, and basic income is distributed via a Refundable Tax Credit. By integrating the tax and benefit systems, we analyzed the implications of effective tax rates, participation tax rates (PTR), and effective marginal tax rates (EMTR) to demonstrate how our model outperforms traditional social assistance.

Our core findings and arguments are summarized as follows:

(1) **Basic Income as Foundational Social Insurance**: In the spirit of the "veil of ignorance," risk-averse individuals can agree on basic income as a foundational form of social insurance that smooths consumption and maintains income across the life cycle. It does not replace contribution-based social insurance; rather, it effectively eliminates its "blind spots" by subsidizing premiums for precarious, low-income workers. In the South Korean context, we demonstrated that a Universal EITC (UEITC), which corrects the regressivity of current earned income deductions, is the ideal mechanism for this role.

(2) **Overcoming the Failures of Social Assistance:** While traditional social assistance is often criticized for stigmatizing recipients and discouraging labor, we provided empirical evidence of even deeper structural issues: the "marriage penalty" and incentives for household dissolution, and the unfairness of income reversals between recipients and non-recipients. In contrast, basic income encourages stable household formation and alleviates the economic burden of raising children. This makes it particularly effective for nations facing ultra-low birth rates like South Korea. A partial basic income expands "real freedom," increases economic efficiency, and enhances demographic sustainability.

(3) **Long-term Fiscal Sustainability Amidst Aging:** By combining Common Wealth and NIT-type Basic Incomes, and the universal EITC, we designed a policy that effectively mitigates inequality while remaining fiscally sustainable even amidst rapid population aging. By providing higher guaranteed income for children and seniors, our model almost entirely eradicates child poverty and significantly reduces elderly poverty. While it may not solve Korea's

high elderly poverty rate overnight, it improves the inefficiency of the current Basic Pension and supports the expansion of public pension coverage.

(4) **Supporting a Just Energy Transition:** Our model supports a "just transition" to address the climate crisis through Carbon Dividends supplemented by Renewable Energy Dividends. We demonstrated that even as carbon emissions decrease and carbon dividends subsequently decline, the shortfall can be compensated by the rising dividends from renewable energy production.

(5) **Enhancing Work Incentives through Negative Marginal Tax Rates:** We clarify that a "Full Basic Income" meeting all basic needs is currently unfeasible; instead, we propose a Partial Basic Income. To encourage labor, we offer low-income earners a negative marginal tax rate of -2% (combining the 10% NIT clawback with the -12% universal EITC rate). For working seniors, we promote "active aging" by applying a low combined tax rate of only 8% (20% NIT clawback plus -12% UEITC).

This is a stark departure from traditional NIT proposals that, while providing high guaranteed income, impose high marginal tax rates that trigger labor disincentives through income and substitution effects. Our approach dispels concerns about slowed economic growth and ensures that low-income earners are not dependent on welfare but are empowered to escape poverty through higher real wages.

(6) **Universal Principles and Social Solidarity:** Unlike traditional NIT models that only target the poor, our model embodies the universal principle where everyone receives a flat dividend and everyone pays a flat-rate tax on all income. Consequently, about 70% of individuals—including the middle class—become net beneficiaries, with redistribution naturally favoring those with lower incomes.

We call upon the top 30% of earners to make additional contributions. Since the burden increases progressively, the impact on those just above the 70th percentile remains minimal. However, we ask the top 10% to contribute an additional amount equivalent to nearly 10% of their disposable income. Given the extreme concentration of wealth and income at the top, and the potential for AI-driven polarization, we believe this request is both just and necessary.

**An Invitation to Debate:** Our proposal may face opposing criticisms: some may find the guaranteed income level too low to drastically reduce poverty, suggesting a household-based model instead; others may find the 10% additional burden on the top tier too radical. We welcome open debate on both fronts. We assert the necessity and legitimacy of our individual-based, modest-level basic income model and the 10% contribution from the elite, but we eagerly invite new policy proposals that can further refine the path toward a more equitable society.

## 10.2 On Universal Basic Capital (Minimum Inheritance)

Some argue that Basic Capital, or a Basic Endowment, is a more effective tool than basic income for addressing the structural inequalities of capitalism. For example, Bruce Ackerman and Anne Alstott (1999) proposed a 'stakeholder grant' of $80,000 in the U.S. Thomas Piketty (2019) proposed a minimum inheritance of 60% of average wealth per adult. We agree that providing a capital endowment to every individual upon reaching adulthood is an excellent policy for promoting equality of opportunity.

However, while Basic Capital can significantly mitigate initial inequalities, its role is inherently limited. In the pursuit of equal opportunity, preventing child poverty and ensuring equality in early childhood care and education are arguably more critical. Empirical studies show that cognitive development gaps in infancy persist through adulthood, and that the quality of primary education and residential environment are decisive factors in future earnings. Furthermore, no matter how equal educational opportunities are, a parent's socioeconomic status continues to exert a profound influence on a child's professional and financial success—a challenge that a one-time capital grant alone cannot fully resolve.

Moreover, even with identical initial endowments, individuals will experience vastly different outcomes due to differences in talent and luck. If an individual falls into debt due to unsuccessful business ventures, poor management, or simple misfortune, can society justify withdrawing all protection on the grounds that equal opportunity was provided? Ultimately, even if Basic Capital reduces the disparity at the starting line, the necessity of Basic Income as a foundational social insurance—providing a permanent floor for income—remains paramount. Reducing the gap at the start of adulthood is essential, but it must not overshadow the importance of mitigating income volatility throughout an individual's entire life.

We propose two primary methods for implementing Basic Capital or a Minimum Inheritance:

**The Negative Capital Acquisitions Tax Model**: Modeled after the Negative Income Tax (NIT), this approach utilizes a Negative Capital Acquisitions Tax. An individual's lifetime receipts of inheritances and gifts would be accumulated and taxed at a progressive rate. If the total value of assets received by the time an individual reaches adulthood is below the national average, the government would provide a capital grant equal to 50% of the shortfall. Conversely, any lifetime acquisitions exceeding the average would be subject to a flat tax of 50% or an appropriately progressive tax rate (e.g., ranging from 30% to 70%).

**The Child Trust Fund (CTF Model**: The second strategy involves depositing the Common Wealth Dividend for children (set at 5% of average income or 3% of GNI per capita; approx. 1.5 million KRW annually in 2024) into a Child Trust Fund. If accumulated for 20 years from birth to age 19, the principal alone would equal the national average annual income (approx. 30 million KRW in 2024). Including interest, this sum could be withdrawn for specific purposes—such as marriage, home purchase, or business startup—after age 20, and becomes available for unrestricted use after age 30.

Furthermore, if half of the guaranteed income from the NIT-type basic income for children (10% of average income) is added to this CTF for 20 years, the principal would reach three times the average annual income (approx. 90 million KRW in 2024). This amount represents nearly half of the average net wealth per capita in Korea (188 million KRW as of 2024), providing a substantial economic foundation for every young citizen.

## 10.3 Applicability to Other Nations

Can the three basic income policies proposed within the South Korean context be implemented in other countries? We believe that Common Wealth basic income and NIT-type Basic Income are universally applicable. While the universal EITC may be difficult to replicate in its exact Korean form, it can be adapted into various modified versions.

- Adaptation to Existing Tax Structures: Countries with generous standard deductions like the United States could convert them into refundable Standard Tax Credits and extend them to everyone. Nations like Canada, which already utilize basic tax credits, could transition them into a refundable format and universalize it. Countries like Japan, which maintain generous but regressive employment income deductions similar to Korea's, could consider adopting the UEITC model. Designing a transition that leverages existing institutional frameworks increases both political and administrative feasibility.

- Land, Carbon, and Renewable Energy Dividends: Land and carbon dividends are well-established concepts within the global basic income community. The Renewable Energy Dividend, though theorized based on the Korean experience, is equally valid for other nations. Carbon dividends, in particular, enjoy broad support among economists as a key tool for a "just transition." However, the recent setbacks of the Canadian carbon dividend policy serve as a cautionary tale; we must be prepared to counter disinformation campaigns and political attacks through transparent information sharing and strategic communication.
- The UEITC and Work Incentives: The core of the UEITC is to convert work-linked benefits (like the US EITC) into an individual-based system while eliminating the "phase-out" range. While eliminating phase-out ranges requires significant fiscal resources, Korea achieves this by reforming its regressive employment income deduction. In countries where such funding is limited, a "Quasi-universal EITC" could be sought by lowering the phase-out rate and extending the income threshold.

## 10.4 An Invitation to Solidarity: Realizing Freedom and Equality

We do not claim that our proposal is the single "perfect" policy. However, we firmly believe it provides a vital pathway to simultaneously enhancing substantive freedom and equality.

Our proposal is fiscally and administratively feasible. In the context of South Korea—a nation facing the existential threat of "population extinction" due to extreme low birth rates and worrying about the sustainability of social spending—our model offers a definitive solution. Contrary to fears that basic income would impose an unbearable fiscal burden, we demonstrate that it provides a breakthrough for an otherwise bleak fiscal outlook.

We hope our proposal sparks vigorous debate within the government, political circles, and civil society. We welcome deliberative public debates and rigorous scientific policy experiments. Should other serious policy alternatives emerge, we invite them to be tested alongside ours in comparative experiments. Through such processes, we hope to see basic income realized at a meaningful level in South Korea.

Furthermore, our research continues. We will pursue follow-up studies on the evaluation of the Stepping Stone Income and Rural Basic Income pilots, strategies to overcome the challenges of carbon dividends, the implementation of Basic Capital, and methods to harmonize elderly poverty alleviation with the fiscal stabilization of public pensions.

Supplementary materials and updated research findings will be available on this book's appendix page. We conclude by inviting you, the readers, to join us in solidarity to realize the ideals of freedom and equality.

# Appendix

## Appendix to Chapter 7

### *Appendix 7.1 Simulation of Basic Deduction Amount and Tax Increase from Abolishing the Basic Deduction*

The 5% income tax micro-sample from the National Tax Statistics Center (2026) provides information on the basic deduction and the taxable income base. Using these data, one can easily estimate additional tax revenue at the individual level by calculating the increase in tax liability that would result from raising the taxable base by the amount of the basic deduction. However, the KGH'BOK data do not contain direct information on the basic deduction or the taxable base. Instead, they provide data on income tax and household members. We therefore use these variables to estimate the basic deduction and the resulting tax increase that would occur if the basic deduction were abolished.

1. Individuals who do not file a comprehensive income tax return or undergo year-end wage settlement do not receive the basic deduction. Accordingly, among those whose income tax is greater than zero, we grant a personal basic deduction of 1.5 million won to



J. S. You et al., *UBI from Idea to Reality*, Exploring the Basic Income Guarantee,
https://doi.org/10.1007/978-3-032-26200-4

individuals whose *estimated earned income amount* or *estimated comprehensive income amount* is at least 1 million won.

- The **earned income amount** is estimated by taking labor income (total wage and salary income) from KGH'BOK and subtracting the earned income deduction amount calculated using the formula in Table 5.10 of Chapter 5.
- The **comprehensive income amount** is estimated as follows. We first estimate business income, property income, and pension income, and then classify as comprehensive income tax filers those whose business income amount is greater than zero, whose property income amount exceeds 15 million won, or whose pension income amount exceeds 1 million won. For these individuals, we define the comprehensive income amount as the sum of business, property, and pension income plus the above estimate of the earned income amount.
- The **business income amount** is estimated by comparing the distribution of "business income" in KGH'BOK with the distribution of "business income amount" in the income tax micro-data and deriving an approximate formula: we multiply business income in KGH'BOK by 0.7, subtract 1 million won, and set negative values to zero.
- The **property income amount** (interest income amount + dividend income amount + real-estate rental income amount) is estimated as follows. In KGH'BOK, "property income" is defined as interest + dividends + rental income. Considering that financial income (interest + dividends) up to 20 million won is generally subject to separate taxation, and that rental income is mostly above 10 million won (78.3% of rental income amounts among comprehensive-taxation rental income taxpayers in the National Tax Statistical Yearbook exceed 10 million won), we assume that "property income" of 15 million won or less is generally not subject to comprehensive income taxation and therefore treat the property income amount as zero in such cases. If "property income" exceeds 15 million won, we treat the full amount as the property income amount.
- The **pension income amount** is estimated by assuming that roughly half of public pension income in KGH'BOK is non-taxable, and then applying the pension income deduction formula to the remaining half (full deduction for amounts up to 3.5 million won; 40% deduction for 3.5–7 million won; 20% for 7–14 million won; and 10% for any amount above 14 million won).

2. Among the above recipients of the personal basic deduction, we grant a dependent basic deduction of 1.5 million won to dependents of the household head who are the spouse, unmarried children aged 20 or under, parents, or grandparents, provided that both their earned income amount and comprehensive income amount do not exceed 1 million won.
3. Among those eligible for the basic deduction (personal and dependent), we grant an additional elderly deduction of 1 million won to individuals aged 70 or over, an additional disability deduction of 2 million won to registered persons with disabilities, an additional deduction of 1 million won to single-parent households, and an additional deduction of 500,000 won to married women whose spouse qualifies as a dependent for deduction purposes and whose comprehensive income amount and earned income amount are both 30 million won or less.
4. We then calculate the current taxable income base and tax liability as follows. The taxable base is defined as the comprehensive income amount, as estimated above, minus the basic deduction, additional deductions, and social insurance contributions. If the comprehensive income amount exceeds 10 million won but does not exceed 60 million won, we further subtract 5% of the comprehensive income amount; if it exceeds 60 million won, we subtract an additional 3 million won. Applying the tax rates in Table 5.9 of Chapter 5 to this taxable base yields the current tax liability.
5. Next, we add the basic deduction amount to the taxable base obtained in step 4 to derive a new taxable base, and we again apply the tax rates in Table 5.9 of Chapter 5 to compute the new tax liability.
6. Subtracting the tax liability in step 4 from the new tax liability in step 5 gives the increase in national income tax resulting from abolishing the basic deduction for comprehensive income tax filers. Finally, we multiply this increase by 1.1 to add local income tax (10% of national income tax) and thus obtain the total increase in income tax.
7. For wage and salary earners whose income tax is greater than zero, whose earned income is at least 5 million won, and who have no comprehensive income amount, we treat them as year-end-settlement wage earners. For these individuals, we estimate the taxable base as earned income amount minus personal deductions (basic

and additional) and minus social insurance contributions and other income deductions. We estimate **other income deductions** as 2% of earned income amount if it is 5 million won or less; 5% if it exceeds 5 million won but does not exceed 10 million won; 8% if it exceeds 10 million won but does not exceed 80 million won; and 6.4 million won if it exceeds 80 million won.

8. Applying the tax schedule to the taxable base obtained in step 7, we compute the initial tax liability. We then recalculate the tax liability using a new taxable base that adds the basic deduction amount to the taxable base in step 7. The difference between these two tax liabilities is taken as the increase in national income tax resulting from abolishing the basic deduction for year-end-settlement wage earners. Multiplying this amount by 1.1 yields the estimated increase in income tax including local income tax for this group.

### *Appendix 7.2 Simulation of Tax Increases from Replacing Existing Public Assistance with a Negative-Income-Tax-Type Basic Income and Abolishing the Child Tax Credit and Additional Elderly Deduction*

The proposal in this book replaces, through a negative income tax, the child allowance, child bonus, child tax credit, additional elderly deduction, and basic pension in their entirety, and replaces cash benefits under the Basic Livelihood Security Program within the range of the negative income tax payment.

In the income tax micro-data, the amounts of the child tax credit and the child bonus are available, but there is no information on the child allowance, the additional elderly deduction, the basic pension, or benefits under the Basic Livelihood Security Program, nor is there information that would allow these amounts to be inferred indirectly.

By contrast, the KGH'BOK data provide information on cash benefits from the Basic Livelihood Security Program and on basic pension benefits. For children, they report the combined amount of the child allowance and the child-rearing allowance, and for the child bonus they report the combined amount of the earned income tax credit and the child bonus. They do not provide information on the child tax credit or the additional elderly deduction. When using the KGH'BOK data, therefore, we cannot distinguish between the child allowance and the child-rearing allowance, and we thus treat the combined amount of the two as being replaced, within the range of the negative income tax payment. Because the earned income tax credit accounts for a much larger share than the child bonus, we treat the full amount of the combined earned-income-and-child bonus in KGH'BOK as the earned income tax credit, which serves as the funding base for the universal earned income tax credit in our model.

To estimate the revenue gain that could be used as a funding source for the negative income tax by abolishing the child tax credit and the additional elderly deduction, we conduct the following simulation.

1. **Eligibility for the child tax credit.**
   Children eligible for the child tax credit are defined as unmarried children of the household head aged 8–20 (children under 8, who are eligible for the child allowance, do not receive the child tax credit) whose comprehensive income amount and earned income amount are each 1 million won or less; in these cases, the child tax credit is applied to the household head. Grandchildren of the household head aged 8–20 whose comprehensive income amount and earned income amount are each 1 million won or less are treated as dependents of the married child of the household head, and the child tax credit is applied to that married child.
2. **Amount of the child tax credit.**
   If there is one eligible child, the child tax credit is 150,000 won; if there are two, 350,000 won; if three, 650,000 won; and if four, 950,000 won.
3. **Additional elderly deduction.**
   Among those eligible for the basic deduction defined earlier, individuals aged 70 or above receive an additional income deduction of 1 million won. The tax-reducing effect of this additional deduction is calculated, as in Appendix 7.1, as the difference between (i) the tax liability obtained by applying the tax schedule to the taxable base calculated earlier and (ii) the higher tax liability obtained by adding 1 million won to that taxable base and reapplying the tax schedule.

### *Appendix 7.3 Simulation of the Amounts of the Earned Income Deduction and Earned Income Tax Credit and of Tax Increases from Their Abolition*

The 5% income tax micro-sample from the National Tax Statistics Center (Please note that the cross-reference "National Tax Statistics Center (2026)" has not been provided in the reference list. Please provide the same.2026) provides the amounts of the earned income deduction and the earned income tax credit. Using these data, one can estimate the additional tax revenue from abolishing the earned income deduction simply by calculating the increase in tax liability caused by the corresponding increase in the taxable income base. However, the KGH'BOK data do not provide the amounts of the earned income deduction or the earned income tax credit. Accordingly, we proceed as follows.

1. Using wage and salary income (total earned income) reported in KGH'BOK, we calculate the amount of the earned income deduction by applying the formula in Table 5.10 of Chapter 5.
2. Using the household-member information in KGH'BOK, we estimate the amount of personal deductions (basic and additional) as in Appendix 7.1. We then use the information on social insurance contributions, and—because we lack information with which to estimate income deductions other than personal deductions and social insurance contributions—we apply the average amount of other income deductions by income bracket reported in the National Tax Statistical Yearbook to estimate the taxable income base for each individual.
3. We calculate the tax liability corresponding to this estimated taxable base.
4. We then add the earned income deduction amount calculated in step 1 to the taxable base and compute the tax liability corresponding to this higher taxable base.
5. The difference between the tax liability computed in step 4 and that in step 3 is taken as the increase in tax revenue resulting from the abolition of the earned income deduction.
6. Finally, because the amount of the earned income tax credit is determined by total earned income and the tax liability, we estimate the amount of the earned income tax credit by applying the formula in Table 5.10 of Chapter 5, using the earned income information in KGH'BOK and the tax liability obtained in step 3.

# Appendix to Chapter 8

**Table 8.A1** Redistributive Effects of a Common Wealth Basic Income Based on Equivalized Disposable Income (Unit: 10,000 KRW, %)

| *Decile* | *Equivalized disposable income* | *Equivalized basic income* | *Equivalized tax from basic deduction* | *Equivalized land-value tax* | *Equivalized increase in carbon expenditure* | *New equivalized disposable income* | *Equivalized net benefit* | *Share of net beneficiaries (%)* |
|---|---|---|---|---|---|---|---|---|
| 1 | 1130.6 | 194.9 | -9.1 | -39.9 | -41.6 | 1235.0 | 104.4 | 91.0% |
| 2 | 1993.1 | 222.9 | -18.9 | -65.2 | -56.5 | 2075.4 | 82.3 | 85.0% |
| 3 | 2611.1 | 237.7 | -26.0 | -68.9 | -64.6 | 2689.4 | 78.3 | 85.5% |
| 4 | 3146.2 | 241.5 | -30.0 | -78.2 | -69.8 | 3209.6 | 63.5 | 82.4% |
| 5 | 3662.6 | 245.7 | -32.7 | -87.1 | -77.0 | 3711.6 | 49.0 | 79.6% |
| 6 | 4227.8 | 246.8 | -34.8 | -107.2 | -80.4 | 4252.1 | 24.3 | 72.2% |
| 7 | 4832.4 | 251.9 | -38.2 | -122.4 | -85.7 | 4838.1 | 5.7 | 68.2% |
| 8 | 5605.7 | 253.1 | -41.7 | -137.2 | -91.9 | 5587.9 | -17.7 | 60.8% |
| 9 | 6782.2 | 253.3 | -48.2 | -179.2 | -101.4 | 6706.7 | -75.6 | 44.6% |
| 10 | 10701.6 | 253.6 | -60.8 | -336.3 | -123.9 | 10434.1 | -267.5 | 24.5% |
| Total | 4468.6 | 240.1 | -34.0 | -122.1 | -79.3 | 4473.3 | 4.7 | 69.4% |

**Table 8.A2** Comparison of the Redistributive Effects of Existing Income-Security Programs and Basic Income Policies by Equivalized Market-Income Decile (Including Imputed Rent) (Unit: 10,000 KRW, %)

| *Decile* | *Equivalized market income* | *Equivalized disposable income* | *Equivalized redistribution* | *Current share of net beneficiaries (%)* | *Equivalized benefit amount* | *Equivalized tax increase* | *Equivalized reduction of existing benefits* | *New equivalized disposable income* | *Equivalized net benefit* | *Share of net beneficiaries (%)* |
|---|---|---|---|---|---|---|---|---|---|---|
| 1 | 492.0 | 1361.9 | 869.9 | 94.4% | 769.3 | -110.1 | -357.1 | 1664.0 | 302.1 | 88.2% |
| 2 | 1557.0 | 2085.1 | 528.0 | 77.7% | 799.5 | -199.0 | -206.8 | 2478.8 | 393.7 | 92.5% |
| 3 | 2384.9 | 2645.8 | 260.8 | 55.5% | 846.4 | -298.6 | -132.8 | 3060.7 | 415.0 | 92.4% |
| 4 | 3053.4 | 3157.4 | 104.1 | 40.7% | 843.9 | -381.3 | -90.7 | 3529.2 | 371.8 | 90.9% |
| 5 | 3706.3 | 3633.7 | -72.6 | 29.0% | 870.7 | -464.7 | -70.8 | 3968.9 | 335.2 | 86.8% |
| 6 | 4351.6 | 4209.5 | -142.1 | 27.2% | 866.1 | -557.0 | -69.0 | 4449.7 | 240.1 | 80.0% |
| 7 | 5100.4 | 4802.9 | -297.4 | 18.8% | 865.7 | -667.6 | -52.7 | 4948.3 | 145.3 | 73.5% |
| 8 | 6042.0 | 5528.1 | -513.9 | 13.0% | 864.2 | -813.4 | -40.3 | 5538.6 | 10.5 | 55.4% |
| 9 | 7563.6 | 6725.1 | -838.5 | 9.2% | 848.4 | -1064.4 | -35.3 | 6473.8 | -251.3 | 19.7% |
| 10 | 12817.6 | 10543.8 | -2273.7 | 4.7% | 840.3 | -1888.7 | -22.8 | 9472.6 | -1071.2 | 1.3% |
| Total | 4705.9 | 4468.6 | -237.3 | 37.0% | 841.4 | -644.3 | -107.9 | 4557.9 | 89.2 | 68.1% |

**Table 8.A3** Comparison of the Redistributive Effects of Existing Income-Security Programs and Basic Income Policies by Equivalized Market-Income Decile (Excluding Imputed Rent) (Unit: 10,000 KRW, %)

| *Decile* | *Equivalized market income* | *Equivalized disposable income* | *Equivalized redistribution* | *Current share of net beneficiaries (%)* | *Equivalized benefit amount* | *Equivalized tax increase* | *Equivalized reduction of existing benefits* | *New equivalized disposable income* | *Equivalized net benefit* | *Share of net beneficiaries (%)* |
|---|---|---|---|---|---|---|---|---|---|---|
| 1 | 399.4 | 1285.4 | 885.9 | 94.4% | 756.2 | –125.8 | –348.3 | 1567.5 | 282.2 | 87.5% |
| 2 | 1429.8 | 1978.9 | 549.1 | 78.7% | 790.8 | –206.6 | –209.4 | 2353.7 | 374.8 | 91.8% |
| 3 | 2247.8 | 2518.9 | 271.1 | 55.8% | 831.4 | –304.0 | –129.8 | 2916.6 | 397.7 | 91.2% |
| 4 | 2908.4 | 2992.2 | 83.8 | 41.7% | 842.0 | –378.1 | –95.8 | 3360.3 | 368.1 | 91.7% |
| 5 | 3555.5 | 3474.8 | –80.7 | 27.6% | 881.6 | –466.7 | –69.4 | 3820.3 | 345.5 | 88.4% |
| 6 | 4192.5 | 4048.5 | –144.0 | 27.5% | 852.1 | –561.9 | –66.2 | 4272.4 | 224.0 | 78.9% |
| 7 | 4909.1 | 4600.1 | –309.1 | 18.3% | 872.6 | –665.5 | –56.2 | 4750.9 | 150.9 | 72.5% |
| 8 | 5827.2 | 5314.7 | –512.5 | 13.0% | 864.2 | –805.4 | –41.1 | 5332.3 | 17.6 | 57.7% |
| 9 | 7289.3 | 6446.8 | –842.5 | 9.0% | 850.5 | –1059.7 | –35.0 | 6202.6 | -244.1 | 20.1% |
| 10 | 12403.1 | 10125.7 | –2277.4 | 4.2% | 852.9 | –1858.9 | –23.5 | 9096.2 | -1029.5 | 1.5% |
| Total | 4514.9 | 4277.6 | –237.3 | 37.0% | 839.4 | –643.1 | –107.5 | 4366.5 | 88.9 | 68.1% |

**Table 8.A4** Comparison of the Redistributive Effects of the Stepping-Stone Income and Our Model Based on Equivalized Market Income (Unit: 10,000 KRW)

| *Decile* | *Equivalized market income* | *Equivalized disposable income* | *Equivalized disposable income with Stepping Stone Income* | *Equivalized net benefit from Stepping Stone Income* | *Share of net beneficiaries from Stepping Stone Income (%)* | *Equivalized disposable income with Basic Income System* | *Equivalized net benefit from Basic Income System* | *Share of net beneficiaries from Basic Income System (%)* |
|---|---|---|---|---|---|---|---|---|
| 1 | 399.4 | 1285.4 | 1661.4 | 376.0 | 75.7% | 1567.5 | 282.2 | 87.5% |
| 2 | 1429.8 | 1978.9 | 2209.1 | 230.2 | 56.4% | 2353.7 | 374.8 | 91.8% |
| 3 | 2247.8 | 2518.9 | 2597.1 | 78.2 | 36.3% | 2916.6 | 397.7 | 91.2% |
| 4 | 2908.4 | 2992.2 | 3002.1 | 9.9 | 5.7% | 3360.3 | 368.1 | 91.7% |
| 5 | 3555.5 | 3474.8 | 3477.5 | 2.7 | 0.5% | 3820.3 | 345.5 | 88.4% |
| 6 | 4192.5 | 4048.5 | 4049.3 | 0.9 | 0.3% | 4272.4 | 224.0 | 78.9% |
| 7 | 4909.1 | 4600.1 | 4600.1 | 0.0 | 0.0% | 4750.9 | 150.9 | 72.5% |
| 8 | 5827.2 | 5314.7 | 5314.7 | 0.0 | 0.0% | 5332.3 | 17.6 | 57.7% |
| 9 | 7289.3 | 6446.8 | 6446.8 | 0.0 | 0.0% | 6202.6 | −244.1 | 20.1% |
| 10 | 12403.1 | 10125.7 | 10125.7 | 0.0 | 0.0% | 9096.2 | −1029.5 | 1.5% |
| Total | 4514.9 | 4277.6 | 4347.4 | 69.8 | 17.5% | 4366.5 | 88.9 | 68.1% |

# Glossary of Terms

**Basic Deduction/Basic Personal Allowance** An income-tax deduction of 1.5 million won per person currently applied to the taxpayer and dependents under the Income Tax Act. Because deductions are more valuable to high-income earners facing higher marginal tax rates, they are regressive: low-income individuals below the tax-free threshold receive no benefit. The authors propose "basic-incomizing" the basic allowance by abolishing it and instead paying all residents the same amount in cash through a refundable tax credit.

**Break-even Income/Threshold** In a negative income tax system, the income level that separates net beneficiaries (who receive payments) from net contributors (who pay net taxes). The authors set the break-even income for the NIT-type basic income at the "national average income," i.e. about 60% of per-capita GNI, thereby providing broad benefits at a level above the median income.

**Capital Income and Capital Gains** Capital income refers to recurring income such as interest, dividends, and rent generated by capital (e.g. financial assets and real estate) without labor. Capital gains refer to realized gains from selling assets whose value has increased. Increases in asset values prior to sale are unrealized capital gains.

**Capitalization** The process of converting future streams of income or costs into their present value and reflecting them in asset prices.



J. S. You et al., *UBI from Idea to Reality*, Exploring the Basic Income Guarantee,
https://doi.org/10.1007/978-3-032-26200-4

- **Capitalization of a land-value tax:** Because an annual land-value tax is a future liability, it tends to reduce land prices (a negative asset effect).
- **Capitalization of a land dividend:** Conversely, an annual land dividend is a future stream of income, which functions as a new "common asset" for individuals (a positive asset effect).

**Carbon Dividend** An equal per-capita payment of all revenues from a carbon tax on fossil-fuel use.

**Carbon Tax** A policy that places a price on carbon emissions, which can be interpreted as a user fee for exploiting the atmosphere's limited capacity to absorb carbon—a depletable common asset. Carbon taxes are effective for addressing the climate crisis but may increase energy costs and thus burdens on low-income households.

**Climate Bonds** Bonds issued to finance large-scale infrastructure investments needed for the energy transition.

**Comprehensive Income** An income concept that includes not only realized cash income but also imputed rental income and unrealized capital gains. It is often defined as "consumption plus the net increase in wealth."

**Earned Income Tax Credit (EITC) / Work Incentive Payment (Korean-style EITC)** A work-based welfare program first introduced in the United States in the 1970s, which has become the country's largest anti-poverty program since 1996 and has inspired similar schemes in many other countries. It pays benefits to low-income workers with earnings in the form of a refundable tax credit, typically with a phase-in, plateau, and phase-out range.

**Effective Tax Rate (ETR)** Not the statutory tax rate, but the ratio of a person's net burden to income: actual taxes paid (income tax, social-insurance contributions, etc.) minus cash benefits received from the government (basic income, public assistance, etc.), divided by total income.

- **Negative effective tax rate:** When transfers from the government exceed taxes paid. Negative income tax and basic income apply negative effective tax rates to low-income individuals, thereby raising their real incomes.

**Effective Marginal Tax Rate (EMTR)** The proportion of an additional unit of income that is lost due to higher taxes and the withdrawal or reduction of benefits. When EMTRs are very high, additional work yields little or no gain, trapping people in poverty. One key economic effect of basic income is to lower the extremely high EMTRs (often above 100%) in current public assistance programs, thereby strengthening work incentives.

**Employment Income Deduction** A system that deducts a certain amount as necessary expenses from a worker's total wage and salary income, thereby reducing taxable income (the tax base). Because higher-income earners face higher marginal tax rates, this deduction gives them larger tax reductions and thus weakens the progressivity of the income tax and reduces overall tax revenue.

**Employment Income Tax Credit** A system that subtracts a fixed amount directly from the calculated tax liability of wage and salary earners. Its limitation is that workers with income below the tax-free threshold—who owe no tax—cannot benefit from it.

**Flat Tax** A tax levied at a single rate regardless of income level. When a flat tax is used to finance an equal basic-income payment to all, the overall redistribution effect—measured by effective tax rates—becomes highly progressive.

- **Full vs. Partial Basic Income Full basic income:** A benefit level high enough to secure a decent standard of living (for example, 50% of the median income) and to replace much of the existing welfare system.
- **Partial basic income:** A lower payment that coexists with existing welfare programs and does not fully replace them.

**Grid Parity** The point at which the unit cost of generating electricity from renewable sources such as solar and wind equals the unit cost of generation from fossil fuels (coal, gas)—the "break-even" cost of power generation.

**Imputed Rent/Imputed Rental Income** The monetary value of the housing services that an owner-occupier enjoys from living in their own home, treated as income.

- **Income Deduction vs. Tax Credit Income deduction:** Reduces taxable income (the tax base). Under a progressive rate structure, the same deduction yields larger tax savings for higher-income taxpayers, making deductions inherently regressive.
- **Tax credit:** Subtracts a fixed amount from the calculated tax liability. Credits are more equitable than deductions but their benefit is limited when the calculated tax is smaller than the credit amount.

**Just (Energy) Transition** Ensuring that, in the process of moving toward a carbon-neutral society to address the climate crisis, low-income and vulnerable groups are protected from disproportionate burdens such as higher energy prices. Carbon dividends and renewable-energy dividends such as "sunlight income" can share the gains from the energy transition and compensate for its costs, thereby enabling a just transition.

**Land Value Tax (LVT)** A tax levied on the value of bare land, excluding buildings. Because the supply of land is fixed, taxing land does not reduce its supply and therefore does not create deadweight loss; it is often regarded as the most efficient form of taxation.

**Land Dividend** An equal per-capita distribution of revenues from a land-value tax. By reclaiming unearned land income (economic rent) and making most citizens net beneficiaries, it is proposed as a strategy for curbing speculation and overcoming political resistance to land-value taxation.

**National Pension "A value" and "B value"** Two components that determine National Pension benefits.

- **A value (flat-rate component):** The average income of all National Pension contributors. It provides the income-redistribution function.
- **B value (earnings-related component):** The contributor's own average income over the contribution period. It provides benefits in proportion to contributions.

**Participation Tax Rate (PTR)** For someone who is not working, the proportion of the extra income from taking up work that is lost through higher taxes and reduced benefits.

**Participation Income** An income scheme similar to basic income but conditional on some form of social contribution ("participation"). Participation is broadly defined to include not only paid work but also child-rearing, elder care, volunteering, job search, education and training, and other socially valuable activities. It is an alternative model that responds to criticisms of the unconditionality of basic income.

**Pigouvian Tax** A tax imposed to reduce activities that impose negative externalities on society, such as pollution. The carbon tax is a representative example. The term derives from the British economist Arthur Pigou.

**Precariat** A neologism combining "precarious" and "proletariat," referring to a new working class exposed to low wages and job insecurity.

**Recognized Income** The income concept used to determine eligibility for public assistance programs such as the National Basic Livelihood

Security System. It is calculated as the sum of "assessed income" and the income value imputed to assets.

**Standard Median Income** The income level of the person in the exact middle when all individuals are ordered by income, calculated separately by household size and officially announced each year for use as an eligibility standard in social programs. For example, 32% or less of the standard median income is the threshold for basic livelihood benefits, and 40% or less for medical benefits.

**Stepping Stone Income** A household-based negative income tax (formerly "Safety Income") promoted by Seoul Mayor Oh Se-hoon. It is a "progressive from the bottom" income-security scheme that tops up 50% of the shortfall for households whose income falls below 85% of the standard median income.

**Sunlight Income/Sunlight Pension, Wind Income/Wind Pension** Dividend income that local residents receive by investing in, or participating as members of cooperatives that operate, renewable-energy projects such as solar or wind power. By returning the profits from using common natural resources such as sunlight and wind to residents, these schemes provide key funding for rural basic income and help overcome local opposition (NIMBY) to renewable-energy facilities, thereby accelerating a just energy transition.

**Sustainable Efficiency** An understanding of efficiency that goes beyond short-term cost minimization to encompass long-term economic growth and ecological and demographic sustainability.

**Tax Expenditure** Measures that reduce tax liability (exemptions, reductions, deductions, etc.) and thereby have effects similar to direct subsidies, even though no budgetary outlay is made. Tax expenditures such as income deductions are often regressive, conferring larger benefits on high-income groups.

**Tax Wedge** The difference between total labor costs to the employer and the worker's take-home pay, consisting of taxes plus social-insurance contributions.

**Work Incentive Payment (WIP/Korean-style EITC)** Modeled on the US EITC, South Korea's Work Incentive Payment (근로장려금) was introduced in 2008 to provide financial support to both employees and the self-employed. In contrast, the nation's Employment Income Tax Credit (근로소득세액공제) provides tax credits solely to wage earners.

# References

Ackerman, Bruce and AnneAlstott. 1999. *The Stakeholder Society*. New Haven, CT: Yale University Press.

Andersson, J. O. 2009. "Basic income from an ecological perspective." *Basic Income Studies* 4(2).

Atkinson, Anthony B. 1995. *Public Economics in Action: The Basic Income/Flat Tax Proposal*. Cambridge, MA: Oxford University Press.

Atkinson, Anthony B. 1996. "The Case for a Participation Income." *Political Quarterly* 67(1): 67–70.

Atkinson, Anthony B. 2015. *Inequality: What Can Be Done?* Cambridge, MA: Harvard University Press.

Averch, Harvey and Leland L. Johnson. 1962. "Behavior of the Firm Under Regulatory Constraint." *American Economic Review* 52(5): 1052–1069.

Baek, S., & Seo, J. (백승호·서정희). 2021. "Limitations of the Existing Welfare State and Directions for Reform (기존 복지국가의 한계와 개혁방향)." In BIKN (기본소득한국네트워크), *The Welfare State with Basic Income* (기본소득이있는 복지국가). Seoul, Korea: Park Jong-cheol Publishing (박종철출판사).

Bargain, O., H. Immervoll, and H. Viitamäki. 2012. "No claim, no pain: Measuring the non-take-up of social assistance using register data." *The Journal of Economic Inequality* 10(3): 375–395.

Bartels, Larry M. 2005. "Homer Gets a Tax Cut: Inequality and Public Policy in the American Mind." *Perspectives on Politics* 3(1): 15–31.

Basic Income Korean Network (기본소득한국네트워크). 2021. *The Welfare State with Basic Income* (기본소득이 있는 복지국가). Seoul, Korea: Park Jong-cheol Publishing (박종철출판사).



J. S. You et al., *UBI from Idea to Reality*, Exploring the Basic Income Guarantee,
https://doi.org/10.1007/978-3-032-26200-4

Bennett, Hayley. 2025. "Automation, data-sharing, and algorithmic opportunities in Universal Credit." Presentation at the Institute for Welfare State Research, Yonsei University.

Bollier, David. 2025. *Think Like a Commoner, Second Edition: A Short Introduction to the Life of the Commons*. Gabriola Island, BC: New Society Publishers.

Boyce, James K. 2018. "Carbon Pricing: Effectiveness and Equity." *Ecological Economics* 150: 52–61.

Boyce, James K. 2019. *The Case for Carbon Dividends*. Cambridge, UK: Polity.

Boyce, James K. 2020. "Distributional Issues in Climate Policy." In Chichilnisky & Rezai (eds.), *Handbook on the Economics of Climate Change*. Cheltenham, UK: Edward Elgar.

Buettner, Thiess. 2003. "Tiebout Visits Germany: Land Tax Capitalisation in a Sample of German Municipalities." *Third Norwegian-German Seminar on Public Economics*.

Burman, L. E. 2019. "A Universal EITC: Sharing the Gains from Economic Growth." *Tax Policy Center*.

Burman, L. E. 2020. "A Universal EITC: Making Work Pay in the Age of Automation." *National Tax Journal* 73(4): 1187–1218.

California Energy Commission. 2021. *Petroleum Watch*, September 2021.

Chang, Yong-sung, J.S. Han, and S.B. Kim. 2024. "NIT and UBI in the eyes of Aiyagari." *Macroeconomic Dynamics* 28: 813–825.

Cho, Dong-hee, Yoon, Yeo-joon, and Moon, Seong-man (조동희·윤여준·문성만). 2019. *Impact Assessment and Implications of EITC Systems in Major Advanced Countries* (주요 선진국 근로장려금 제도의 영향평가 및 시사점). Sejong, Korea: KIEP (대외경제정책연구원).

Choi, Byeong-hwa and Yesola Kweon. 2025. "From Meritocracy to Uncertainty: AI, White-Collar Insecurity, and the Demand for Universal Basic Income." Presented at the Welfare State Research Group seminar.

Choi, Hye-eun and You, Jong-sung (최혜은·유종성). 2022. "The Impact of Public and Basic Pensions on Income Inequality Among the Elderly." (공적연금과 기초연금이 노인의 소득불평등에 미치는 영향). *Journal of Pension Studies* (연금연구) 12(1): 21–50.

De Wispelaere, J. 2016. "The Struggle for Strategy: On the Politics of the Basic Income Proposal." *Politics* 36(2): 131–141.

De Wispelaere, J. and L. Morales. 2021. "Emergency Basic Income during the Pandemic." *Cambridge Quarterly of Healthcare Ethics* 30(2): 248–254.

De Wispelaere, Jurgen and Lindsay Stirton. 2007. "The Public Administration Case against Participation Income." *Social Service Review* 81(3): 523–549.

Dixson-Declève, S. et al. 2022. *Earth for All: A Survival Guide for Humanity*. Gabriola Island, BC: New Society Publishers.

Downs, Anthony. 1957. "An Economic Theory of Political Action in a Democracy." *Journal of Political Economy* 65(2): 135–150.

Economists' Statement on Carbon Dividends. 2019. https://clcouncil.org/economists-statement/ (Accessed on March 1, 2025).

Eurofound. 2015. *Access to social benefits: Reducing non-take-up.* Publications Office of the European Union.

European Commission. 2021. "The 2021 Ageing Report: Economic & Budgetary Projections for the EU Member States (2019–2070)".

France Stratégie. 2014. *Quelle France dans Dix Ans. Les chantiers de la decennie.* Paris: Commissariat general a la strategie et a la prospective.

Friedman, Milton. 1962. *Capitalism and Freedom.* Chicago, IL: University of Chicago Press.

Friedman, Milton. 1966. "The Case for the Negative Income Tax: A View from the Right." *Proceedings of the National Symposium on Guaranteed Income.*

Friedman, Milton. 1978. "An Interview with Milton Friedman." *Human Events* 38(46).

Fuchs, M. et al. 2020. "Falling through the social safety net? Analysing non-take-up of minimum income benefit and monetary social assistance in Austria." *Social Policy & Administration* 54: 827–843.

George, Henry. 1879. *Progress and Poverty.* San Francisco, CA: W.M. Hinton & Co.

Gilens, Martin and Benjamin I. Page. 2014. "Testing Theories of American Politics: Elites, Interest Groups, and Average Citizens." *Perspectives on Politics* 12(3): 564–581.

Goedemé, T. and J. Janssens. 2020. "The concept and measurement of non-take-up." *InGRID-2 project.*

Goodstein, E. and S. Polasky. 2020. *Economics and the Environment*, 9th Edition. Hoboken, NJ: Wiley.

Google Trends (구글 트렌드). 2026. Available at https://trends.google.co.kr/trends/ (Accessed on March 1, 2026).

Green, Christopher. 1967. *Negative Taxes and the Poverty Problem.* Washington, DC: The Brookings Institution.

Hankook Research (한국리서치). 2019. *Public Opinion within Public Opinion: Survey Report (January)* (여론 속의 여론 조사보고서 1월).

Hardin, Garrett. 1968. "The Tragedy of the Commons." *Science* 162(3859): 1243–1248.

Hartwick, John M. 1977. "Intergenerational Equity and the Investing of Rents from Exhaustible Resources." *American Economic Review* 66: 972–974.

Hiilamo, Heikki. 2022. *Participation Income: An Alternative to Basic Income for Poverty Reduction in the Digital Age.* Cheltenham, UK: Edward Elgar Publishing.

Hong, Se-hyun, Nak-Nyeon Kim et al. 2024. "Income Inequality in South Korea, 1933–2022: Evidence from Distributional National Accounts." *halshs-04424085.*

Hong, Soon-man (홍순만). 2021. *The Future of Taxation and Finance: Directions of Tax Increases for Sustainable Welfare* (조세와 재정의 미래: 지속 가능한 복지를 위한 증세 방향). Goyang-si, Korea: Moonusa (문우사).

Hotelling, Harold. 1931. "The Economics of Exhaustible Resources." *Journal of Political Economy* 39(2): 137–175.

Howard, Christopher. 1997. *The Hidden Welfare State: Tax Expenditures and Social Policy in the United States.* Princeton, NJ: Princeton University Press.

Howard, M. and J. Pinto. 2019. "Ecological effects of basic income." In M. Torry ed., *The Palgrave International Handbook of Basic Income.* Cham, Switzerland: Springer.

Howard, M. W. 2012. "A cap on carbon and a Basic Income: A Defensible Combination in the U.S.?" In Widerqist, K & M. Howard eds., *Exporting the Alaska model.* New York, NY: Palgrave Macmillan.

Idel, Robert. 2022. "Levelized Full System Costs of Electricity." *Energy* 259(15): 124905.

Jeon, Kang-soo and Kang, Nam-hoon (전강수·강남훈). 2017. "Basic Income and Land Value Tax: Background, Implementation, and Expected Effects. " (기본소득과 국토보유세). *Historical Criticism* (역사비평)120.

Jeong, Eun-ha (정은하). 2022. "Current Status of Seoul Stepping Stone Income (Ansim Sodeuk) Pilot Project." (서울시 안심소득 시범사업 추진현황). Presentation at the *Korea Association of Public Finance Policy Fall Conference* (한국재정정책학회 추계 학술대회).

Kahneman, Daniel. 2013. *Thinking, Fast and Slow.* New York, NY: Farrar, Straus and Giroux.

Kahneman, Daniel and Amos Tversky. 1979. "Prospect Theory: An Analysis of Decision under Risk." *Econometrica* 47(2): 263–291.

Kahneman, D., & Tversky, A. 1984. "Choices, values, and frames." *American Psychologist* 39(4): 341.

Kang, Nam-hoon (강남훈). 2019a. *Economics of Basic Income* (기본소득의 경제학). Seoul, Korea: Park Jong-cheol Publishing (박종철출판사).

Kang, Nam-hoon (강남훈). 2019b. "Redistributive Effects of Replacing Employment Income Deductions with Basic Income." (근로소득세 공제 없애고 기본소득을 지급할 때의 재분배 효과). *Social and Economic Review* (사회경제평론) 58(1): 1–27.

Kangas, Olli. 2016. *From idea to experiment: Report on universal basic income experiment in Finland.* Kela Working papers 106.

Kangas, Olli et al. 2016. *Basic Income in the Finnish Context.* Prime Minister's Office Helsinki.

KIHASA (Korea Instituter for Health and Social Affairs, 한국보건사회연구원). 2024. 2024 Survey Research of Public Perception on Social Policy (2024년 사회정책 국민 인식조사 연구). Sejong, Korea: Korea Institute for Health and Social Affairs.

Kim, Dani, Young-seong Yoo, and Insik Bang. Forthcoming. "Understanding Young Adults' Attitudes toward Basic Income Scheme in South Korea." *Social Policy and Administration.* https://doi.org/10.1111/spol.70049

Kim, Nak-hui et al. (김낙회·변양호·이석준·임종룡·최상목). 2021. *Economic Policy Agenda 2022* (경제정책 어젠다 2022). Paju, Korea: 21st Century Books (21세기북스).

Kim, Nak Nyeon. 2018. "Top Incomes in Korea: Update, 1933–2016." *World Inequality Lab Working Papers.*

Kim, Nak Nyeon (김낙년). 2019. "Estimating the Distribution of Individual Wealth in Korea." (우리나라 개인자산 분포의 추정). *Economic History Review* (경제사학) 43(3): 437–482.

Kim, Nak Nyeon (김낙년). 2020. "Correction of Household Survey Data using Administrative Records." (가계조사의 행정자료에 의한 보정). *Korea Social Policy Review* (한국사회정책) 27(1): 39–61.

Kim, Nak Nyeon. 2022. "Redistributive Effect of Imputed Rents in Korea: International Comparison." *KIRL Working Paper 2022-02.*

Kim, Nak Nyeon (김낙년). 2023. "Functional Income Distribution in Korea." (한국의 기능별 소득분배). *Korean Economic Forum* (한국경제포럼) 16(2): 1–36.

Kim, Yeon-myung (김연명). 2013. "The Characteristics and Prospects of the Korean Welfare State." (한국 복지국가의 성격과 전망). *Korean Journal of Social Welfare Studies* (한국사회복지조사연구) 36: 27–59.

Kobayashi, H. 2014. "The future of social assistance reform in Japan: Workfare versus basic income?". In Vanderborght, Y & T. Yamamori eds., *Basic income in Japan.* New York, NY: Palgrave Macmillan.

KOSIS(국가통계포털). 2025. "National Accounts: Key Indicators (국민계정 주요지표)." https://kosis.kr/statHtml/statHtml.do?orgId=301&tblId=DT_200Y101&conn_path=I3 (Accessed on July 27, 2025).

Ku, In-hoe, Kang, Seong-ho, Park, Hyung-jon, Son, Byung-don, Hae-bong Woo, and Lee, Won-jin (구인회·강성호·박형존·손병돈·우해봉·이원진). 2021. *In-depth Analysis of the Multi-layered Old-age Income Security System using Administrative Data* (행정데이터를 활용한 다층노후소득보장체계 심층분석). Ministry of Health and Welfare (보건복지부).

Kwon, Pil-seok et al. (권필석·강남훈·안진걸·오준호·기혁·함일찬). 2023. *Carbon Neutrality and Basic Income* (탄소중립과 기본소득). Basic Society Foundation (사단법인 기본사회).

Lee, K. & Lim, D. (이근대·임덕오). 2022. *LCOE Forecasting System for Renewable Energy Expansion* (재생에너지 공급확대를 위한 중장기 발전단가(LCOE)전망 시스템 구축).KEEI (에너지경제연구원).

Lee, Jungmin et al. 2025. "The Stepping Stone Income Project and Welfare Reform: Final Report on Three-Year Outcomes." Presentation at the Seoul International Forum on Stepping Stone Income 2025.

Lee, Sang-jun (이상준). 2025. "Community, Lifestyle Politics, and Participation Income." (공동체, 생활정치 그리고 참여소득). *Citizens and the World* (시민과세계): 111–148.

Lee, Seungju. 2025. "Examining the potential impact of universal basic income on labor supply." *International Journal of Social Welfare* 34(1): 1–19.

Lee, Seungju and Jong-sung You (이승주·유종성). 2025. "Changing public opinion and the politics of basic income in South Korea." Presented at the *26th IPSA World Congress.*

Lee, Seungju and You, Su-jin (이승주·유수진). 2021. "The Impact of Disaster Basic Income Discussions on Media Attitudes Toward Basic Income." (재난기본소득의 논의가 기본소득에 대한 언론의 보도 태도에 미친 영향). *The Korean Journal of Public Administration* (한국행정연구) 30(4): 177–207.

Lee, Soomi. 2021. "Politics of Universal and Unconditional Cash Transfer." *Basic Income Studies* 16(2).

Lee, Soomi. Forthcoming. "Beyond the Prototype, Towards the Varieties of Basic Income Experience." In Merrill & Neves eds., *Determining the Value of Universal Basic Income* (Palgrave Macmillan), 171-192.

Lee, Sophia Seung-yoon. 2023. *Varieties of Precarity: Melting Labour and the Failure to Protect Workers in the Korean Welfare State.* Bristol, UK: Policy Press.

Lee, Tae-jin et al. (이태진·이봉주 외). 2023. *2023 Korea Welfare Panel Study Analysis Report* (2023년 한국복지패널 조사·분석 보고서). KIHASA (한국보건사회연구원).

Lee, Won-jin, No, Dae-myung, and Ha, Eun-sol (이원진·노대명·하은솔). 2024. *Development of NBLSS Simulation Model and Analysis of Major Reform Effects* (국민기초생활보장제도 시뮬레이션 모델 개발 및 주요 개편방안 효과 분석). KIHASA (한국보건사회연구원).

Leff, Benjamin M. 2020. "EITC for All: A Universal Basic Income Compromise Proposal." *Wash. & Lee J. Civ. Rts. & Soc. Just.* 26(1): 84-145.

Macartney, Suzanne and RobinGhertner. 2021. "Participation in the U.S. Social Safety Net: Coverage of Low-Income Families, 2018." *ASPE Research Brief.* U.S. Department of Health & Human Services.

Mankiw, N. Gregory. 2016. *Principles of Microeconomics* (8th ed.). Boston, MA: CENGAGE Learning.

Mankiw, N. Gregory. 2021. "How to Increase Taxes on the Rich (If You Must)." In Blanchard O. & D. Rodrik eds., *Combating Inequality.* Cambridge, MA: The MIT Press.

Miller, Annie. 2017. *A Basic Income Handbook.* London, UK: Luath Press.

Miller, David. 1992. "Distributive Justice: What the People Think." *Ethics* 102(3): 555–593.

Ministry of Data and Statistics [MODS] (국가데이터처/통계청). 2020. *Understanding the Integration of Survey and Administrative Data in the SHFLC* (가계금융복지조사에서의 조사자료와 행정자료의 통합방법 이해).

Ministry of Data and Statistics [MODS] (국가데이터처/통계청). 2025a. *Survey of Household Finances and Living Conditions (SHFLC) 2024* (가계금융복지조사 2024).

Ministry of Data and Statistics [MODS] (국가데이터처/통계청). 2025b. *Press Release: 2023 Pension Statistics Results* (2023년 연금통계 결과 보도자료).
Ministry of Health and Welfare (보건복지부). 2024. *The 5th Mid-to-Long-term Fiscal Projection for Social Security* (제5차 사회보장 중장기 재정추계).
Ministry of Health and Welfare (보건복지부). 2025. *Current Status of NBLSS Recipients in 2023* (2023년 국민기초생활보장 수급자 현황).
Mirrlees, J. et al. 2011. *Tax by Design*. Oxford, UK: Oxford University Press.
Myles, John and Paul Pierson. 1997. "Friedman's Revenge: The Reform of 'Liberal' Welfare States in Canada and the United States." *Politics & Society* 25(4): 443–472.
Nam, Chan-seob and Kim, Yeon-myung (남찬섭·김연명). 2023. "For Pension Reform Centered on the National Pension." (국민연금 중심의 연금개혁을 위하여). *Journal of Pension Studies* (연금연구) 13(2): 125–150.
Nam, Yun-min and Kang, Myung-se (남윤민·강명세). 2025. "Support for the People's Livelihood Recovery Consumption Coupons in an Era of Affective Polarization (정서적 양극화시대, 누가 소비쿠폰 정책을 지지하는가?)". Presented at the *Welfare State Research Association Seminar*.
National Tax Service (국세청). 2024. *Statistical Yearbook of National Tax* (국세통계연보).
National Tax Statistics (국세청). 2026. *5% Random Sample Micro-data of Income Tax for 2023* (국세통계센터 2023년 귀속 소득세 5%임의 샘플 미시자료).
Naver Data Lab (네이버 데이터랩). 2026. Available at https://datalab.naver.com/ (Accessed on February 10, 2026).
OECD. 2017. "Basic income as a policy option: Can it add up?", No. 2017/01, OECD Publishing, Paris.
OECD. 2025. *OECD calculator of taxes and benefits*. https://www.oecd.org/en/data/tools/oecd-calculator-of-taxes-and-benefits.html (Accessed on November 1, 2025).
OECD. 2025. *Social Expenditure Database (SOCX)*. https://www.oecd.org/en/data/datasets/social-expenditure-database-socx.html (Accessed on December 10, 2025).
Olson, M. 1965. *The Logic of Collective Action*. Cambridge, MA: Harvard University Press.
Ostrom, E. 1990. *Governing the Commons*. Cambridge, UK: Cambridge University Press.
Paine, T. (2004). Agrarian Justice (1797). In: Cunliffe, J., Erreygers, G. (eds) *The Origins of Universal Grants*. Palgrave Macmillan.
Park, Hyung-jon (박형존). 2022. "Income Information Construction using Administrative Data." (행정자료를 이용한 소득정보 구성). *Korea Social Policy Review* (한국사회정책) 29(2): 79–113.
Park, Ki-seong and Byun, Yang-gyu (박기성·변양규). 2017. "The Effects of Stepping Stone Income (Safety Income) System." (안심소득제의 효과). *Quarterly Journal of Labor Economics* (노동경제논집) 40(3): 57–77.

Pierson, Paul. 1994. *Dismantling the Welfare State?*. Cambridge, UK: Cambridge University Press.

Piketty, Thomas. 2020. *Capital and Ideology*. Cambridge, MA: Harvard University Press.

Piketty, Thomas and Emmanuel Saez. 2003. "Income Inequality in the United States, 1913–1998." *Quarterly Journal of Economics* 118(1): 1–39.

Piketty, Thomas, Emmanuel Saez, and Stefanie Stantcheva. 2014. "Optimal Taxation of Top income." *American Economic Journal: Economic Policy* 6: 230–271.

Ranalli, Brent. 2021. *Common Wealth Dividends: History and Theory*. Cham, Switzerland: Palgrave Macmillan.

Rawls, John. 1971/1999. *A Theory of Justice*. Cambridge, MA: Harvard University Press.

Rawls, John. 1988. "The Priority of Right and Ideas of the Good." *Philosophy and Public Affairs* 17: 251–276.

Reuters. 2023. "Denmark to take 20% ownership of new offshore wind farms." Available at https://www.reuters.com/business/energy/denmark-take-20-ownership-new-offshore-wind-farms-2023-05-30/ (Accessed on March 1, 2025).

Rodrik, Dani. 1995. "Getting Interventions Right: How South Korea and Taiwan Grew Rich." *Economic Policy* 20: 55–107.

Roosma, Femke and Wim Van Oorschot. 2020. "Public Opinion on Basic Income." *Journal of European Social Policy* 30(2): 190–205.

Seoul Institute (서울연구원). 2018. *Seoul Welfare Survey Data* (서울시 복지실태조사자료).

Sheahen, Al and Karl Widerquist. 2004. "A Proposal to Transform the Standard Deduction into a Refundable Tax Credit." *USBIG Discussion Paper No. 93*.

Simon, Herbert A. 2000. "A Basic Income for All: UBI and the Flat Tax." *Boston Review* 25(5): 9–10. Available at https://www.bostonreview.net/forum/ubi-van-parijs/herbert-simon-ubi-and-flat-tax/ (Accessed on March 1, 2015).

Society for Health Equity (한국건강형평성학회). 2018. *Health Inequality Profile: National, Provincial, and Municipal Levels* (건강격차 프로파일-전국, 광역시도, 시군구).

Standing, Guy. 2011. *The Precariat: The New Dangerous Class*. London, UK: Bloomsbury.

Standing, Guy. 2017. *Basic Income: A Guide for the Open-Minded*. New Haven, CT: Yale University Press.

Standing, Guy. 2019. *Plunder of the Commons*. London, UK: Penguin.

Standing, Guy. 2022. "This South Korean Election is Vital." *BIEN*. Available at https://basicincome.org/news/2022/01/this-south-korean-presidential-election-is-vital/ (Accessed on March 1, 2025).

Standing, Guy. 2023. *The Politics of Time*. London, UK: Penguin.

Stevens, Harvey and Wayne Simpson. 2017. "Toward a National Universal Guaranteed Basic Income." *Canadian Public Policy* 43(2): 120–139.
Stiglitz, Joseph E. 2015. *The Great Divide*. New York, NY: W. W. Norton & Company.
Suplicy, Eduardo Matarazzo and Milton Friedman. 2000. "THE SUPLICY-FRIEDMAN EXCHANGE." *BIEN NewsFlash* No. 3.
Tideman, T. N. and Trustees of the Robert Schalkenbach Foundation. 1991. "Open letter to Mikhail Gorbachev." *Challenge*, 34(2): 4–6.
Tietenberg, Tom and Lynne Lewis. 2024. *Environmental and Natural Resource Economics*, 12th edition. New York, NY: Routledge.
Tobin, James, Joseph A. Pechman, and Peter M. Mieszkowski. 1967. "Is a Negative Income Tax Practical?" *Yale Law Journal* 77: 1–27.
Torry, Malcolm. 2017. *Citizen's Basic Income: A Christian Social Policy*. Bristol, UK: Policy Press.
Torry, Malcolm. 2018. *Why We Need a Citizen's Basic Income*. Bristol, UK: Policy Press.
Torry, Malcolm. 2020. "Evaluation of a Recovery Basic Income." *EUROMOD Working Paper Series*.
Ummel, Kevin. 2020. "Household Impact Study II (HIS2)." *Working Paper*.
United Nations. 2025. *World Population Prospects 2024*. Available from https://population.un.org/wpp/ (Accessed on December 20, 2025).
Van Parijs, Philippe. 1995. *Real Freedom for All*. Oxford, UK: Oxford UniversitynPress.
Van Parijs, Philippe and Yannick Vanderborght. 2017. *Basic Income: A Radical Proposal for a Free Society and a Sane Economy*. Cambridge, MA: Harvard University Press.
Varian, H. R. (2014). *Intermediate Microeconomics: A Modern Approach*. New York, NY: W Norton & Co Inc.
Weinzierl, Matthew. 2011. "The Surprising Power of Age-Dependent Taxes;" *The Review of Economic Studies*, 78(4): 1490–1518.
Widerquist, Karl. 2005. "A Failure to Communicate: What (If Anything) Can We Learn from the Negative Income Tax Experiments?" *Journal of Socio-Economics* 34(1): 49–81.
Widerquist, Karl and Michael W. Howard (eds.). 2012. *Exporting the Alaska Model*. New York, NY: Palgrave Macmillan.
World Bank. 1993. *The East Asian Miracle*. Oxford, UK: Oxford University Press.
World Bank Group. 2023. *State and Trends of Carbon Pricing 2023*. Washington, DC: The World Bank.
Yang, Jae-jin. 2017. should be dropped.
Yang, Jae-jin. 2020. should be dropped.
Yoo, Hee-won et al. (유희원·류재린·김혜진·김아람). 2022. *Current Status of Blind Spots in the National Pension System and Countermeasures* (국민연금제도의

사각지대 현황과 대응방안). Korea National Pension Research Institute (국민연금연구원).

Yoo, Young-seong and Young-ju Ma (유영성·마영주). 2020. "Estimation of Adequate Basic Income Amount for Gyeonggi-do." (경기도 적정 기본소득액 추정). In *Basic Income for Everyone's Economic Freedom*. Seoul, Korea: Dahal Media (다할미디어).

Yoo, Young-seong, Choi, Kwang-eun, and Yoo, Ik-jin (유영성·최광은·유익진). 2021. *What People Think About Basic Income* (사람들은 기본소득을 이렇게 생각한다). GRI (경기연구원).

You, Jong-sung. 2014. "Land Reform, Inequality, and Corruption." *The Korean Journal of International Studies* 12: 191–224.

You, Jong-sung. 2015. *Democracy, Inequality and Corruption: Korea, Taiwan and the Philippines Compared*. Cambridge, UK: Cambridge University Press.

You, Jong-sung (유종성). 2018. "A Study on the Fiscal Feasibility and Redistributive Effects of Basic Income." (기본소득의 재정적 실현가능성과 재분배효과에 대한 고찰). *Korea Social Policy Review* (한국사회정책) 25(3): 3–35.

You, Jong-sung (유종성). 2020a. "Why Universal Basic Income is Needed." (왜 보편적 기본소득이 필요한가?). *Trends and Prospects* (동향과전망) 110: 60–113.

You, Jong-sung (유종성). 2020b. "Need for a Life-Cycle Tailored Basic Income (생애주기형 전국민기본소득제 도입의 필요성과 실현방안)." In *Asking the Way for the Korean Welfare State after the Candlelight Revolution* (촛불 이후 한국 복지국가의길을 묻다). Paju, Korea: Hanul (한울아카데미).

You, Jong-sung (유종성). 2021 "Distributive justice and basic income." In Lee, H. et al. *New Social Welfare for a Fair Society*, Seoul: Sigongsa (이한주 외, 공정사회를 만드는 새로운 복지, 시공사), 92–114.

You, Jong-sung (유종성). 2023. "Cases of Utilizing Social Security Administrative Data (사회보장행정데이터의 활용사례와 향후과제)." *Health and Welfare Forum* (보건복지포럼), November issue.

You, Jong-sung (유종성). 2025. "A Reform Plan for the National Pension as an Income-based Social Insurance." (국민연금의 소득기반 사회보험으로의 개혁방안). *Korean Social Security Studies* (사회보장연구) 41(3): 85–115.

You, Jong-sung and Jieun Choi. 2022. "Will South Korea Be the First Country to Introduce Universal Basic Income?" *KIRL Working Paper 2022-01*.

Yun, Hong-shik (윤홍식). 2019. *The Origin and Trajectory of the Korean Welfare State 3* (한국복지국가의 기원과 궤적 3). Seoul, Korea: Social Review Academy (사회평론아카데미).

Zelleke, Almaz. 2007. "Targeting Benefit Levels to Individuals or Families?" *Basic Income Studies* 2(1): 1–10.

# Index






J. S. You et al., *UBI from Idea to Reality*, Exploring the Basic Income Guarantee,
https://doi.org/10.1007/978-3-032-26200-4

## C

**D**

E

**T**



**U**

FSC
www.fsc.org
MIX
Papier | Fördert gute Waldnutzung
FSC® C083411

Kolibri 360 GmbH
Ferdinand-Jühlke-Straße 7
99095 Erfurt, Deutschland
produktsicherheit@kolibri360.de